"What does it mean to follow Jesus in the twenty-first century? Wright provides a stimulating account of what this might look like through a close reading of three of Jesus' primary spiritual practices in Luke's Gospel. She sets forth Jesus' spiritual practices through convincing exegesis, situating Jesus in his historical context, and through examining the reception of Jesus' teachings in the early church. Wright successfully shows how Jesus is the supremely good king and teacher who calls his people to a distinctive way of life. We need more books like this helping to point the way forward to how Jesus' practices—specifically simplicity, humility, and prayer—can shape the lives of would-be disciples of Jesus."

Joshua W. Jipp, associate professor of New Testament at Trinity Evangelical Divinity School, author of *Reading Acts*

"With *Spiritual Practices of Jesus*, Catherine J. Wright has given a gift both to church and academy. Looking at Jesus' teaching and deeds of simplicity, humility, and prayer, she follows a similar pattern: she traces the theme in the Gospel narrative; then she contextualizes its practice within the views expressed in the larger Jewish and Greco-Roman environment of antiquity; finally, she explores the ways in which the teachings of the Lukan Jesus on simplicity, humility, and prayer were received in the early church. Wright is fully conversant with the pertinent primary and secondary literature, and along the way, she sprinkles examples from popular culture to present in bold relief the countercultural claims of Jesus. Pastors and lay Bible teachers will find here a kind of evangelical version of Ignatius's *Spiritual Exercises*, a treasure trove intended to encourage modern believers to adopt a simpler, humbler, and more prayerful way of life."

Mikeal C. Parsons, professor and Macon Chair in Religion at Baylor University

"There's a lot going on in this well-crafted book. Catherine Wright wants us to read Luke's Gospel as Christian Scripture. She wants us to learn habits of reading Luke faithfully from the early church. She wants us to take seriously first-century expectations for a narrative like Luke's lest we overwhelm the text with twenty-first-century assumptions. Above all, though, she wants us to be shaped decisively through encountering Jesus in Luke's Gospel. Focusing on the coherence of Jesus' life and teaching around spiritual practices, Wright invites us to apprentice ourselves to Jesus, our teacher and royal model. Here is a book you will want to read slowly, perhaps with others, taking in and becoming like the scriptural Jesus."

Joel B. Green, professor of New Testament at Fuller Theological Seminary

"Wright combines careful exegesis and painstaking research into the ancient writers with refreshingly authentic reflections from her own Christian community and experience. By expanding the notion of spirituality beyond prayer into the Lukan emphases on simplicity of life and the humility that flows from an understanding of the true self, Wright has found in the Third Gospel resources that could, if taken seriously, restore the Western church to authenticity."

Sharyn Dowd, New Testament scholar and pastor

"In *Spiritual Practices of Jesus*, Catherine Wright invites readers into a delightful place where biblical studies and spiritual formation meet, a rare space that allows for Luke's Gospel and his literary world to embrace. I enthusiastically recommend this book. Wright's work not only expanded my understanding of how Luke's audience would have first heard his Gospel, but it also inspired me to double down in my own pursuit to imitate his Christ in simplicity, humility, and prayer."

Joseph R. Dodson, associate professor of New Testament at Denver Seminary

"Catherine Wright looks back with a prophetic edge, inviting us to read Luke through the eyes of the early church, taking on our tendencies to keep Scripture at a safe distance or to spiritualize Jesus' most difficult commands. She invites us to encounter the gift of freedom in the unlikeliest of places by worldly standards—through simplicity, humility, and prayer—knowing that Jesus has the power to unburden and transform our hearts for the sake of this world God loves so much."

Karna Marks, reverend at Immanuel in Pepin, Wisconsin

"*Spiritual Practices of Jesus* situates simplicity, humility, and prayer squarely within Jesus' life, the literary world of the early church, and the writings of early Christian leaders. Rather than being abandoned to guess at their meaning or how to implement them, Wright guides her readers through the many literary sources unpacking concrete dimensions of each practice for the world we live in today. Wright's conversation with Luke and other writers fully describes the ancient context for what many dismiss as a modern addition to Christianity."

Stan Harstine, professor in religion at Friends University

Catherine J. Wright

SPIRITUAL PRACTICES of JESUS

LEARNING SIMPLICITY, HUMILITY,
AND PRAYER WITH LUKE'S
EARLIEST READERS

ivp
Academic

An imprint of InterVarsity Press
Downers Grove, Illinois

InterVarsity Press
P.O. Box 1400, Downers Grove, IL 60515-1426
ivpress.com
email@ivpress.com

InterVarsity Press® is the book-publishing division of InterVarsity Christian Fellowship/USA®, a movement of students and faculty active on campus at hundreds of universities, colleges, and schools of nursing in the United States of America, and a member movement of the International Fellowship of Evangelical Students. For information about local and regional activities, visit intervarsity.org.

Scripture quotations, unless otherwise noted, are from the New Revised Standard Version Bible, copyright © 1989 National Council of the Churches of Christ in the United States of America. Used by permission. All rights reserved worldwide.

Cover design and image composite: David Fassett
Interior design: Daniel van Loon
Images: pastel shades of color © andipantz / DigitalVision Vectors / Getty Images
         white marble texture © undefined undefined / iStock / Getty Images Plus

ISBN 978-0-8308-5226-0 (print)
ISBN 978-0-8308-7364-7 (digital)

Printed in the United States of America ∞

InterVarsity Press is committed to ecological stewardship and to the conservation of natural resources in all our operations. This book was printed using sustainably sourced paper.

Library of Congress Cataloging-in-Publication Data
A catalog record for this book is available from the Library of Congress.

P 25 24 23 22 21 20 19 18 17 16 15 14 13 12 11 10 9 8 7 6 5 4 3 2 1

Y 37 36 35 34 33 32 31 30 29 28 27 26 25 24 23 22 21 20

To my children, Ron and Natalie, to my mother Barbara,

and in memory of my father, Ronald Wright

CONTENTS

ACKNOWLEDGMENTS

THIS BOOK HAS BEEN A LONG TIME IN THE MAKING. I am indebted to Charles Talbert, my dissertation advisor, who many years ago took my interest in spiritual formation and pointed me toward the study of Luke's spiritual practices within Luke's literary world. His significant impact has shaped not only this book but the content of countless lectures over the past twenty years.

I am grateful to Dan Reid who first caught the vision for a book that would fill the niche between biblical scholarship and spiritual formation. I had actually approached Dan many years ago about a different version of the book. At the time, I was pregnant with my first child and thought it perfectly feasible to write a book while my infant napped beside me in his bassinette. Twelve years later, fueled by desires to extend the project in the direction of reception criticism, I approached him again. The meeting felt serendipitous, and this time I had the mental space to write. I am also thankful for Anna Gissing who inherited the project, and whose encouragement moved the book along to its finish line.

I wrote a large portion of the book at St. Benedict's Monastery in St. Joseph, MN, where I participated in Studium as a visiting scholar. I remain incredibly grateful for the sisters' friendship and hospitality, and for the helpful feedback I received from a presentation to the Studium community. I am particularly thankful for Sister Theresa Schumacher, one of the most loving and gracious people I have known, who we lost to ALS last summer, and Sister Ann Marie Biermaier for their love, encouragement, and support over the years.

I am deeply appreciative of colleagues who gave me comments on the manuscript: Juan Hernández, Jenell Paris, Bernon Lee, Sara Shady, Marion

Larson, and Angela Sabates. Sara Shady and Marion Larson read early drafts
of the manuscript, coaching me to develop a more conversational writing
voice. Angela Sabates provided encouraging feedback as the book was
nearing its final stages. Jenell Paris read both early and late drafts, providing
extensive handwritten comments that she then mailed to me from across
the country. Juan Hernández challenged my middle-class perspectives on
the simplicity unit, helping me to allow the biblical text to retain its unset-
tling message. Bernon Lee provided helpful comments, particularly on the
methodology section. Any failures in the manuscript remain my own, but
I am so thankful for my colleagues' support and encouragement.

I am grateful for classes who have been my audience and conversation
partners for portions of this book over the last several years. I would especially like to thank the students who worked on the bibliography, appen-
dices, and footnotes: Steven Meissner, Matt Barton, Rylee Forshee, Ian
Jerzyk, and David Felsch, all of whom have promising futures in the church
and in academia.

Finally, I want to express my gratitude to my family—to my father,
whose faith prompted stories in this book, to my mother, for her constant
love and support, and to my children for whom I have almost more love
and pride than a heart can contain.

ABBREVIATIONS

1 En.	1 Enoch
ANF	*Ante-Nicene Fathers*
Apoc. Mos.	Apocalypse of Moses
Bar	Baruch
Did.	Didache
Ep. Barn.	Epistle of Barnabas
FC	Fathers of the Church
Jub.	Jubilees
LCL	Loeb Classical Library
Let. Aris.	Letter of Aristeas
Lif. Sec.	Life of Secundus the Philosopher
NPNF^1	*Nicene and Post-Nicene Fathers*, Series 1
NPNF^2	*Nicene and Post-Nicene Fathers*, Series 2
Pr. Azar.	Prayer of Azariah
Pr. Man.	Prayer of Manasseh
Ps.-Phoc.	Sentences of Pseudo-Phocylides
Pss. Sol.	Psalms of Solomon
Sib. Or.	Sibylline Oracles
Syr. Men.	Sentences of the Syriac Menander
T. Ab.	Testament of Abraham
T. Isaac	Testament of Isaac
T. Jac.	Testament of Jacob
T. Jud.	Testament of Judah
Vis. Ezra	Vision of Ezra

Ambrose

Exp. Luc.	*Exposition of the Holy Gospel According to Saint Luke*

Aristotle

Eth. nic.	*Nicomachean Ethics*

Athanasius
Ep. fest.   *Festal Letters of Fasting, and Trumpets and Feasts*
Vit. Ant.   *Life of Antony*

Augustine
Conf.   *Confessions*
WSA   *Works of Saint Augustine*

Cassian, John
Conf.   *Conferences*

Chrysostom, John
Hom. Act.   *Homilies on the Acts of the Apostles*
Hom. Heb.   *Homilies on the Epistle to the Hebrews*
Hom. Jo.   *Homilies on the Gospel of Saint John*
Hom. Matt.   *Homilies on the Gospel of Saint Matthew*
Hom. Phil.   *Homilies on the Epistle to the Philippians*
Hom. Rom.   *Homilies on the Epistle to the Romans*
Sac.   *Priesthood*
Theod. laps.   *Exhortation to Theodore After His Fall*

Clement of Alexandria
Paed.   *Paedagogus*, or *Christ the Educator*
Quis div.   *Salvation of the Rich*
Strom.   *Stromata*, or *Miscellanies*

Cyprian
Dom. or.   *The Lord's Prayer*
Eleem.   *On Works and Almsgiving*
Fort.   *To Fortunatus: Exhortation to Martyrdom*
Zel. liv.   *Jealousy and Envy*

Cyril of Alexandria
Comm. Luke   *A Commentary on the Gospel of Saint Luke*

Diogenes Laertius
Vit. phil.   *Lives of the Philosophers*

Diotogenes
Ep.   *Epistles*

Epictetus
Ench.   *Enchiridion*
Frag.   *Fragments*

Isocrates
Dem.   *To Demonicus*

Jerome
Pelag.   *Against the Pelagians*

Josephus
Ant.   *Jewish Antiquities*

Lactantius
Inst.   *The Divine Institutes*

Lucian
Demon.   *Demonax*
Perger.   *The Passing of Peregrinus*
Rhet. praec.   *A Professor of Public Speaking*

Origen
Cels.   *Against Celsus*
Fr. Matt.   *Commentary on Matthew*
Fr. prin.   *First Principles: Book IV*
Hom. Num.   *Homily XXVII on Numbers*
Mart.   *An Exhortation to Martyrdom*

Philo
Abraham   *On the Life of Abraham*
Joseph   *On the Life of Joseph*
Migration   *On the Migration of Abraham*
Moses 1, 2   *On the Life of Moses* 1, 2
Sobr.   *On Sobriety*
Spec. Laws 1, 2, 3, 4   *On the Special Laws* 1, 2, 3, 4
Virtues   *On the Virtues*

Plato
Apol.   *Apology of Socrates*
Ep.   *Epistles*

Euthyphr.	*Euthyphro*
Leg.	*Laws*
Phaed.	*Phaedo*
Phaedr.	*Phaedrus*
Pol.	*Statesman*
Resp.	*Republic*
Symp.	*Symposium*
Tim.	*Timaeus*

Pliny the Elder

| *Nat.* | *Natural History* |

Plutarch

Adul. amic.	*How to Tell a Flatterer from a Friend*
Ag. Cleom.	*Agis and Cleomenes*
Alex.	*Alexander*
Cam.	*Camillus*
Cim.	*Cimon*
Cleom.	*Cleomenes*
Comp. Cim. Luc.	*Comparison of Cimon and Lucullus*
De laude	*On Praising Oneself Inoffensively*
Luc.	*Lucullus*
Lyc.	*Lycurgus*
Mor.	*Moralia*
Num.	*Numa*
Tim.	*Timoleon*
Virt. prof.	*How a Man May Become Aware of His Progress in Virtue*

Seneca

Ben.	*On Benefits*
Brev. vit.	*De brevitate vitae*
Ep.	*Epistles*
Vit. beat.	*De vita beata*

Stobaeus

| *Flor.* | *Florilegium* |

Suetonius

| *Cal.* | *Gaius Caligula* |

Tertullian

Idol.	*Idolatry*
Marc.	*Against Marcion*
Or.	*Prayer*
Pud.	*Modesty*

Vergil

Aen.	*Aeneid*

Xenophon

Cyr.	*Cyropaedia*
Mem.	*Memorabilia*
Oec.	*Oeconomicus*

INTRODUCTION

WHY DOES LUKE'S STORY
of JESUS MATTER?

AS I SAT DOWN TO EDIT THIS MANUSCRIPT, I paused briefly for a quick prayer, a practice which I am still trying to form into habit. I had a refrain on my mind, one that has lingered before many a significant task over the past few years. Surprisingly, perhaps, it was not a line of Scripture but rather a bit of advice from Plato's Socrates to Timaeus, reminding him that all "who possess even a small share of good sense call upon God always at the outset of every undertaking, be it small or great."[1] In Luke also, Jesus prays before the critical events in his life, but my thoughts were drawn first to Plato. Why? Socrates's pithy advice rings in my ears, bringing Jesus' example to life. Sometimes texts can become almost too familiar—so much so that their messages lose their initial punch. Socrates's simple line has enabled me to begin to put Jesus' teachings into practice. Particularly when we are dealing with the ancient and familiar text of Scripture, we sometimes need the help of other ancient voices to hear the text in the way that its first hearers might have experienced it. This book invites readers into the practice of reading Luke's portrait of Jesus within its ancient context and with its earliest readers in the hopes that our own understanding and experience of the text will be enlarged.

Jesus' practices of simplicity, humility, and prayer are fitting to explore because they are profoundly Lukan emphases and have been foundational spiritual practices in the church's life of faith since its inception. They remain critical, if not always adequately present, characteristics of the

---

[1] Plato, *Tim.* 27c.

church today. I have been exploring Lukan texts in these three areas with my students for nearly twenty years and know that for those who are able to really hear Luke's invitation to imitate Jesus' spiritual practices, the experience can be transformative. My desire for my readers is for them to have their understandings of these biblical texts expanded in order that they too might accept Luke's invitation into a life of simplicity, humility, and prayer. Luke's story of Jesus' spiritual practices is important for the church's life of faith because Luke has set Jesus up as a pattern for us to follow. As we individually and corporately imitate Jesus, we live lives of greater authenticity, we are oriented toward his kingdom, and we are transformed by his manner of life.

READING LUKE THROUGH FIRST-CENTURY EYES:
IMITATION AS A MEANS FOR TRANSFORMATION

Those of us who study the Bible academically often approach it as a repository of historical and cultural information about the ancient world. Our intent is to analyze the text as objectively as possible in order to more fully understand its context, history, and message. We typically reserve discussions about its application for Sunday school and assume that questions about the practicalities of faith might only confuse a more objective reading of the text. But this attitude would have been alien to Luke's earliest interpreters.

We often read a modern biography because the figure piques our interest, or we want to possess more information about that individual or the period in which he or she lived. Biographies in Luke's cultural world, however, typically aimed to do more than inform or entertain. Charles Talbert points out that ancient biography was designed "to reveal the character or essence of the individual often with the purpose of affecting the behavior of the reader."[2] While a discussion of the genre of Luke's Gospel is beyond the purview of this book, and while the Gospel was likely written with many purposes, Luke shares with ancient Mediterranean biographies an intent to impact the life of the reader. For instance, Lucian,

---

[2]Charles H. Talbert, *What Is a Gospel?: The Genre of the Canonical Gospels* (Philadelphia: Fortress Press, 1977), 17.

a popular second-century writer, provides an idealized portrait of the philosopher Demonax, observing that character is not best formed by laws or moral guidelines but through an actual example of a virtuous person. In his *Life of Demonax*, Lucian writes, "It is now fitting to tell of Demonax . . . that young men of good instincts who aspire to philosophy may not have to shape themselves by ancient precedents alone, but may be able to set themselves a pattern from our modern world and to copy that man, the best of all the philosophers I know about."[3] Biographies like this might lead others to virtue through their emulation of the literary hero. We see this same goal in Plutarch, a biographer roughly contemporary with Luke. Plutarch's purpose in writing was not so much to give a straightforward account of the actions or internal life of his subjects, as we might expect from a modern biographer, but to give character studies and moral examples. He writes,

> I began the writing of my "Lives" for the sake of others, but I find that I am continuing the work and delighting in it now for my own sake also, using history as a mirror and endeavouring in a manner to fashion and adorn my life in conformity with the virtues therein depicted.[4]

Plutarch's practice of setting up his characters as virtuous models for readers to follow is so effective that he finds himself transformed by them as well! Luke's earliest readers may also have recognized Jesus as a person of virtue who was worthy of emulation, responding to Luke's invitation to pattern their lives after Jesus.

THE MODEL OF THE IDEAL KING

In order to read Luke well, we should try to understand what his first readers might have been thinking. Biographers from Luke's historical and cultural world would sometimes write about virtuous kings to inspire their audiences to greater virtue. In order to benefit from the power of that model, however, we must understand a few things about ideal kingship in the wider thought world of Luke's day.

---

[3]Lucian, *Demon.* 2.
[4]Plutarch, *Tim.* 1.1.

From the time of Plato, many people felt that the best form of law was the exemplary leadership of an ideal king who actually embodied divine law. Plato felt that the "best thing is not that the laws be in power, but that the man who is wise and of kingly nature be ruler."[5] This idealized philosopher-king was known as a *living law*, and the example of his virtuous life was thought to provide a law higher than that of any written code. Such a king, who was "regarded as a law with eyes for men," had the ability to apply the divine law that he had internalized to a great variety of circumstances,[6] and his personal example was thought to effect transformation in the lives of his subjects. Plato despaired of ever finding such a person, however. He says, "At present such a nature exists nowhere at all, except in small degree; wherefore we must choose what is second best, namely, ordinance and law, which see and discern the general principle, but are unable to see every instance in detail."[7] While Plato was disillusioned with the models before him, the persisting idealization of this philosopher-king in the centuries after him creates an important context for understanding the ways in which Luke's intended audience would have responded to his portrait of Jesus.

An ideal king's ability to embody the law of God meant that such an individual was uniquely capable of effecting transformation in others. Ecphantus, the legendary Greek philosopher, says that of all people "a king alone is capable of effecting this good in human nature."[8] Such a king, "assimilating himself to one . . . will beneficently endeavour to render all whom he governs similar to himself."[9] Isocrates, a Greek rhetorician, counsels Demonicus to "pattern after the character of kings, and follow closely their ways," to go beyond obedience to their written laws, considering "their manner of life your highest law."[10] For Plutarch, Numa's exemplary character and unique ability to transform his people is due to his embodiment of divine law:

---

[5]Plato, *Pol.* 294a.
[6]Xenophon, *Cyr.* 8.1.22.
[7]Plato, *Leg.* 9.875c.
[8]Ecphantus, *On a Kingdom*, in *Political Fragments of Archytas, Charondas, Zaleucus, and Other Ancient Pythagoreans Preserved by Stobaeus*, trans. Thomas Taylor (Chiswick: C. Whittingham, 1822).
[9]Ecphantus, *Kingdom*, 34.
[10]Isocrates, *Dem.* 36.

> Either fear of the gods, who seemed to have him in their especial care, or reverence for his virtue, or a marvellous felicity, which in his days kept life free from the taint of every vice, and pure, made him a manifest illustration and confirmation of the saying which Plato, many generations later, ventured to utter regarding government, namely, that human ills would only then cease and disappear when, by some divine felicity, the power of a king should be united in one person with the insight of a philosopher, thereby establishing virtue in control and mastery over vice.[11]

For Plutarch, when people "see with their own eyes a conspicuous and shining example of virtue in the life of their ruler, they will of their own accord walk in wisdom's ways . . . attended by righteousness and temperance. Such a life is the noblest end of all government, and he is most a king who can inculcate such a life and such a disposition in his subjects."[12] Plutarch's point to his readers is clear: similar to Numa's subjects, they too can aspire to righteousness through their imitation of this ideal king.

Jewish literature also speaks of the yearning for a leader who will legislate through personal example. Hope for a just king lies behind the Israelites' initial request for a king, since Samuel's sons went after personal gain and perverted justice (2 Kings 8:3). Frustrated hope for a righteous king is also apparent in descriptions of Saul's kingship, which fails due to his refusal to obey God's laws.[13] David, however, is portrayed as an ideal king: 2 Samuel records that David "administered justice and equity to all his people" (8:15). The fact that many kings did not live up to this ideal of righteousness did not diminish the expectation for such a leader. Isaiah speaks of a future king who "will bring forth justice to the nations" (Is 42:1). This ideal is also found in royal psalms. Psalm 72:1-2 is a prayer that God will produce a king who will rule through God's own righteous example:

> Give the king thy justice, O God,
>   and thy righteousness to the royal son!
> May he judge thy people with righteousness
>   and thy poor with justice! (RSV)

---

[11]Plutarch, *Num.* 20.7-8.

[12]Plutarch, *Num.* 20.7-8.

[13]He refuses to devote all the spoils of war to destruction as God had commanded (1 Sam 15:1-34).

By the time of the first century, the Greek ideal of the philosopher-king was so widespread and influential that it also influenced Jewish ideas.[14] Philo adopts the Hellenistic ideal that a king's legislation should come out of his own being. He notes: "the king is a living law, and the law a just king."[15] Abraham, who "did the divine law and the divine commands," was "himself a law and an unwritten statute."[16] For Philo, Moses is a "reasonable and living impersonation of law"[17] who instructed his subjects by "setting before them the monument of his own life like an original design to be their beautiful model."[18] Moses' unique capacity as living law came from his relationship with God. He was able to penetrate "into the darkness where God was," which enabled his life to be "beautiful and godlike, a model for those who are willing to copy it."[19] Those who imitate Moses are, in effect, imitating God, whom Moses himself imitates so well. Philo notes that Moses' ability to save his subjects extended even after his death: "Thus all future rulers would find a law to guide them right by looking to Moses as their archetype and model."[20]

The pervasive idealization of the philosopher king in the first-century Mediterranean world would have certainly shaped the expectations of Luke's intended readership. Luke's earliest readers would have been primed to look for a righteous king with an ability to legislate from personal example. If Luke's readers recognized in Jesus the characteristics of an ideal king, they would have had heightened expectations for their encounter with Jesus to be a transforming experience.

The Model of the Ideal Teacher

In today's society, we typically judge the merits of a teacher on his or her grasp of subject matter, ability to lecture well, and capabilities in

---

[14]Glenn Chesnut, "The Ruler and the Logos in Neopythagorean, Middle Platonic, and Late Stoic Political Philosophy," in *Aufstieg und Niedergang der römischen Welt: Geschichte und Kultur Roms im Spiegel der neueren Forschung*, part 2, *Principat*, ed. Hildegard Temporini and Wolfgang Haase (Berlin: de Gruyter, 1972–), 16.2:1310-32, 1326.

[15]Philo, *Moses* 2.1.4.

[16]Philo, *Abraham* 46.276.

[17]Philo, *Moses* 1.28.162.

[18]Philo, *Virtues* 9.51.

[19]Philo, *Moses* 1.28.158.

[20]Philo, *Virtues* 11.70.

facilitating student learning. Luke's audience would have had somewhat different expectations for ideal teachers. In Luke's literary world, philosophy was seen as a "guide to life": it was not just an intellectual conversation but also a mandate for living.[21] The study of philosophy for the exercise of the mind alone was a thought alien to the minds of early philosophers. Seneca, a contemporary with Paul, notes that philosophy "is not devised for show. It is not pursued in order that the day may yield some amusement." Rather, it "moulds and constructs the soul; it orders our life, guides our conduct, shows us what we should do."[22]

The ancient world carried such an expectation for philosophers to demonstrate a unity of thought and action that the worthiness of a philosopher was judged on the basis of the practical results of his or her lifestyle. In a Cynic letter, the philosopher Diogenes makes it clear that he thinks an introduction to a certain philosopher is unnecessary since "you will know that he is a man from his portraits, and from his life and words whether he is also a philosopher."[23] Epictetus, a first-century philosopher, similarly demands, "Show me a man fashioned according to the judgments which he utters!"[24] The expectation that an ideal philosopher would instruct through his or her lifestyle was so strong that for ancient Mediterranean people an ideal philosophical education involved spending time in the company of a genuine sage, rather than merely studying a philosopher's teachings in an academy. The ancient Greek philosopher Xenophon accordingly notes that "nothing was more useful than the companionship of Socrates, and time spent with him in any place and in any circumstances." Indeed, even "the very recollection of him in absence brought no small good to his constant companions and followers."[25] We see a similar

---

[21]M. L. Clarke, *The Roman Mind: Studies in the History of Thought from Cicero to Marcus Aurelius* (Cambridge: Harvard University Press, 1965), 72.

[22]Seneca, *Ep.* 16.3.

[23]Diogenes, *Ep.* 18, in Malherbe, Abraham J. *The Cynic Epistles: A Study Edition*. Missoula, MT: Scholars Press for the Society of Biblical Literature, 1977. The dating of the pseudonymous letters of Diogenes is complicated. The individual letters fall into groups that were written in different periods by different authors. The eighteenth letter is considered to be composed earlier than the late second century.

[24]Epictetus, *Discourses* 2.19.

[25]Xenophon, *Mem.* 4.1.1.

idea in Seneca when he counsels a disciple to "choose a master whose life, conversation, and soul-expressing face have satisfied you; picture him always to yourself as your protector or your pattern."[26] Seneca counseled those looking for a teacher to choose those "who teach us by their lives, men who tell us what we ought to do and then prove it by practice, who show us what we should avoid, and then are never caught doing that which they have ordered us to avoid."[27]

Much Jewish literature similarly mirrors the Hellenistic ideal for a teacher to instruct through his or her lifestyle. In the Wisdom of Solomon, likely written in the first century BCE, for instance, the wicked complain that a righteous man

> became to us a reproof of our thoughts;
> the very sight of him is a burden to us,
> because his manner of life is unlike that of others. (Wis 2:14-15 RSV)

Just keeping company with the wise was thought to be a great benefit. Sirach, probably written in the second century BCE, thus encourages those seeking wisdom to "let righteous men be your dinner companions" (Sir 9:16 RSV).

Within first-century Judaism, we also find the idea that an ideal teacher will instruct through personal example.[28] Philo notes that Joseph's companions in prison "were rebuked by his wise words and doctrines of philosophy, while the conduct of their teacher effected more than any words." Joseph, "by setting before them his life of temperance and every virtue, like an original picture of skilled workmanship . . . converted even those who seemed quite incurable."[29] Philo, like other writers in Luke's literary world, idealizes wise teachers who are able to move their students to virtue through their own exemplary lifestyles. Luke's readership might well have had similar expectations for Jesus.

Luke's intended audience lived in a cultural environment that idealized teachers and kings who were able to lead through their own virtuous

---

[26]Seneca, *Ep.* 11.10.

[27]Seneca, *Ep.* 52.8.

[28]Charles H. Talbert accordingly has noted that "it takes no argument to establish what everyone knows, namely, that Judaism's concern for the Law was a concern for it as a guide for life." *Literary Patterns, Theological Themes, and the Genre of Luke-Acts* (Missoula, MT: Scholars Press, 1974), 92.

[29]Philo, *Joseph* 16.86-87.

example. They may have, with Plato, longed for a virtuous philosopher-king who could save his people through effective, exemplary leadership. Luke writes his narrative of Jesus' life in a way that clearly sets Jesus up as this kind of teacher. His Gospel concerns "all that Jesus did and taught" (Acts 1:1). Repeatedly, Luke connects Jesus' teaching with the pattern of his life.[30] Luke's intended audience would also have resonated with the power of this kind of portrait to effect transformation. They might well have come to the reading of Luke's Gospel expecting to be changed through the lifestyle and teaching of Jesus. As contemporary readers, we want to try to read Luke's portrait of Jesus with a similar set of expectations, not just so that we can gain a fuller appreciation of an ancient text but so that we can be similarly formed by our own interaction with Jesus' character.

HOW CAN WE AS A PEOPLE OF FAITH UNDERSTAND LUKE'S NARRATIVE?

One of the first things that we must realize when reading Luke is that we are dealing with a piece of ancient narrative, and as such, it will be more challenging for us to hear the text on its own terms and to make sense of it in a way that is relevant for the concerns of our own time. Interpreting an ancient text is not an exact science.[31] Meaning comes as a result of the dance between text and interpreter, as our horizons of understanding intersect with the horizon of the text. Meaning is not located in the mind of the real author of the text, nor is it entirely dependent on the reader, as if the text were a series of inkblots onto which we posit our own under-standings. We try to follow the directions of the text, even as we look at the world and at history through the lenses of our own experiences, his-tories, presuppositions, and understandings.

Imagine all of time and history on a long continuum. Somewhere along that continuum you are located. Picture a set of imaginary brackets at that

---

[30]Luke 4:1-13; 22:39-46.

[31]Modern literary theory has abandoned the illusion of assuming that we can somehow objectively view the past from an unbiased perspective. Historical context is not an "independent series of events that exists apart from an observer," and a literary work "is not an object that stands by itself and that offers the same view to each reader in each period." Hans Robert Jauss, *Toward an Aesthetic*, trans. Timothy Bahti (Minneapolis: University of Minnesota Press, 1982), 21.

point that provide the parameters of your perspective. This is your horizon, or your range of vision that includes everything that you can see from your vantage point. Your horizon includes your understandings, beliefs, presumptions, culturally dictated assumptions—everything that gives you your own perspective within time. As you grow and mature, your horizon expands. Your knowledge base grows, your perceptions change, your attitudes mature. Your "horizon" of understanding, therefore, is continually changing. Because we are located at ever-changing points along the horizon of time and history, we cannot step outside of our own locatedness to objectively view another period in history. Instead, when we look at another point in history, we are attempting to fuse our horizons of understanding with the horizon of that point in history. How might we do that? To that question, we now turn.

A First Reception

Modern readers of ancient literary works face a greater challenge than the original readers since today's perspectives can be so distant from those of the first audience. If we are unfamiliar with the contextual concerns of author and audience, we may inadvertently impose contemporary understandings and attitudes onto an ancient text. Looking at the possible expectations that Luke's intended audience might have brought to the text introduces a starting place to enter into a conversation with Luke's portrait of Jesus.[32] Our reading of Luke and our ability to be spiritually formed through Luke's portrait of Jesus will be enhanced by our ability to ask the kinds of questions that Luke's Gospel was written to answer.[33]

Luke wrote with intended readers in mind that he expected would be able to understand and be transformed by his portrait of Jesus. The *intended* readers or the *authorial audience* are the readers that the text

---

[32]Peter J. Rabinowitz, "Whirl Without End: Audience Oriented Criticism," in *Contemporary Literary Theory*, ed. G. Douglas Atkins and Laura Morrow (Amherst: University of Massachusetts Press, 1989), 85.

[33]As Rabinowitz observes, "If historically or culturally distant texts are hard to understand it is often precisely because we do not possess the knowledge required to join the authorial audience." Peter J. Rabinowitz, "Truth in Fiction: A Reexamination of Audiences," *Critical Inquiry* 4 (1977): 127.

was written for and that the text to some degree assumes. They are the readers presupposed by the text, sometimes called *"contextualized implied readers."*[34] Our exploration of the hypothetical *first reception* of the Lukan text requires that we ask what type of audience Luke had in mind. What were their assumptions? How might Luke's portrait of Jesus have resonated with them, given their cultural environment? What patterns do we see in Luke's literary world that might help us to understand the expectations, and therefore the reading experience, of Luke's intended audience? Luke writes for a particular audience and the closer we can get to their reading experience, the better we will be positioned to respond to Luke's invitations.

Studying the intended readers' horizons of understanding is part of a literary theory that is known as reception theory. Reception theory was developed in the late 1960s in Germany by a group of literary scholars at the University of Constance who sought to bring ancient texts to life for contemporary readers. One of them, Hans Robert Jauss, argues that this method is "indispensable" for understanding ancient literature. When dealing with an ancient text in which the author's intent is unknown, readers can use this method to try to discover the questions that the text answers. This helps contemporary readers get closer to understanding how the intended audience might have understood the text.

Jauss advocated familiarizing oneself with other literary works that share a similar cultural context with the work being studied.[35] By doing this, we explore the hypothetical *first* reception of the text by trying to comprehend the understandings, beliefs, presumptions, and culturally dictated assumptions that the text and its first readers might have made. This can enable us to understand the expectations that may have existed when the work first appeared and read with the kinds of questions and

---

[34]Rabinowitz, "Whirl Without End," 84-85.

[35]Jauss observes, "The method of historical reception is indispensable for the understanding of literature from the distant past. When the author of a work is unknown, his intent undeclared, and his relationship to sources and models only indirectly accessible, the philological question of how the text is 'properly'—that is, 'from its intention and time'—to be understood can best be answered if one foregrounds it against those works that the author explicitly or implicitly presupposed his contemporary audience to know." *Toward an Aesthetic*, 28.

expectations that the text was written to answer. In this way, author and reader will be speaking a similar cultural and historical language. Practically, this means that if Luke's intended audience would have been familiar with expectations for ideal philosophers and kings to be virtuous and to lead others to righteousness, they might approach Luke's biography of Jesus with an expectation for formation. Since contemporary scholarly readers value objective distance in their reading of biblical texts, we might not then "deal with texts in the act of interpreting in the same way as the author dealt with them in the act of writing."[36]

Some qualifications are in order. First, we of course cannot assume that we can maintain some objective standpoint from which to view the conceptual world of the readers.[37] Reading against the background of the works the author presupposed his contemporary audience to know does not assume that the author's real readers would have been consciously aware of these particular texts.[38] Instead, "these texts help to establish the *most likely conceptual world* of the readers, the authorial audience," and to understand the "broader societal ways of looking at the world."[39] As we remind ourselves that this is not an exact science and that the boundaries of these categories may be hazier than we would like, we can still move a few steps closer to entering into this conceptual world. Second, if we cannot read with complete objectivity, we also are unable to assume an objective first audience for a text. It is also important to note that by "authorial audience we are not necessarily referring to a particular, localized community from which and for which a text is alleged to have originated. Rather the authorial audience refers to the larger cultural milieu within which a document was read/heard."[40] We also cannot assume that the original readers came from a completely homogenous background or that they would have all read in identical ways.

---

[36]Joel Green's definition of Umberto Eco's "model reader" in *Seized by Truth: Reading the Bible as Scripture* (Nashville: Abingdon, 2007), 57.

[37]As Parris notes, "The reconstructed question is never identical with the original question the text sought to answer because any reconstruction of a past horizon is always enveloped in the present horizon of the interpreter." David Paul Parris, *Reception Theory and Biblical Hermeneutics*, Princeton Theological Monographs 107 (Eugene, OR: Pickwick, 2009), 139.

[38]Charles H. Talbert, *Reading Luke-Acts in Its Mediterranean Milieu* (Leiden: Brill, 2003), 16.

[39]Talbert, *Reading Luke-Acts*, 16 (emphasis added).

[40]Talbert, *Reading Luke-Acts*, 17.

READING LUKE WITH AND FOR THE CHURCH

Starting with the Enlightenment, biblical scholars thought that it was appropriate to bracket out issues of faith and formation in order to have a more objective approach to the text. Today, understanding that there is no such thing as a purely objective reading of any text, some scholars try to read the Bible from an intentionally *interested* position,[41] with and for the church. This theological interpretation of Scripture sometimes adopts reception theory as a means of expanding the interpretive conversation to include not only contemporary scholarship on the Bible but voices from the early church as well.

The richness of our past interpretive tradition promises not only to uncover fresh interpretations but also to transform our attitudes. Reading Jesus' injunction against worry (Lk. 12:22-34) through the lens of the early church's great confidence in God's provision has promise to expand our own limits of faith. Learning that the early church saw humility as the foundation for the life of faith can revive for us what has become a forgotten virtue. Reading through the eyes of early Lukan interpreters can challenge our self-sufficiency and perhaps for the first time enable us to really believe in the efficacy of prayer. We engage with our forefathers and foremothers who approached the text as their Scripture and whose motivation for study stemmed from a desire to know and love God more deeply and to communicate scriptural portraits of that God to the church. We inherit from them not only new interpretations but a fundamentally new attitude toward Scripture. They call us back to a position of reverent submission to the Word of God and enjoin us to interpretive habits that are dependent on prayer, listening for the voice of God in solitude, and displacing our deified selves in a practiced humility. In other words, they reorient us to the priority of Christ and his kingdom. Reading Scripture with the early church does not mean that we adopt all of their perspectives as our own or that we forget the wealth of contemporary scholarship. It does not have to be pitted against the interpretive methods to which we

---

[41]Theological interpretation of Scripture may be seen as an example of an "interested" reading. Green, *Seized by Truth*, 17.

have become accustomed. It does mean, however, that we prioritize the text as the church's Scripture. As those who seek to interpret Scripture within the long tradition of the church, we come to our task with a desire to be transformed into the image of Christ. This book assumes that it is possible for us as contemporary readers to make sense of Scripture in a way that honors the formative intent of the texts that we study and that stretches our understandings. It assumes that the scriptural portrait of Jesus has inherent power to conform us, as willing readers, to the image of Christ. Plutarch tells his readers that the study of his heroes has transformed his own life by giving him models of virtue to emulate.[42] We, however, stand with the church in reception of the Word of God, formed in Christ by the power of the Spirit. We recognize the power of imitation but also that we do not imitate Jesus through our own abilities. Luke has given us a portrait of Jesus to emulate with the knowledge that this is made possible through the Holy Spirit, working within us and among us.

This book invites readers to explore the spiritual disciplines of simplicity, humility, and prayer with Luke's earliest readers. Simplicity rejects greed, embraces a nonmaterialistic lifestyle, practices generosity, and understands true value in life apart from money or possessions. Humility, rooted in an accurate self-assessment, rejects arrogant pride, which is seen in a desire to gain or maintain status, glorying in undeserved honors, and self-praise. Prayer is communion with God, oriented toward God's will, grounded in confidence in God's provision, and essential for spiritual strength. The book is organized in three major sections. Chapters 1, 4, and 7 provide a brief exegetical discussion of Lukan texts on simplicity, humility, and prayer, respectively. Chapters 2, 5, and 8 explore the way in which these texts might have been understood by Luke's intended audience. Chapters 3, 6, and 9 trace conversations about these texts in the early church through the post-Nicene era. This book is written with the hopes that the practice of reading with Luke's earliest interpreters will expand the horizons of our understanding, enabling us to embrace the power of Jesus' example.

---

[42]Plutarch, *Tim.* 1.1.

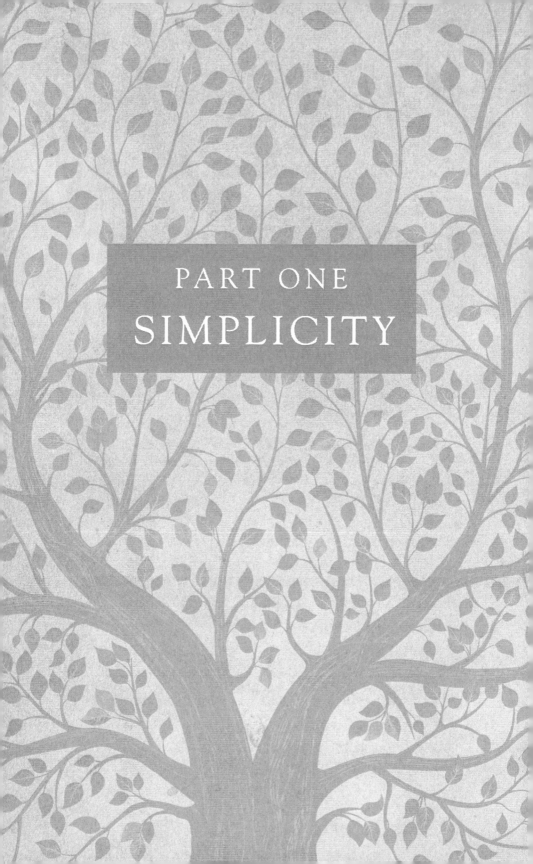

PART ONE
SIMPLICITY

1

SIMPLICITY IN THE GOSPEL NARRATIVE

AT SOME TIME OR ANOTHER, most of us have worried about money. We have fretted over how to pay off higher-than-expected bills, credit card debt, and student loans, or perhaps have even exchanged our dream career for one that promises more security. As I write, these fears are particularly acute: the crisis resulting from the coronavirus pandemic has cratered the global economy and many have lost or are terrified of losing their jobs. We are realists. We know that Jesus doesn't want us to live lives oriented around money, but the bills still need to be paid. How do we make sense of Jesus' teachings on money, given the financial realities of our lives? In Luke, Jesus promotes a lifestyle oriented around the kingdom of God instead of money, releasing us from a preoccupation with money that stems from need as well as greed. Jesus invites those who are anxious about putting food on the table, paying the rent, or even finding a safe place to sleep at night into a daily dependence upon God's provision, and urges the rest of us to step up to care for them.

GIVE TO EVERYONE WHO ASKS (LUKE 6:27–38)

In this text, Jesus teaches his disciples that they must extend themselves in love and generosity, not only to their friends but to everyone in imitation of God. Often when we engage in missions with those less economically advantaged than we are, we will travel to a mission site, do some act of service, and then return to our comfortable homes. We often operate with an "us-them" mentality, regardless of how well-intentioned we may be. For Jesus, however, the poor are friends with whom we share our possessions.[1] When we exercise this kind of practical love toward others, we imitate God's own generosity (Lk 6:33).[2] God gives like a generous merchant who, without care for personal profit, fills the measuring cup until it overflows (Lk 6:38).[3] Any magnanimity we demonstrate is ultimately rooted in the nature of God and shows that we are children of our great Benefactor (Lk 6:35-36).[4]

It is difficult to understand Jesus' teaching on money in Luke without a little insight into the conversations about money that were taking place in the first century. The language of "doing good" (Lk 6:27) should be understood within the context of ancient benefaction.[5] In Luke's day, there was an expectation that those who had money would be benefactors for those less fortunate. However, along with that came an expectation for some sort of reciprocation. If a patron gave a gift, the client knew that there were strings attached—even if that was measured in loyalty. For Luke, however, those who give in anticipation of reciprocation do not exhibit the kind of love Jesus demands (Lk 6:32-34).[6] Rejecting the normative patterns of reciprocity, Jesus here makes clear that simplicity involves the ability to give with no expectation of return (Lk 6:33). His disciples should not even expect gratitude as a return for their benefactions.[7] The behavior of God's children should not be governed by the actions of others but by God's character.[8] The only reward that members of the kingdom can expect for their gifts comes from God, the source of their benefaction.[9]

Such generosity should not be limited to our closest social circles either but distributed to "everyone." These instructions aren't just for the very wealthy. The description of Jesus' audience indicates that the disciples had

[1]Joel B. Green, *The Gospel of Luke*, New International Commentary on the New Testament (Grand Rapids: Eerdmans, 1997), 270.

[2]James R. Edwards, *The Gospel According to Luke* (Grand Rapids: Eerdmans, 2015), 198.

[3]Green, *Gospel of Luke*, 275.

[4]Green, *Gospel of Luke*, 271. We will act like God's children; not, we will become God's children (274).

[5]In Acts, Jesus is a benefactor who is "doing good" (Acts 10:38). Mikeal C. Parsons, *Luke* (Grand Rapids: Baker Academic, 2015), 108.

[6]Charles H. Talbert, *Reading Luke-Acts in Its Mediterranean Milieu* (Leiden: Brill, 2003), 75.

[7]Halvor Moxnes, *The Economy of the Kingdom: Social Conflict and Economic Relations in Luke's Gospel* (Philadelphia: Fortress, 1988), 133.

[8]Edwards, *Gospel According to Luke*, 198.

[9]Green, *Gospel of Luke*, 270.

at least some possessions, such as an outer cloak or money that might be lent (Lk 6:29, 35).[10] Jesus points out that love for enemies (Lk 5:27–6:11, 22-23) is also expressed through giving.[11] Such generosity is an essential element of the lifestyle of members of the kingdom of God.

THE RICH MAN AND HIS BARNS (LUKE 12:13–21)

In Luke's story of the rich man and his barns, the rich man tears down his barns and replaces them with larger ones that can store his bumper crop of a harvest. If we looked at this story outside of its context of greed in Luke, we might describe this character simply as a shrewd businessperson. By way of analogy, we might think of a real estate developer in a highly desirable area who bulldozes a few small shops to make room for a lucrative shopping mall. The context, however, juxtaposes a lifestyle of greed, a desire to have more than others, with that of utter dependence on God.[12] In both the Jewish and Greco-Roman worlds, greed was considered to be a form of moral corruption.[13] Jesus, directing his teaching to the crowd, places "life" in direct contrast to "possessions" (Lk 12:15), suggesting that genuine life is not obtainable when one has an abundance of possessions.[14]

In language that recalls the Pharisaic propensity for greed (Lk 11:39),[15] someone from the crowd[16] abruptly interrupts Jesus' teaching in an effort to urge Jesus to assist him in obtaining his share of the family inheritance. Although the Mosaic law allowed for an inheritance to be divided, keeping the inheritance intact by having the inheritors share the estate together was the ideal.[17] While religious teachers sometimes arbitrated in such legal matters, Jesus rejects this role.[18]

---

[10]Green, *Gospel of Luke*, 271.

[11]Green, *Gospel of Luke*, 272.

[12]François Bovon, *Luke 2: A Commentary on the Gospel of Luke 9:51–19:27*, Hermeneia (Minneapolis: Fortress, 2013), 198.

[13]Green, *Gospel of Luke*, 489.

[14]Thomas E. Schmidt, *Hostility to Wealth in the Synoptic Gospels* (Sheffield, England: JSOT Press, 1987), 146.

[15]Green, *Gospel of Luke*, 488.

[16]Jesus' teachings on simplicity are not a behavioral norm for only a select group of disciples but for the crowds as well (Lk 12:13).

[17]Bovon, *Luke 2*, 195.

[18]Joseph A. Fitzmyer, *The Gospel According to Luke*, 2 vols., Anchor Bible 28-28A (Garden City, NY: Doubleday, 1985), 968-69 (pages are numbered sequentially throughout the two vols.).

Jesus then introduces a parable about "a rich man"[19] whose primary orientation is possessions (Lk 12:15). His speech and actions show that he is self-sufficient, having no need for God,[20] but likely mask a motivation of fear.[21] Jesus calls him a "fool," recalling images from the Wisdom literature of the Hebrew Bible, where a "fool" acts as if God does not exist (see Ps 14:1).[22] With no ability to see God's provision, he feels the need to secure his own future. Ironically, another reason for his "foolishness" is that he has apparently forgotten the second part of the idiom, "Let us eat and drink, *for tomorrow we die.*"[23]

The decision to replace barns in order to store the abundant crop also is based in greed (Lk 12:17-18). Rather than building additional barns on land that could be used for farming, or selling his grain to a presumably glutted market, he chooses to store it for a less profitable season when he can charge a greater price for his grain.[24] His wealth is evident in his ability to afford to build new barns for the additional grain and his other "goods" (Lk 12:18). His monologue shows no thought for the welfare of others; rather, he uses a common idiom to describe the hedonistic lifestyle he desires.[25]

In the movie *You've Got Mail*, Meg Ryan's character, Kathleen Kelly, owns a small, independent bookstore that is run out of business by the mega-bookstore Fox Books. Her little bookstore just can't compete with the nearby mega-store. Just as Joe Fox (played by Tom Hanks) has not considered the effect his business will have on smaller bookstores in the area, so in Luke's story the landowner's decision to hold back the surplus of grain seems to be made with only his own financial health in mind. Such a decision would have affected the village's economy[26] and been extremely

---

See also Robert C. Tannehill, *Luke*, Abingdon New Testament Commentaries (Nashville: Abingdon, 1996), 205.

[19]This has a verbal parallel with Lk 16:19; both rich men are unconcerned about anyone else. Parsons, *Luke*, 205.

[20]Green, *Gospel of Luke*, 487.

[21]Bovon, *Luke 2*, 198.

[22]Fitzmyer, *Gospel According to Luke*, 972.

[23]Tannehill, *Luke*, 206.

[24]Green, *Gospel of Luke*, 490.

[25]Tannehill, *Luke*, 206.

[26]Green, *Gospel of Luke*, 491.

distasteful to those struggling to meet daily needs. The wealthy were expected to engage in benefactions,[27] but this landowner's wealth comes at the cost of those around him. His primary orientation is money, but he is not "rich toward God," meaning that he is stingy with both his resources (Lk 14:33) and himself (Lk 9:23) and has thereby excluded himself from the kingdom.[28] If we are to have the characteristics of God, our primary orientation must be toward God's kingdom, clearly evident in both our attitudes and the way in which we allocate our resources.

GOD'S PRACTICAL PROVISION (LUKE 12:22–34)

In these next few verses, Jesus supplies a commentary on the parable of the rich fool, emphasizing the need to rely on the beneficence of God (Lk 12:22-34).[29] This text is one that we might struggle with. As many students have told me, it just doesn't seem realistic. Are we really supposed to rely on God for our needs as much as the birds or the lilies? Wouldn't this make us financially irresponsible? However, if we can catch Jesus' logic here, this text has the power to release us from the power that money can have over us.

First, the command to cease from anxiety (Lk 12:22) is balanced with the reason (Lk 12:23): "For life is more than food, and the body more than clothing."[30] Our culture promotes a lifestyle utterly oriented around the pursuit of money. Such a mentality chokes the beauty from life and reduces relationships to business transactions. Jesus would have more than that for us.

Second, Jesus points to our value to God. People are worth far more to God than birds and vegetation, and God will provide for us with even more care than God gives to the rest of creation.[31] The argument is "how

---

[27]Aristotle says that illiberality "takes two forms, stinginess and inordinate acquisitiveness." *Eth. nic.* 4.1.38, in Frederick W. Danker, *Benefactor: Epigraphic Study of a Graeco-Roman and New Testament Semantic Field* (St. Louis: Clayton, 1982), 248. It is interesting that many ancient commentaries on beneficence take for granted that the wealthy are expected to engage in general benefactions. The wealthy appear to be judged on their motives for giving rather than the act itself since the virtues of beneficence are assumed.

[28]Bovon, *Luke 2*, 203.

[29]Fitzmyer, *Gospel According to Luke*, 976.

[30]Talbert, *Reading Luke*, 141.

[31]Talbert, *Reading Luke*, 142.

much more." If God cares even for ravens, who were considered unclean by Jews and generally despised, or the grass that is trampled underfoot, how much more will God care for us (Lev 11:15; Deut 14:14)?[32]

Third, Jesus points to God's trustworthiness. Proof of God's gracious benefaction is all around us. Confidence in God is what has the power to free us to adopt a lifestyle of complete dependence on God. In contrast with the landowner, who must secure his own future, we are to place our confidence in God, freeing us from the fear that prohibits us from imitating God's generosity. Although the disciples are among the peasant class who must struggle for daily bread, they have already learned that God will supply their needs (Lk 11:1-13). Without faith, such dependence on God seems rash.[33] However, Jesus wants his disciples to be free from material concerns so that they can devote themselves to God's kingdom, knowing that life is more than obtaining basic necessities (Lk 12:23).[34]

Finally, Jesus points to the futility of worry. Fretting over the future could not help the wealthy landowner; neither will it add a single hour to one's life (Lk 12:25).[35] Instead of seeking material security, true disciples should seek spiritual security (Lk 12:31). Jesus reminds the disciples that God delights in making them a part of the kingdom, which is a far greater treasure than any material possessions they might accumulate.[36] He reassures them that those who seek the kingdom will receive God's provision for daily necessities and the release from anxiety that will enable them to practice almsgiving.[37] The appropriate alternative to preoccupations with wealth is benefaction.[38] Such generosity is an indication of righteousness and treasure in heaven.[39]

---

[32]Pliny the Elder, *Nat.* 35.7.23.

[33]Green, *Gospel of Luke*, 494.

[34]Fitzmyer, *Gospel According to Luke*, 978. Luke drops Matthew's "all" (Mt 6:33), noting simply that God is aware that they need "these things" (12:31). God does not know that they need all these things; God knows that they need necessities. Schmidt, *Hostility to Wealth*, 147.

[35]"Cubit" occurs in a temporal sense in Diogenes Laertius, *Plato* 3.11, and seems to fit the context of this discussion. Fitzmyer, *Gospel According to Luke*, 978; Bovon, *Luke 2*, 217.

[36]Fitzmyer, *Gospel According to Luke*, 980.

[37]Green, *Gospel of Luke*, 487. The worry in view here, *meteōrizomai*, refers to being "tossed about" on the waves, shaken about by life's concerns if one's primary orientation is not in God. Bovon, *Luke 2*, 220.

[38]Schmidt, *Hostility to Wealth*, 148

[39]Talbert, *Reading Luke*, 142.

The logic of this passage makes sense. If we are fearful of our financial futures, we will cling tightly to our possessions, generosity will be extremely difficult for us, and money will be the preoccupying center of life. Trust in God's ability to care for us releases us from our anxious preoccupation with money and frees us up to experience the fullness of kingdom life in imitation of God. For many of us, living into this may be a process. It may also be necessary to bring our values more in line with God's. Most of us are probably more concerned with living comfortably than with having life's necessities. Using this text to promote a gospel of prosperity is an utter misrepresentation of the cross and Jesus' teachings about wealth. Christianity isn't about personal fulfillment but about getting on board with God's vision for the world's needs.

DISPOSSESSION FOR JESUS' SAKE (LUKE 14:1-33)

The context of this story furthers Luke's growing characterization of the Pharisees as lovers of money. Jesus is invited to a Sabbath meal and heals a man with dropsy, a disease often used as a metaphor for greed.[40] Diogenes compared money lovers to people with dropsy because just as those who suffer from this disease desire to drink more in spite of their already bloated bodies, those who love money crave more even though it leads to further destruction of their souls.[41] At the dinner, Jesus rebukes his host for inviting only those wealthier guests who might reciprocate.[42] The guest list Jesus suggests instead includes "the poor, the crippled, the lame, and the blind"—in other words, those incapable of reciprocation.[43]

Jesus then outlines excuses that those laden with possessions might give that exclude them from the kingdom (Lk 14:18-20). Since those weighed down with their possessions and obligations reject the invitation to the banquet, the offer is extended to those who will gladly accept it. They are "compelled" to come and not expected to reciprocate.[44] Jesus finally says

---

[40]Willi Braun, *Feasting and Social Rhetoric in Luke 14* (Cambridge: Cambridge University Press, 1995), 30-42.

[41]Stob. flor. 3.10.45, comparison provided by Green, *Gospel of Luke*, 547.

[42]Moxnes, *Economy of the Kingdom*, 130.

[43]Moxnes, *Economy of the Kingdom*, 132.

[44]David E. Garland, *Luke*, Zondervan Exegetical Commentary on the New Testament (Grand Rapids: Zondervan, 2011), 591.

that radical dispossession is necessary for discipleship (Lk 14:33). The kings of the world attempt their tasks with great resources (Lk 14:31), useless in God's kingdom. Jesus' disciples, instead, must abandon their sources of security and seek heavenly treasure by thrusting themselves into God's care in a way that enables them to dispossess themselves.

Does this text imply that anyone who is serious about their faith needs to sell all of his or her possessions in order to follow Christ? Some have thought so. Athanasius tells the story of the desert father Anthony, who in response to the gospel message of dispossession quite literally gave away all of his belongings and went to the desert to live a monastic life.[45] Many contemporary interpreters understand Jesus' teaching to mean that the kingdom of God must be the ordering priority of our lives, not money. In this line of thought, just as we aren't literally intended to hate family members (Lk 14:26) but to prioritize Christ above all relationships, we aren't all necessarily called to complete dispossession but must be willing to dispossess ourselves for the sake of Christ if necessary. After all, there are wealthy individuals in both Luke and Acts who use their resources to advance God's kingdom work. Theophilus is likely Luke's wealthy bene-factor also. However, this perspective makes Jesus' teaching more about attitude than action, and if we consistently interpret Luke's teachings on wealth in this way, we will mute the transformative shock value of the text. Jesus' teachings probably made his first audience uncomfortable, and if we are reading Luke the way we should be, it will do the same for us. Acts gives us a picture of the earliest church putting Jesus' teachings into action. They aren't simply convincing themselves that money has no power over them while maintaining the comfort of their lifestyles; they are selling their belongings to take care of the poor so that Luke can actually say there was no one in need among them (Acts 4:34).

THE DISHONEST MANAGER (LUKE 16:1-9)

In this story, a dishonest manager is accused of squandering his master's property. Faced with the loss of his job and the unlikelihood of another

---

[45]Athanasius, *Vit. Ant.* 2-3.

one (Lk 16:3), he devises a plan to provide for his future (Lk 16:3-7). He decides to reduce the bills of each of his master's clients, hoping that when he is out of a job, they will take him in and provide for him. The extent of the debt highlights the extreme wealth of the master and shows that he is dealing with wealthy business clients.[46]

There are a couple of different ways to interpret the manager's plan. Some think that he gave up his commission in the hopes of attaining the favor of those whose debts he had reduced.[47] It is unlikely that his commission could be considered part of the amount that was owed to the master, however.[48] Another interpretation is that the termination of the manager's employment was not yet widely known. The length of time needed to fire the manager (by collecting his records and reviewing them) is reflected in the present tense "is taking . . . away" (16:3) and "when I am removed" (16:4).[49] During that time, the manager reduces the debts of his master's clients, pretending that he is doing so with the full knowledge and approval of his master.[50] Some commentators feel that since he is still acting as his master's manager, his arrangements are binding.[51] Others believe that although the master could object to the manager's agreements, the manager correctly assumes that his master would not want to risk his clients' hatred by undoing the manager's actions.[52] Through his cunning plan, the manager wins the favor of his master's clients, hoping that they will exercise hospitality toward him in the future when he is unemployed and homeless.

---

[46]For instance, the amount of oil owed would be the annual yield for a large olive grove; the wheat would represent the produce of almost two hundred acres. John Nolland, *Luke*, 3 vols., Word Biblical Commentary 35A-C (Dallas: Word, 1989–1993), 799. Bovon suggests that a laborer would need to work five hundred to six hundred days to pay for such a vast amount of oil. *Luke 2*, 448.

[47]See Fitzmyer, *Gospel According to Luke*, 1098, who does not wish to read the parable as "an approval of the dishonesty of the manager or an approval of any falsification of accounts." Also Moxnes, *Economy of the Kingdom*, 140.

[48]Parsons, *Luke*, 247.

[49]Green, *Gospel of Luke*, 592.

[50]Nolland, *Luke*, 797-98.

[51]Nolland, *Luke*, 800.

[52]Kenneth Ewing Bailey, *Poet and Peasant: A Literary Cultural Approach to the Parables in Luke* (Grand Rapids: Eerdmans, 1976), 102.

When Jesus teaches his disciples to "make friends" through dishonest wealth, he is telling them to make friends with the poor (by canceling debts or giving alms) so that their welcome may be into eternal homes (Lk 16:9). For this, they should not expect reciprocation but an eternal reward.[53] In the parable, the "friends" are the poor, and the provision of homes to the manager is analogous to the provision of heaven/the kingdom of God to the almsgivers. The mention of friendship recalls discussions of ideal friendship found in Luke's cultural world. Ideal friendship was supposed to occur between equals, and true friends were to share possessions. When Luke speaks of friendship, he envisions a relationship of equality—far removed from the obligations of a patron-client relationship and the patronizing charity that we sometimes bestow on the "less fortunate."[54] Looking at this text through the lens of friendship can revitalize our giving. If I give to you as an act of charity, I may question whether you deserve the gift, whether you have the proper degree of appreciation and gratitude, and may have opinions about how you choose to spend it. If the money bestowed is money shared between friends, these sorts of expectations dissolve. If the gift ceases to be "mine" and becomes "ours," the patron-client relationship disappears.

YOU CANNOT SERVE GOD AND WEALTH (LUKE 16:10-18)

What follows is an application of Luke 16:1-9.[55] "True riches" (Lk 16:11) are obtained through almsgiving (12:33).[56] The first part of Luke 16:13 gives a proverb that is explained in the latter half of the verse: it is impossible to serve God and mammon equally.[57] We cannot submit to the material values of this world and simultaneously exhibit the values of the kingdom

---

[53]The point of comparison between the steward and Jesus' followers may be that as the steward provided for his future, aware of his impending judgment, so Christians should provide for theirs, knowing that they too will face judgment. Walter Grundmann, *Das Evangelium nach Lukas* (Berlin: Evangelische Verlagsanstalt, 1961), 320.

[54]Moxnes, *Economy of the Kingdom*, 142.

[55]Lk 16:1-13 is "composed of a parable with some interpretations." Talbert, *Reading Luke*, 153. Others see a "clear separation" between Lk 16:1-8 and Lk 16:9-13. Bailey, *Poet and Peasant*, 111; Joachim Jeremias, *The Parables of Jesus* (New York: Charles Scribner's Sons, 1963), 46.

[56]Green, *Gospel of Luke*, 595. This wealth does not need to be seen as possessions acquired dishonestly (Fitzmyer, *Gospel According to Luke*, 1110). Dishonest wealth is merely part of the contrast with "true riches." Dishonest wealth does not last because it belongs to the present realm, not because it can't bring one through all crises (Fitzmyer, *Gospel According to Luke*, 1110).

[57]Nolland, *Luke*, 804.

of God. Money is not under our private ownership but under the ownership of God.[58] God grants true (spiritual) wealth to those of us who can handle material wealth with kingdom principles.[59] This treasure that God gives can then be said to be our "own" (Lk 16:12).[60]

The second part of Luke 16 (Lk 16:14-31) is addressed to the Pharisees. It is connected to Luke 12:34,[61] indicating that those who accumulate possessions prove their lack of worthiness for the kingdom of God. In Luke 16:14-15, the Pharisees ridicule Jesus' teaching about wealth since they believed that wealth is a sign of God's favor. In contrast to Jesus' followers who are to make "friends" by giving to the poor in Luke 16:9, Luke notes that the Pharisees are "friends" of money (Lk 16:14).[62] Their desire for honor and status precludes their friendship with the poor.[63] The Pharisees are self-sufficient, like the rich fool of Luke 12:16–20. Jesus implies that their desire for money is rooted in a desire for a good image (Lk 16:15). However, God, who knows their hearts, is aware of their self-deception. Borrowing from the prophetic tradition that highlights the poor as recipients of God's favor and the wealthy who oppressed them as degenerates (Amos 2:6-8), Jesus tells the Pharisees that prosperity itself is no indication of righteousness.[64]

LAZARUS AND THE RICH MAN (LUKE 16:19-31)

In 2014, Nick Cannon sported a pair of two-million-dollar diamond-encrusted shoes for the season finale of *America's Got Talent* (which he eventually donated to charity). While ostentation to this degree created a flurry in the media, our culture is no stranger to flaunting wealth. In Luke's narrative, Jesus tells a story of a man who leads an ostentatious lifestyle, detailing the themes of Luke 16:14-15.[65] Refusing to help Lazarus, he exemplifies the pride of the wealthy who are judged by God.[66]

---

[58]Nolland, *Luke*, 807.
[59]Nolland, *Luke*, 807.
[60]Nolland, *Luke*, 807.
[61]Schmidt, *Hostility to Wealth*, 156.
[62]Green, *Gospel of Luke*, 601.
[63]Green, *Gospel of Luke*, 601.
[64]Talbert, *Reading Luke*, 156.
[65]Talbert, *Reading Luke*, 156.
[66]Talbert, *Reading Luke*, 157.

In keeping with Luke's penchant for reversals, the selfish isolation of the wealthy man is pitted against Lazarus's favored position before God. In the next life, the rich man is in torment, separated from Lazarus, who is in the bosom of Abraham, by a great chasm. He asks Lazarus to dip the tip of his finger in water to cool his tongue, which ironically he would never have done during his lifetime since he would have avoided contact with unclean beggars.[67] The Pharisees would never have thought of Lazarus as righteous. His lifestyle of begging made him unclean, as did his sores and the dogs who licked them. However, even Lazarus's name (he whom God helps) indicates his piety.[68] Lazarus depends on God for his salvation,[69] so locating himself within realm of God's kingdom. That Lazarus is named at all is noteworthy: he is the only person to receive a name in a Gospel parable.[70] The fact that Lazarus has a name and the rich man has none also highlights the folly of the wealthy man's assumptions about the worth of the poor and foreshadows the reversal of fortune.[71]

The contrasts between Lazarus and the rich man could not be greater. The rich man is dressed like royalty,[72] while Lazarus is clothed in sores, which evoke images of righteous Job.[73] The wealthy man enjoys daily lavish feasts (Lk 16:19), while Lazarus is starving. The rich man receives a decent burial (Lk 16:22), while Lazarus, presumably, is cast aside. In the next life, the situations of Lazarus and the wealthy man are reversed. Lazarus is carried away by angels to be with Abraham who is "at his side" (Lk 16:23), enjoying both comfort and honor while the rich man is in torment.

The rich man's wealth was no indication of God's blessing but rather ensured his condemnation. Failing to grasp that Lazarus no longer has the

---

[67]Talbert, *Reading Luke*, 157.

[68]Talbert, *Reading Luke*, 157.

[69]Schmidt, *Hostility to Wealth*, 157.

[70]Nolland, *Luke*, 828.

[71]Nolland, *Luke*, 828.

[72]Bovon notes that in the Roman Empire purple was the color of emperors. *Luke 2*, 478. It was a costly process to create white wool and to obtain Tyrian purple dye from which the rich man's clothing is made. Green, *Gospel of Luke*, 605.

[73]This story mirror's Job's theology that poverty is no indication of God's judgment. Green, *Gospel of Luke*, 605.

status of a servant, the rich man asks for him to fetch him a drink (Lk 16:24) and asks that he may be dispatched to warn his brothers (Lk 16:27). His requests betray that he still sees himself as worthy of preferential treatment. That the rich man knows Lazarus's name heightens his callousness.[74] The rich man calls Abraham "father," recalling John's admonition in Luke 3:8 to those who might justify themselves by calling on Abraham.[75] Abraham's remark that the brothers would not even listen to one who comes from the dead (Lk 16:30) heightens the rich man's condemnation.[76] The reference to Moses and the prophets recalls Jesus' observation in Luke 16:16-17 and points to the Pharisees' guilt.

Lazarus dies of his illness and possibly starvation. Ironically, his name means "he whom God helps." Recalling Jesus' promise in Luke 12:31, we might wonder how exactly God helped Lazarus. If this is the sort of help we can expect from God, anxiety over the future seems appropriate! First of all, this teaching is aimed at lovers of money who are failing in their duty to care for the poor. They need to understand that their actions matter. Lazarus might have survived if the wealthy man had cared for him as the good Samaritan cared for the injured man in Luke 10:25-37. What we might glean from this text is a bit of reality—what we do makes a concrete difference, and if we do nothing to help people in need, they will not be okay, and God will hold us accountable for that. If this story had ended differently—for instance, if God had sent an angel to preserve Lazarus's life—we might assume that what we do for others doesn't actually matter; God will always cover for us. But Lazarus dies. Second, as difficult as it may be for us to understand, God *does* care for Lazarus: he is in the bosom of Abraham. Our culture is obsessed with youth and longevity. We get a different perspective from the Gospels. The orientation is not this-worldly but is toward the kingdom, extending our perspective beyond our own needs and even our own survival to the care of all. It also understands that richness, blessing, joy, relationship, and the care of God are not limited to our earthly lives.

---

[74]Fitzmyer, *Gospel According to Luke*, 1133.
[75]Moxnes, *Economy of the Kingdom*, 149.
[76]Fitzmyer, *Gospel According to Luke*, 1128.

The Rich Ruler (Luke 18:18-30)

In Luke's story, the rich ruler faces a choice that has lasting consequences. Jesus recites the commandments that have to do with relationships between people,[77] and the ruler claims that he has obeyed these since his youth (Lk 18:21).[78] His words evoke images of Zechariah, Elizabeth, Simeon, and Anna, and are a strong statement of his piety.[79] Jesus then clearly tells the man that if he wants to enter into the kingdom, he must dispossess himself.[80] Just as it is impossible for the largest known animal to pass through the smallest known space,[81] it is impossible to simultaneously follow the kingdom and seek wealth. The parallel between "to enter the kingdom" and "to enter through the eye of a needle" indicates how utterly impossible it is for one to follow wealth and mammon at the same time.[82] The ultimatum reveals the man's true priorities. For Luke, the heart of human relationships and proof of one's qualification for the kingdom include a willingness to dispossess oneself and practice almsgiving.[83] Inability to do this shows that mammon and not God is master (Lk 16:13), and disqualifies one for the kingdom.

Jesus' radical ultimatum reverberates among his disciples. "Then who can be saved?" they ask (Lk 18:26). Those listening may have assumed that the ruler's wealth was proof of God's pleasure (Lk 16:14-15).[84] Jesus reminds them that salvation is from God, who is able to bring even the wealthy into the kingdom.[85] Peter then announces that he and the other disciples have left "everything" to follow him—they have done both things that Jesus asked the ruler to do (Lk 18:22). They have imitated Jesus, who has already declared himself homeless (Lk 9:58), by leaving their homes to follow him

---

[77]Fitzmyer, *Gospel According to Luke*, 1197.

[78]We have no reason to doubt that his reply is truthful. Bovon, *Luke 2*, 567.

[79]Nolland, *Luke*, 886.

[80]Grundmann, *Das Evangelium nach Lukas*, 354-55; Karl Heinrich Rengstorf similarly observes that Jesus challenges the external securities of the rich man's life. *Das Evangelium nach Lukas* (Göttingen: Vandenhoeck & Ruprecht, 1965), 210.

[81]Fitzmyer, *Gospel According to Luke*, 1204.

[82]Green, *Gospel of Luke*, 658.

[83]Green, *Gospel of Luke*, 656.

[84]Green, *Gospel of Luke*, 657.

[85]Fitzmyer, *Gospel According to Luke*, 1205.

(Lk 18:28). Jesus therefore affirms that they are members of the kingdom and in the age to come will have eternal life.

Zacchaeus (Luke 19:1-10)

The rich man's failure to respond to Jesus' invitation stands in contrast to Zacchaeus's positive response. At first glance, Zacchaeus's generosity seems measured, particularly when one considers Jesus' mandate for complete dispossession in Luke 12:33, Luke 14:33, or Luke 18:22.[86] Actually, with the exception of the poor widow in Luke 21:1-4, he is probably the most generous character in Luke and Acts. Zacchaeus retains half of his possessions not for his own use but in order to make restitution.[87] In response to his actions, Jesus declares his salvation (Lk 19:9), including him in the company of the formerly lost who are coming into the kingdom (Lk 19:9-10). The passage answers the question of Luke 18:26 by showing that if even a tax collector can dispossess himself to follow God, salvation truly comes only from God.

The Poor Widow's Offering (Luke 21:1-4)

Given the Lukan emphasis on dispossession as a quality of discipleship, although the poor widow gives "all she had to live on," Jesus' words should not be taken as a rebuke that she has been wrongly persuaded to give up her livelihood.[88] The woman is an ideal disciple and a foil against the relative stinginess of the "rich people" (Lk 21:1).[89] Luke drops from his source the indication that the rich people's gifts were "large,"[90] a sign that he is unimpressed with their lack of self-sacrifice. The size of the widow's gift would not have been large enough to even place in one of the thirteen

---

[86]Bovon, *Luke 2*, 599.

[87]Schmidt, *Hostility to Wealth*, 159.

[88]This has been suggested by Addison G. Wright, "The Widow's Mites: Praise or Lament?—A Matter of Context," *CBQ* 44 (1982), 256-65. See also Fitzmyer, *Gospel According to Luke*, 1320. But Luke focuses here on the widow as an ethical subject. François Bovon, *Luke 3: A Commentary on the Gospel of Luke 19:28–24:53*, Hermeneia (Minneapolis: Fortress, 2012), 95.

[89]Rengstorf notes that Luke's portrait of this woman is especially significant since she had freed herself from possessions in the same carefree manner that Jesus had. *Das Evangelium nach Lukas*, 232.

[90]Nolland, *Luke,* 978.

trumpet-shaped offering containers in the temple.[91] Instead, the widow would have had to place her meager funds in another chest intended for "voluntary" giving.[92] Luke, however, emphasizes the quality of the widow's gift—complete dependence on God with no thought for security.[93] The story provides another example of Jesus calling his disciples to radical dispossession, leaving concerns about the practicalities of life to faith.[94]

Faith like the widow's might seem irresponsible to us. However, Luke's audience might have seen this text within the context of a faith-inspiring story. In 1 Kings 17: 7-16, the widow of Zarephath gives Elijah her and her son's last meal. God then miraculously ensures that the flour jar and the olive jug don't run dry. Today, Christians sometimes tell the story of George Müller (1805–1898), whose ministry to orphans was sustained almost entirely by prayer. He never asked anyone for money and did not take a salary. He didn't take out loans or go into debt. He simply trusted that God would supply whatever was necessary for his ministry. My family has our own stories of God's provision. When my parents were in their twenties, my father felt the call of God on his life to pursue an education for ministry in the United States. He and my mother immigrated from South Africa to Canada, but because she could not obtain a US work visa, they could not come to the States together. They initially planned to work for a few years in Canada before trying to immigrate to the United States later. Here is the story, in my mother's words, which she once wrote out for my son:

> While we were looking for jobs in Toronto, Canada, we were walking down a busy street downtown, silently, both deep in our thoughts. Grandfather actually had an appointment for a job in a building which we just passed when he said to me, "Let's go and have a cup of coffee." I nodded my head and we crossed the road and went into a coffee shop and sat down at a table. We were not talking, just silently going through the motions, when he put his hand over mine and said he knew that I knew. I just looked at him and tears started falling down my cheeks. It was like the voice of God within us both, at the

---

[91]Bovon, *Luke 3*, 93.
[92]Bovon, *Luke 3*, 94.
[93]Gerhard Schneider, *Das Evangelium nach Lukas* (Würzburg: Echter-Verlag, 1984), 413-14.
[94]Nolland, *Luke*, 979.

same time, telling Grandfather that our plans were not His plans. He wanted grandfather not to waste any more time but to go immediately to the States and get on with it. I knew this too without any further explanation. God told us both at the same time.

Within a few days, my mother had obtained a job as a nanny, living in a household with her expenses paid in exchange for childcare duties on Saturdays, a position that she held (in addition to her job in a law firm) for the next two years until my father graduated from college in the United States. They saw each other on breaks and during the summers. For the next forty years of their married lives, this narrative was for both a concrete example of God's care and provision.

The Correlation of Jesus' Life and Teaching Regarding Wealth and Simplicity

Whenever Luke mentions Jesus' lifestyle, he shows it to be fully consistent with Jesus' teachings about simplicity.[95] Jesus teaches his disciples that even food and clothing are not worth striving for (Lk 12:23). He urges them to dispossess themselves (Lk 12:33) and abandon themselves to the kingdom (Lk 12:32), with all confidence in God (Lk 12:28) and with no worries about their future (Lk 12:29).

Without food (Lk 6:1) or money (Lk 9:13), Jesus relies completely on God and devotes himself entirely to proclaiming God's kingdom. Luke 6:1 narrates that Jesus and his disciples were going through the fields picking heads of grain. Hebrew law dictated that landowners leave the gleanings for the poor (Lev 23:22). Jesus and his disciples clearly have no property. They are the poor for whom God has made provision. Similarly, in Luke 9:13, Jesus tells his disciples to give the crowds something to eat. Of course they do not have the food or the money to purchase food. However, Jesus demonstrates his faith in the providence and care of God, blesses the five loaves and fish, and multiplies the food for the multitudes. Finally, Jesus himself carries no money and forbids the disciples to carry any

---

[95]"The daily events, the journeys, and the celebrations in which Jesus participated with the disciples were characterized by simplicity." Richard Cassidy, *Jesus, Politics, and Society: A Study of Luke's Gospel* (Maryknoll, NY: Orbis, 1978), 26.

possessions whatsoever: "Carry no purse, no bag, no sandals; and greet no one on the road" (Lk 10:4). Instead they are to rely on the provision of God (Lk 10:5) through the benefaction of others. In Luke 9:58, Jesus warns a potential disciple, "Foxes have holes, and birds of the air have nests; but the Son of Man has nowhere to lay his head." When his followers imitate his lifestyle, Jesus praises them for their willingness to embrace the kingdom: "Truly I tell you, there is no one who has left house or wife or brothers or parents or children, for the sake of the kingdom of God, who will not get back very much more in this age, and in the age to come eternal life" (Lk 18:29-30). Jesus, then, proclaims the simplicity of life in the kingdom of God through both his actions and his teachings.

We can also see the unity of Jesus' life and teaching regarding generosity. As we have seen, Jesus emphasizes that we must exercise generous almsgiving (Lk 12:33). We might wonder how one who has no place to lay his head can practice generosity. Jesus, of course, has dispossessed himself so completely that he has no material goods with which to share with the poor. He himself is numbered among the "poor" who must survive from the alms of others (Lk 6:1). However, he is not without ability to practice benefaction. In fact, Jesus possesses the most fabulous treasure of all: the treasure of the kingdom (Lk 12:32). He has devoted his entire life to the mission of bringing people from the realm of the world into the kingdom of God (Lk 19:10). Members of his society might have expected itinerant preachers to require pay. Jesus, however, bestows the greatest treasure at no cost.

SUMMARY

Luke depicts simplicity, a lifestyle characterized by complete dependence on God, willingness to share possessions, and habits of almsgiving and generosity as an indicator of one's participation in the kingdom of God. Jesus teaches out of his own lifestyle, as one who has no home and requires no fee for his instruction. Jesus' teaching on the wealthy man who replaces his barns in Luke 12:13-21, the rich man's treatment of Lazarus in Luke 16:19-31, and the wealthy ruler who refuses discipleship by refusing to dispossess himself in Luke 18:18-30 illustrate his principles on the moral bankruptcy of greed (Lk 12:13-15; 16:14-15; 18:24-30). The examples of Zacchaeus's (Lk 19:1-9) and the destitute widow's (Lk 21:1-4) giving provide portraits of generosity and dependence on God's provision (Lk 12:22-34). Luke contrasts two lifestyles, one of luxury and self-indulgent wealth, and another of sharing possessions, trust in God's provision, and radical generosity. The benefits of the latter bring spiritual rewards: God trusts heavenly wealth to those who demonstrate their ability to handle material wealth with kingdom values (Lk 12:32-34).

Luke's intended audience would have understood the implications of the unity of Jesus' teachings on poverty, wealth, and generosity and his own lifestyle of simplicity. The fact that Luke sums up his Gospel as being about all that Jesus "did and taught" (Acts 1:1) suggests that the presentation is intentional. As we will see in the next chapter, Luke's cultural world reveals an expectation for ideal heroes to show a unity of teaching and action with respect to simplicity. Such integrity was the mark of a true philosopher-king, one who could lead others to virtue through personal example. While we might read Luke's portrait of Jesus as an interesting narrative, Luke's audience would have recognized the power of Jesus' example of simplicity—power to transform even the most anxious about our financial futures into a kingdom people whose habits are marked by a modest lifestyle and generosity to those who are most in need.

2

SIMPLICITY THROUGH FIRST-CENTURY EYES

FIGURING OUT JESUS' TEACHINGS ON MONEY gets a lot easier if we have a better grasp of what Luke's target audience thought about wealth and how Luke was interacting with those understandings. The audience for whom Luke wrote, familiar with cultural ideals for generosity and warnings against greed, would have possessed an ideological framework for grasping Jesus' teachings and putting them into practice. Looking at their views allows us to join the conversation Luke has initiated with them. Because Jesus' teachings and lifestyle of simplicity match models of simplicity among ideal Greco-Roman and Jewish heroes, Luke's portrait of Jesus in similar terms might have caused his intended audience to see Jesus as an ideal leader as well. This would further be emphasized by the unity of his life and teaching in simplicity. Reading this portrait of Jesus as a model and teacher of simplicity through the lens of Luke's cultural world allows us to ask the sort of questions that Luke's narrative invites and stretches the horizons of our own preconceptions about the right use of money.

WEALTH

Wealth can be fleeting. As I make final edits to this manuscript in the Spring of 2020, our country is experiencing the beginning of the coronavirus pandemic. The stock market is in a freefall, ten million Americans have filed for unemployment in the last two weeks, hospitals are in crisis, and the numbers of the dead increase dramatically each day. Americans are reeling from the chaos and loss, and I can't help but wonder about the fate of communities across the globe who were already impoverished and living in cramped, unsanitary conditions before this catastrophe began. Those who are lucky enough to still be healthy are facing a very uncertain economic future. It has become more than clear that we simply can't count on incomes to be there for us when we need them. We can't guarantee that we will be there to spend our money in the future either. The rich man who hoards his grain in Luke 12:13-21 has forgotten this. Seneca could have similarly warned him: "All these possessions that force you to swell with pride, and, exalting you above mortals, cause you to forget your own frailty . . . unconscious of how many arrows Fortune may be preparing for you behind your back."[1] For Seneca, the only kind of wealth that is guaranteed to last is that which is given away. Accordingly, he tells the story of Mark Antony on his deathbed, who exclaimed, "Whatever I have given, that I still possess!" Seneca then asks, "Why do you spare your wealth as through it were your own? You are but a steward. . . . Do you ask how you can make them your own? By bestowing them as gifts!"[2] Similarly, for Jesus, in Luke, generosity, or being "rich toward God" (Lk 12:21), is the only way to ensure lasting wealth. Through almsgiving, one may "make purses for yourselves that do not wear out, an unfailing treasure in heaven" (Lk 12:33). Jesus' plea to care for those in need is directed toward us today also. The uncertainty of the future can only be met with the consistency of Jesus' clear command to provide for the growing poor among us.

Jewish discussions of wealth also emphasized its transient nature. In the Sentences of Pseudo-Phocylides, a sapiential poem written sometime in the first century BCE or the first century CE, we see that "life is a wheel; prosperity is unstable."[3] Baruch, an apocryphal Jewish work, asks,

> Where are the rulers of the nations . . .
>   who hoarded up silver and gold? . . .
> They have vanished and gone down to Hades,
>   and others have arisen in their place. (Bar 3:16-19)

In the Wisdom of Solomon, the fools ask,

---

[1] Seneca, *Ben.* 6.3.
[2] Seneca, *Ben.* 6.3.
[3] Ps.-Phoc. 27.

And what good has our boasted wealth brought us?

All those things have vanished like a shadow . . .

like a ship that sails through the billowy water . . .

or as, when a bird flies through the air,

no evidence of its passage is found. (Wis 5:8-11)

Like us, Luke's audience was acutely aware that money does not last. They would have been primed to hear Jesus' teachings about the kind of wealth that does make a lasting difference.

The cost of a dollar. Plato's Socrates complains that "we are compelled to gain money for the sake of the body. We are slaves to its service. And so, because of all these things, we have no leisure for philosophy."[4] Some of my students, struggling to juggle a job and find time for their studies, can probably relate! They work harder than their peers, often settling down to study only after the long evening shifts that fund their tuition. Others have postponed college to earn money first. Seneca gives advice to one person who wanted to postpone his studies in order to make money:

> Doubtless, your object, what you wish to attain by such postponement of your studies, is that poverty may not have to be feared by you. But what if it is something to be desired? Riches have shut off many a man from the attainment of wisdom; poverty is unburdened and free from care. . . . And yet this ideal, which you are putting off and placing second to other interests, should be secured first of all.[5]

Some things are just more important even than one's needs. For Seneca, that was philosophy.[6] For Jesus, it was the kingdom of God. Seneca points out that the person who puts off the pursuit of philosophy to earn a living has postponed "real life." Someone who is unencumbered with the need to earn money will "with free and happy spirit" . . . "laugh at the bustling of rich men, and the flurried ways of those who are hastening after wealth, and say: 'Why of your own accord postpone your real life to the distant future?'"[7] Seneca compares the pursuit of philosophy with an army's

---

[4]Plato, *Phaed.* 66d.

[5]Seneca, *Ep.* 17.3-5.

[6]Seneca did not count himself among those who had attained wisdom. He might have been talking about himself when he noted that riches have prevented many a person from obtaining it.

[7]Seneca, *Ep.* 17.10.

pursuit of a kingdom, noting that any sacrifice, even of genuine needs, must be made in order to reach one's goal:

> Even though we starve, we must reach that goal. Armies have endured all manner of want, have lived on roots, and have resisted hunger by means of food too revolting to mention. All this they have suffered to gain a kingdom, and,—what is more marvelous,—to gain a kingdom that will be another's. Will any man hesitate to endure poverty, in order that he may free his mind from madness?[8]

Seneca urges, "Therefore one should not seek to lay up riches first. . . . Is philosophy to be the last requisite in life . . . but if you have nothing, seek understanding first, before anything else."[9] The parallels to Luke 12:31 are remarkable both in their similarity and in their difference. Both the Lukan Jesus and Seneca urge their readers to understand that material wealth pales in comparison to the pursuit of the kingdom of God or philosophy. Money simply can't compete with such a great good. Seneca advises that the sacrifice is worth it "even though we starve," however, while the Lukan Jesus promises God's provision (Lk 12:22-31).

I have a deep respect for the difficult financial choices that my students have to make and compassion for those who must juggle a full-time work schedule with their studies. Jesus' practical emphasis on God's provision, however, should be taken seriously. This does not mean that we don't need to be financially responsible or even be willing to shoulder another job along with our work of the kingdom—Paul did this too, as we know, as do many pastors today.

I once had a student with a particular aptitude for biblical studies. She loved her Bible classes. Frederick Buechner talks about calling as the place where our deep gladness and the world's deep hunger meet, and this student lived in that sweet spot with her ministry to youth. She wanted to major in biblical studies, but her father, who wasn't a Christian, was pushing her into another major that promised a greater future income. She could, of course, have served God just as well in that career, but I recognized in her an

---

[8]Seneca, *Ep.* 17.7.
[9]Seneca, *Ep.* 17.8.

unmistakable passion for biblical studies that I felt she was stifling out of a desire to please her father. To me, it felt like Seneca's dilemma—any financial windfall that she might gain from her career or her father would pale in comparison to the joy that comes from living in that sweet spot of ministry.

The moral corruption of greed. Luke's target audience knew about greed and corruption. Suetonius tells us that Caligula once built a two-mile floating bridge across the Bay of Bauli just so that he could gallop back and forth across it.[10] His horse had a marble stall, an ivory manger, a jeweled collar, and his own house.[11] Cassius Dio said that he was fed oats mixed with gold flakes.[12] Luke's authorial audience would have read the caricature of the wealthy man who shuns Lazarus' need (Lk 16:19-31) or the self-preoccupied man consumed with securing his own financial security (Lk 12:13-21) with similar disdain. Such ostentation would have been extremely distasteful to most of the population, struggling to provide for their families. Familiar with ideals for generous benefaction, particularly concerning those with great wealth, they would have quickly noted the greed of those who chose instead to spend their fortunes on personal pleasure. Xenophon's Cyrus notes that "if any man enjoy the reputation of having great wealth and do not appear to help his friends in a manner worthy of his abundance, that, it seems to me at least, fixes upon him the stigma of being a mean sort."[13] Plutarch compares the lives of two kings, one who dispensed his wealth in generous benefaction, and another who spent it on the luxurious lifestyles of himself and his few friends. He notes of Cimon and Lucullus,

> Though both alike were wealthy, they did not make a like use of their wealth. There is no comparing the south wall of the Acropolis, which was completed with the moneys brought home by Cimon, with the palaces and sea-washed

---

[10]Suetonius, *Cal.* 19. In *The Lives of the Twelve Caesars; An English Translation, Augmented with the Biographies of Contemporary Statesmen, Orators, Poets, and Other Associates,* ed. J. Eugene Reed (Philadelphia: Gebbie & Co., 1889).

[11]Suetonius, *Cal.* 55.

[12]Cassius Dio, *Roman History* LIX, 14. Granted, these accounts need to be taken with a grain of salt! Even if such accounts are not accurate, they speak to the distaste of greed in Luke's cultural world.

[13]Xenophon, *Cyr.* 8.4.32.

Belvideres at Neapolis, which Lucullus built out of the spoils of the Barbarians. Nor can the table of Cimon be likened to that of Lucullus; the one was democratic and charitable, the other sumptuous and oriental. The one, at slight outlay, gave daily sustenance to many; the other, at large cost, was prepared for a few luxurious livers.[14]

We could think of contemporary examples. Mswati III, king of Swaziland, has been internationally criticized for his extravagance, with fifteen wives, thirteen royal palaces, fleets of BMWs, and a $17 million private jet, while 80 percent of the Swazi population makes less than $2 per day.[15] While *Forbes* estimated Mswati's wealth to be $100 million in 2009, according to UN data, about two-thirds of Swazis can't meet their daily food requirements. On the other hand, Warren Buffet still lives in the same home he bought for $31,500 in 1958.[16] Luke's cultural world and ours generally respect leaders who embrace simplicity and use their careers to benefit others instead of exploiting those whom they are supposed to serve.

We know that leading a lifestyle of greed and ostentation while one's people starve is wrong. Is it bad to possess a lot of wealth, though? In Luke's literary world there is a fairly extensive tradition marking the potential corrupting power of excessive wealth. Xenophon's Socrates warns that "many by their wealth are corrupted."[17] Jewish literature carries the same warnings. Ahiqar, an ancient wise scribe commands, "[Do not amass wealth], lest you pervert your heart."[18] First Enoch declares, "Those who amass gold and silver; they shall quickly be destroyed. Woe to you, O rich people! For you have put your trust in your wealth."[19] Sirach cautions,

> One who loves gold will not be justified;
> one who pursues money will be led astray by it. (Sir 31:5-7)

---

[14]Plutarch, *Lives, Comp. Cim. Luc.* 1.5-6.

[15]Jonathan W. Rosen, "Last Dance for the Playboy King of Swaziland?," *National Geographic*, October 3, 2014, http://news.nationalgeographic.com/news/2014/10/141003-swaziland-africa-king-mswati-reed-dance/.

[16]See Tanza Loudenback, "Extremely Wealthy People Who Choose to Live Frugally," *Business Insider*, July 14, 2016, www.businessinsider.com/the-habits-of-frugal-billionaires-2016-7.

[17]Xenophon, *Mem.* 4.2.35.

[18]Ahiqar 137.

[19]1 En. 94.7-8.

The Sentences of Pseudo-Phocylides and the Sibylline Oracles declare money as the "mother of all evil."[20] The Psalms of Solomon point out that moderate wealth is adequate—with righteousness, "for with this comes the Lord's blessing." However, "if one is excessively rich, he sins."[21]

In fact, writers in Luke's literary world see the lure of wealth as being so dangerous that it can lead an entire people to destruction. Plutarch talks about riches as a "fatal thing" for Sparta.[22] Greed can hinder the common interests of the state. He points out that the Lacedaemonian state suffered corruption "soon after its subversion of the Athenian supremacy filled it with gold and silver."[23] There is particular danger for a city ruled by a money-loving leader. Plutarch paints this picture of corruption: "The citizens had been lulled to sleep by idleness and pleasure; the king was willing to let all public business go, providing that no one thwarted his desire for luxurious living in the midst of his wealth; the public interests were neglected, while every man was eagerly intent upon his own private gain."[24] In Plutarch's mind, when the rich neglect "the common interests for their own private pleasure and aggrandizement" the entire nation suffers.[25] Josephus too connects individual greed with the ruin of a nation. He has Moses interpret Israel's eventual fall as a consequence of greed: should they be carried away by wealth, they will lose the favor they found with God and "will forfeit the land."[26] In a later volume, Josephus shows how the Israelites have failed to heed Moses' words: "As their riches increased, under the mastery of luxury and voluptuousness," they "no longer hearkened diligently to its laws," but "enslaved to the pleasures of lucre," they "were launched into civil war."[27] Prioritizing individual wealth over the common interests of the people can bring down a nation.

In Luke 16:18-31, the wealthy man who ignores Lazarus ends up in Hades while Lazarus is finally at peace in the bosom of Abraham. For

---

[20]Ps.-Phoc. 42-27; Sib. Or. 2.111-14.
[21]Pss. Sol. 5.16-17.
[22]Plutarch, *Ag.* 9.1.
[23]Plutarch, *Ag.* 5.1.
[24]Plutarch, *Cleom.* 2.1.
[25]Plutarch, *Cleom.* 3.1.
[26]Josephus, *Ant.* 4.189-90.
[27]Josephus, *Ant.* 5.132-35.

Luke's target audience, this would not have been too surprising. The idea finds parallel thought in Isaiah, who observes that God will reverse the fortunes of those who have enjoyed financial security in this life (Is 14:30-32; 29:18-19; 41:17). In the Testament of Judah, part of a collection of pseude-pigraphal writings proposing to contain the last words of the twelve sons of Jacob, we see that "those who died in poverty for the Lord's sake shall be made rich."[28] In the Testament of Isaac, God tells Abraham, "Let him feed the hungry one with bread and I will give him a place in my kingdom."[29] Similarly, in the Testament of Jacob, Jacob tells his sons, "O my sons, do for the poor what will increase compassion for them here and now, so that God will give you the bread of life forever in the kingdom of God."[30] For Luke, simply possessing money isn't necessarily wrong. Excessive wealth can be dangerous, however, particularly if one ignores the needs of the poor. Luke points out that those who have used their good fortune entirely on their own interests can expect a reversal of fortune in the future.

SIMPLICITY

True wealth redefined. For Luke's target audience, Jesus' distinction be-tween material wealth and spiritual treasure would not have been entirely new (Lk 12:32-34). Writers in Luke's literary world often distinguished between material wealth and the kind of riches that have eternal value. In the writings of both Xenophon and Plato, Socrates redefines true wealth, admiring "treasures of wisdom above gold and silver" because "while gold and silver cannot make men better, the thoughts of the wise enrich their possessors with virtue."[31] Plato's Socrates, too, shows his awareness that genuine wealth is nonmaterial when he prays, "O beloved Pan and all ye other gods of this place, grant to me that I be made beautiful in my soul within, and that all external possessions be in harmony with my inner man. May I consider the wise man rich; and may I have such wealth as only the self-restrained man can bear or endure."[32] Seneca similarly redefines true

---

[28]T. Jud. 25.4.
[29]T. Isaac 6.11-12.
[30]T. Jac. 7.22-25.
[31]Xenophon, *Mem.* 4.2.9.
[32]Plato, *Phaed.* 279c.

wealth as the pursuit of wisdom: "Shall you wait for some interest to fall due, or for some income on your merchandise, or for a place in the will of some wealthy old man, when you can be rich here and now? Wisdom offers wealth in ready money, and pays it over to those in whose eyes she has made wealth superfluous."[33]

Jewish literature also shows a tendency to redefine true wealth as that which is immaterial. Baruch defines wisdom as that which is bought for "pure gold" (Bar 3:30). The Wisdom of Solomon asks, "What is richer than wisdom, the active cause of all things?" (Wis 8:5). This redefinition of true wealth as wisdom primed Luke's target audience to receive Jesus' teachings about money. It also can help us to sort out our true values and readjust our habits accordingly. If those who know us best point to entertainment or work as our chief priority, it doesn't necessarily mean that that *is* what we value above all else. It might mean that we are living lives that are out of sync with the values that we do have, however, and that it might benefit us to ask *why* we are immersed in these other things instead of what we truly value. Workaholism, internet addiction, or shopping, for instance, often mask a deeper unwillingness to remain still before God. In my own life, when I have fallen victim to these patterns, I am trying to simply "check out" for a while because I am afraid that the intensity of living in the midst of the kingdom moment to moment will exhaust me—a good indicator of the need to learn both to work and relax in the presence of God.

Praises for the simple lifestyle. A friend of mine comes to mind when I consider the lifestyle of simplicity. As a large family living on a single, modest salary, they live in a smallish home, most of their kids needing to bunk together. They don't have all of the newest electronics. She shops at thrift stores when a member of her family really needs something. They eat at home nearly all of the time, with homegrown fruits and vegetables. She decorates her home with her own artwork. When they go on vacations, they drive to their destination instead of flying and camp instead of staying in hotels. She doesn't stress out about money but lives with the expectation

---

[33]Seneca, *Ep.* 17.10.

that God will continue to provide. In spite of their limited resources and large family, she is generous with her money.

In Luke, Jesus and his followers live a lifestyle of simplicity (Lk 9:58; 18:28-30). This sort of lifestyle was idealized by many philosophers who would have been known in Luke's day. Xenophon's Cyrus, for instance, practiced simplicity throughout his life in spite of his wealth. Once when Cyrus was a youth, his grandfather put on a fancy banquet for him. Instead of enjoying his feast, Cyrus distributed it all to his grandfather's servants.[34] He also refused expensive clothing and was sometimes rebuked for his attire "which was not at all showy."[35]

In spite of his privileged upbringing, Plutarch's Agis was also not one for fine clothes. Plutarch notes, "Indeed the young man himself, owing to his simplicity, his love of hardships, and the pride he took in clothing and arming himself with no more splendour than a common soldier, won the admiration and devotion of the multitudes."[36] Agis, although he had been raised with "wealth and luxury," "set his face against pleasures. He put away from his person the adornments which were thought to benefit the grace of his figure, laid aside and avoided every extravagance."[37]

Socrates was also noteworthy for his simplicity. He had nothing, and wanted nothing, since his desires were so simple. Diogenes Laertius describes him this way: "Often when he looked at the multitude of wares exposed for sale, he would say to himself, 'How many things I can do without!'"[38] Instead, Socrates "prided himself on his plain living. . . . He used to say that he most enjoyed the food which was least in need of condiment, and the drink which made him feel the least hankering for some other drink; and that he was nearest to the gods in that he had the fewest wants."[39] When Socrates, famous for his poor clothing and bare feet,[40] was offered a beautiful garment in which to die, he replied, "Is my own good

---

[34]Xenophon, *Cyr.* 1.3.6-7.
[35]Xenophon, *Cyr.* 2.4.6.
[36]Plutarch, *Ag.* 14.3.
[37]Plutarch, *Ag.* 4.1.
[38]Diogenes Laertius, *Vit. phil.* 2.25.
[39]Diogenes Laertius, *Vit. phil.* 2.27.
[40]Diogenes Laertius, *Vit. phil.* 2.28.

enough to live in but not to die in?"[41] For Diogenes Laertius, that was because Socrates felt that "wealth and good birth bring their possessor no dignity, but on the contrary evil."[42]

Jewish literature echoes this theme. Josephus, who has the difficult task of positing wealth as both blessing from God and potential for greed, nonetheless glorifies the simplicity of his heroes. He notes that Moses "dressed like any ordinary person, in all else he bore himself as a simple commoner, who desired in nothing to appear different from the crowd, save only in being seen to have their interests at heart."[43] Similarly, Daniel, "being superior to considerations of money and scorning any kind of gain and thinking it most disgraceful to accept anything even if it were given for a proper cause," gave those who were envious of him not a single reason for complaint.[44]

We might ask why it is necessary to live a life of simplicity. After all, if God has blessed us with wealth, why not enjoy it? There is a strong Jewish tradition that supports this idea. For instance, Sirach praises the simple lifestyle—for those who can afford no better. Sirach thus notes in a manner recalling Socrates, "How ample a little is for a well-disciplined person!" and "In everything you do be moderate" (Sir 31:19, 22). However, Sirach also says,

> My child, treat yourself well, according to your means,
>   and present worthy offerings to the Lord. . . .
> Give, and take, and indulge yourself,
>   because in Hades one cannot look for luxury. (Sir 14:11, 16)

The Sentences of the Syriac Menander, a collection of ancient proverbs, similarly declare, "Live on your possessions as long as you are alive and your eye can see and your foot can walk. For remember and see: one cannot use his goods in Sheol, and riches do not accompany one into the grave. Therefore, you shall not deny yourself the good things."[45]

---

[41]Diogenes Laertius, *Vit. phil.* 2.35.
[42]Diogenes Laertius, *Vit. phil.* 2.31.
[43]Josephus, *Ant.* 3.212.
[44]Josephus, *Ant.* 10.252.
[45]Syr. Men. 368-74.

It would be difficult to see Luke supporting this perspective, however. Life's shortness is motivation to invest in the kingdom, not hedonism (Lk 12:13-21). For Luke, while money itself is not intrinsically evil, it *is* wrong to make a god of money or to place one's confidence in it. Living in the lap of luxury without giving to those around us who go without is sinful, a violation of God's law (Lk 16:31). Simplicity can also clear a path for our ability to respond to God. It can release us from the motivation to accumulate wealth, which in turn inhibits our ability to prioritize God's kingdom. It can teach us to hold our possessions lightly, making benefaction possible. For Luke, however, simplicity is not just living a modest lifestyle while accumulating millions in the bank. Simplicity avoids ostentation but also calls upon us to care for those in need around us.

The ideal of generous benefaction. Luke's intended audience probably expected people of great wealth to give generously (Lk 12:35; 14:33; 16:9, 19-31; 18:18-30; 19:1-9; 21:1-4). Both Greco-Roman and Jewish streams of literature affirm the practice of generous benefaction. Xenophon describes Cyrus as "most generous of heart."[46] Early in his career, Cyrus points out that he has little money, declaring, "I have spent it upon my soldiers."[47] Later, Cyrus gives generously of his wealth. He says,

> All this, my friends, you must consider mine no more than your own; for I have been collecting it, not that I might spend it all myself or use it up all alone . . . but that I might on every occasion be able to reward any one of you who does something meritorious, and also that, if any one of you thinks he needs something, he might come to me and get whatever he happens to want.[48]

Similarly, Xenophon's Socrates affirms generous benefaction. When an inquirer tells Socrates that he wants to "honour the gods without counting the cost . . . help friends in need, and look to it that the city lacks no adornment that my means can supply," Socrates responds by exclaiming

---

[46]Xenophon, *Cyr.* 1.2.1.
[47]Xenophon, *Cyr.* 2.4.9.
[48]Xenophon, *Cyr.* 8.4.36.

that he has "truly noble aspirations."[49] Plutarch similarly tells the story of Cleomenes, who spent his pension by maintaining "himself and his friends in a simple and modest manner, and spent the greater part in good offices and contributions to the refugees from Greece who were in Egypt."[50]

Seneca writes extensively about benefaction. He says that a true gift should be given without any thought to how the giver may benefit. To do otherwise "is to be, not a benefactor, but a money-lender."[51] Seneca describes his ideal benefactor as one who

> "by his spirit matched the wealth of kings," who bestowed his little, but gave it gladly, who beholding my poverty forgot his own, who had, not merely the willingness, but a desire to help, who counted a benefit given as a benefit received, who gave it with no thought of having it returned, who, when it was returned had no thought of having given it, who not only sought, but seized, the opportunity of being useful.[52]

On the other hand, those benefits that "win no thanks" are those "which, though they seem great from their substance and show, are either forced from the giver or are carelessly dropped."[53] For Seneca, as for Luke's Jesus (Lk 21:1-4), the attitude and motivation behind the act of generosity matters. Seneca thus states that what counts as a benefit is not "what is done or what is given, but the spirit of the action, because a benefit consists, not in what is done or given, but in the intention of the giver or doer."[54]

For Seneca, poverty is no excuse to avoid benefaction. He cites the example of Aeschines, who, since he was poor, had only the gift of himself to offer Socrates. Seneca notes that his gift "surpassed Alcibiades, whose heart matched his riches, and the wealthy youths with all their splendid gifts."[55] He concludes, "You see how even in pinching poverty the heart finds the means for generosity."[56] Luke's intended audience might have seen the poor widow in Luke 21:1-4 in the same light.

---

[49]Xenophon, *Oec.* 11.9-10.
[50]Plutarch, *Cleom.* 32.3.
[51]Seneca, *Ben.* 4.3.
[52]Seneca, *Ben.* 1.7.
[53]Seneca, *Ben.* 1.7.
[54]Seneca, *Ben.* 1.6.
[55]Seneca, *Ben.* 1.8.
[56]Seneca, *Ben.* 1.9.

The Jewish model of generous giving is rooted in the laws of the Hebrew Bible. The Israelites were commanded to sow their land for six years and then, in the seventh, allow it to rest so that the poor could feed from it (Ex 23:10-11). They were also commanded to refrain from fully reaping their harvest, so that the poor could gather the remainder (Lev 23:22; Deut 24:21-24). They knew that the one who has pity for the poor lends to God (Prov 19:17). Later Jewish literature echoes these ideals. The Sentences of Pseudo-Phocylides commands against postponing benefactions: "Give to the poor man at once, and do not tell him to come tomorrow."[57] For Sirach, failure to attend to the poor is foolish because God will hear their cries:

> Do not reject a suppliant in distress,
> > or turn your face away from the poor.
> Do not avert your eye from the needy,
> > and give no one reason to curse you;
> for if in bitterness of soul some should curse you,
> > their Creator will hear their prayer. (Sir 4:4-6)

Jewish literature so highly values acts of benefaction, in fact, that the giving of alms can almost be seen as purifying act. Tobias, whose generosity is marked by his willingness to give half of his possessions away, is told by Raphael that "almsgiving saves from death and purges away every sin" (Tob 12:9). Similarly, on his deathbed, Tobit warns his son Tobias, "If you have many possessions, make your gift from them in proportion; if few, do not be afraid to give according to the little you have. So you will be laying up a good treasure for yourself against the day of necessity. For almsgiving delivers from death and keeps you from going into the Darkness" (Tob 4:8-10). For Sirach, benefactions have atoning power:

> As water extinguishes a blazing fire,
> > so almsgiving atones for sin. (Sir 3:30)

Likewise, in the Vision of the Blessed Ezra, Ezra asks who the people are who are escaping the fires of hell. The angel replies that they are those "who

---

[57]Ps.-Phoc. 22.

gave alms generously" and "clothed the naked."[58] Ezra asks the identity of those who can walk over fire without getting burned and is told that they were the ones "freely bringing alms."[59] In contrast, the ones burning in the fire were those who "did not give alms . . . therefore they are in anguish."[60]

Luke's expectation for benefaction may seem radical to us. Many people in our culture vehemently believe that all of the money that we make or inherit is ours to spend on ourselves as we see fit. Luke, however, affirms our responsibility to care for those around us in desperate need. The parable of the rich man and Lazarus tells us that enjoying our own wealth while refusing to meet the needs of the poor may leave us open for God's judgment. Melinda Gates, noting that "Jesus was always reaching out to the poor," declares that for her "faith is about faith in action." She says, "There is a passage in Luke, that you do not put a light under a bushel basket. You put it up for everybody to see. We at the foundation are trying to shine light on the world, on the world's problems and inequities, so that other people will feel this calling too."[61]

THE CORRELATION OF LIFE AND TEACHING
REGARDING WEALTH AND SIMPLICITY

Luke's literary world yields many examples of people who not only preached an ideal of simplicity but also lived it. Xenophon's Socrates, for instance, did not "encourage love of money in his companions"[62] and "showed himself to be one of the people and a friend of mankind," never exacting a fee from anyone "but of his abundance he gave without stint to all."[63] Plutarch's Alexander chided his friends since he was amazed that they did not see "that it is a very servile thing to be luxurious."[64] His own simplicity was so evident, however, that Olympias complained that he gave

---

[58]Vis. Ezra 4-6.

[59]Vis. Ezra 27.

[60]Vis. Ezra 30-32.

[61]Melinda Gates, interview by Timothy C. Morgan, "Melinda Gates: 'I'm Living Out My Faith in Action,'" *Christianity Today*, July 28, 2015, www.christianitytoday.com/ct/2015/july-august /melinda-gates-high-price-of-faith-action.html.

[62]Xenophon, *Mem.* 1.2.5-6.

[63]Xenophon, *Mem.* 1.2.60.

[64]Plutarch, *Alex.* 40.1-2.

all his possessions away, "whilst thyself thou strippest bare."[65] Plutarch's Lycurgus ordered the use of iron money "since its heaviness rendered it virtually worthless."[66] Gradually, luxury "died away of itself, and men of large possessions had no advantage over the poor."[67] Lycurgus himself was known for the "rigid simplicity of his habits, and his unwearied industry."[68]

Plutarch sees his heroes Agis and Cleomenes as "real" kings because of their simplicity and generosity. For instance, Agis

> put into the common stock his own estate, which included extensive tillage and pasture, and apart from this six hundred talents in money. . . . The people, accordingly, were filled with amazement at the magnanimity of the young man, and were delighted, feeling that after a lapse of nearly two hundred years a king had appeared who was worthy of Sparta.[69]

Plutarch's Cleomenes, who was "magnanimous, and no less prone by nature than Agis to self-restraint and simplicity,"[70] "himself placed his property in the common stock, as did . . . his step-father and every one of his friends besides."[71] because he wanted to put into place a kingdom where "the whole land should be common property, debtors should be set free from their debts" and where the people would live lives of moderation and simplicity.[72] Plutarch sees him as a "real" king because he legislates out of his own example:

> In all these matters Cleomenes was himself a teacher. His own manner of life was simple, plain, and no more pretentious than that of the common man, and it was a pattern of self-restraint for all . . . but when men came to Cleomenes, who was a real as well as a titled king, and then saw no profusion of purple robes or shawls about him, and no array of couches . . . they were charmed and completely won over, and declared that he alone was a descendant of Heracles.[73]

---

[65]Plutarch, *Alex.* 39.5.
[66]Plutarch, *Lyc.* 9.1-2.
[67]Plutarch, *Lyc.* 9.4.
[68]Plutarch, *Lyc.* 11.3.
[69]Plutarch, *Ag.* 9.3-10.1.
[70]Plutarch, *Cleom.* 1.3.
[71]Plutarch, *Cleom.* 11.1-2.
[72]Plutarch, *Cleom.* 10.6; 7.1.
[73]Plutarch, *Cleom.* 13.1-2.

Luke's target audience would have been primed to recognize Jesus as this ideal sort of king. In Luke, Jesus practices what he preaches about simplicity. Homeless, he and his disciples are entirely dependent on God for their sustenance (Lk 6:1; 9:13; 9:58; 10:5). With experiential familiarity of the daily provision of God, Jesus urges his disciples to place their confidence in God's ability to supply their needs, an act that will free them up for generous benefaction.

It may be surprising to learn that for all he had to say about wealth and generosity, Seneca was probably in the top 1 percent of wealth for his own society. While he was generous with his friends, he never gave vast amounts of his personal wealth to the poorest people in his society. Admittedly not a wise man,[74] he sketched out for others what he recognized to be a true path of life. The discrepancy between his life and teachings did not go unnoticed either. If we are really honest with ourselves, however, we will probably admit that we have more in common with Seneca than with Plutarch's Agis or Cleomenes. While the hypocrisy in our own lives may not be quite as flagrant as Seneca's, we probably spend more time worrying about our own finances than about the truly poor in our society, we probably care more about how much we save in our purchases than about the ethical business practices of the stores that we frequent, and we probably spend frivolously on ourselves more than we give. Christians aren't always on the cutting edge of moral change in society, to state the situation mildly. We just need to look around us also: there are those in our society, many of whom aren't even Christians, who put us to shame by their generosity and compassion for the world's poor. Plutarch thought we needed a hero to go before us and model the way to virtue. Luke sets up Jesus as a pattern for us to follow. If that weren't enough, we have in Acts a model of the church putting Jesus' teachings on money into practice. As we will see in the following chapter, Luke's early Christian readers took Jesus' teachings on wealth and generosity very seriously indeed. They invite us to an interpretive posture of submission as we ask ourselves how we too might embrace a lifestyle of simplicity.

---

[74]Seneca, *Vit. beat.* 17.3, 4.

SUMMARY

Readers familiar with Luke's literary culture would have been primed to appreciate his portrait of Jesus' teachings and lifestyle of simplicity. They would have felt appropriate disgust for the rich fool of Luke 12:13-21 and the wealthy man who shuns Lazarus in Luke 16:19-30. They would have understood Jesus' teachings about the values of nonmaterial wealth in Luke 12:21, recognizing Christ's kingdom as far more valuable than any material pursuits. They might have considered Luke's ideal for the church as friends sharing wealth (Lk 16:9) against the best cultural ideals for benefaction between friends. They would probably have held a far greater expectation for wealthy members of the community to practice generous benefaction than we do today. A lifestyle of simplicity would have been recognized as more worthy of the kingdom than a lifestyle of luxury and self-indulgence.

At times, Luke's readers would have been pushed to expand their own horizons of understanding. They might have expected Jesus to urge them to seek God's kingdom even if they suffered privation, as Seneca urged a student to pursue philosophy even if he faced starvation. The promise of God's provision (Lk 12:22-34) might have challenged their assumptions. Those familiar with the cultural warnings against excessive wealth may have wondered whether a wealthy person could be included within the kingdom of God and heard hope in Jesus' promise that what is impossible for mortals is possible with God (Lk 18:27). Those already destitute would have been prompted to greater trust through Luke's portrait of a generous God, concerned with the sustenance of God's people.

Luke's readers might have made assumptions alien to a contemporary Western audience. We might doubt that giving to the poor atones for sin and likely would not assume that generosity strengthens our prayers. However, the Jewish expectation that almsgiving brings spiritual power anticipates similar refrains among Luke's commentators in the third and fourth centuries of the church who see the poor in Luke as special recipients of God's favor (Lk 2:18; 16:19-31). The early church emphasized both our need to depend on God's provision and our responsibility to be that provision for the poor. To that discussion we now turn.

3

LEARNING SIMPLICITY
WITH THE CHURCH

W E H A V E A G R E A T D E A L to learn from the early church about a correct
attitude toward and use of money. I sometimes wonder if the materialism
of our culture blinds us so much that we are incapable of really hearing
Jesus' invitation to a radically different lifestyle. We tend to spiritualize
Jesus' teachings on money and don't take seriously enough his mandate to
care for the poor. Many in the early church, however, understand that the
material things that they have are to be shared. Before we can apply Jesus'
teachings on money, we must first truly understand what Jesus is saying.
If the lifestyle of our own culture obscures Jesus' message, we can look to
the early church for help in understanding it.

"Give to Everyone Who Begs from You"; "Lend, Expecting Nothing in Return" (Luke 6:27–38)

As you approach a stoplight, a man walks toward your car with a cardboard
sign: "Homeless. Hungry." Do you give to him or not? If we hesitate, it may
be in part because we are unsure whether we are being helpful or not—and
unsure how the recipient will spend the money. In fact, many cities have
instituted public campaigns to discourage people from giving to panhandlers, arguing that giving handouts promotes homelessness and drug and
alcohol abuse. Pope Francis weighed in on this issue a couple of years ago.
He said, "Give them money, and don't worry about how they are going to
spend it."[1] It is clear from their interpretation of this Lukan text that

---

[1] Editorial Board, "The Pope and the Panhandler," *New York Times*, March 3, 2017, A18.

several of the patristic writers felt the same way. Clement of Alexandria thought that one should not attempt to "distinguish between the 'worthy' and the 'unworthy,'" for by "pretending to test who will deserve the benefit and who will not, you may possibly neglect some who are beloved of God."[2] Tertullian, a prolific writer of the second and third century, would have agreed, insisting that we are simply required "to give to him that asks,"[3] regardless of need. In other words, just as we would not wonder about how our waiter might spend the tip we give him, so also we do not need to worry about the money we give a panhandler after it leaves our hands. It is no longer ours. Chrysostom also thought judging a person's moral character should not be a factor in a decision to give to a beggar. He says, "Just give." He continues, "The poor man has one plea . . . do not require anything else from him; but even if he is the most wicked of all men and is at a loss for his necessary sustenance, let us free him from hunger."[4] Chrysostom notes, "When you see on earth the man who has encountered the shipwreck of poverty, do not judge him, do not seek an account of his life, but free him from his misfortune. . . . Charity is so called because we give it even to the unworthy."[5] Finally, he simply states, "Need alone is the poor man's worthiness."[6]

Not all ancient Christian interpreters would agree, however. The Didache, a short first-century Christian document, proclaims curses on one who receives alms without genuine need, leading to the mandate, "Let thine alms sweat in thy hands, until thou know to whom thou shouldst give."[7] Whether we give to panhandlers directly or channel that money through charities that seek to end homelessness, our Christian responsibility, however, remains clear. We must give to those in need. As Cyril of Alexandria, a prominent fifth-century church father, observes, such giving is "a proof indeed of love."[8]

---

[2]Clement of Alexandria, *Quis div.* 92:341.
[3]Tertullian, *Marc.* 17, in *ANF* 3:372-73.
[4]Chrysostom, *On Wealth and Poverty* 52.
[5]Chrysostom, *On Wealth and Poverty* 52.
[6]Chrysostom, *On Wealth and Poverty* 53.
[7]*Did.* 1, in *ANF* 7:377.
[8]Cyril of Alexandria, *Comm. Luke* 29, 137.

Giving to those in need is merciful, and the appropriate activity for Jesus' followers. In words that are fitting for today as well, Gregory of Nyssa, the fourth-century bishop of Nyssa, observes, "We have seen in these days a great number of the naked and homeless," and he urges the church to "assist these people."[9] Looking at so many in need around him, he says, "The commandment is vital especially now, with so many in need of basic essentials for survival, and many constrained by need, and many whose bodies are utterly spent from suffering sickness. In caring for them, you will see for yourself the realization of the good news. I think above all of the victims of a terrible illness."[10] Given the distress of our own day, Gregory's words are as appropriate as ever. He urges Christians to live out the gospel through their care of those in need around them.

We tend to think of our personal wealth as *ours* to do with as we please. Gregory of Nyssa points out that we should not "retain everything" for ourselves but "share with the poor, who are favorites of God."[11] In any case our wealth is not our own, but "all belongs to God, our common Father."[12] For many in the early church, failure to give to the poor is akin to robbing them of their due. Augustine, for instance, observes that for the Christian, "failure to share his surplus with the needy is like to theft."[13] This is rooted in the idea that God has blessed the wealthy with more than they need, so that they may care for the poor. Augustine urges his audience, "You be their granaries, so that God may give to you what you can give to them."[14] Those who refuse this task shirk their duties to redistribute wealth to those in need and are thus stealing from the poor and from God.

For the early church, as for Seneca, as we saw in the last chapter, one's attitude in benefaction also matters. Gifts must come from the heart and

---

[9]Gregory of Nyssa, *On the Love of the Poor*: 1 "On Good Works" in Susan Holman, *The Hungry are Dying: Beggars and Bishops in Roman Cappadocia*, Oxford Studies in Historical Theology (New York: Oxford University Press, 2001), 194.

[10]Gregory of Nyssa, *On the Love of the Poor*: 2 "On the saying, 'Whoever Hs Done It to One of These Has Done It to Me'" in Susan Holman, *The Hungry are Dying: Beggars and Bishops in Roman Cappadocia*, Oxford Studies in Historical Theology (New York: Oxford University Press, 2001), 200-201.

[11]Gregory of Nyssa, "On Good Works," 197.

[12]Gregory of Nyssa, "On Good Works," 197.

[13]Augustine, *Sermon* 206.2, in FC 38:87.

[14]Augustine, *Sermon* 376A.3, in WSA III/10:350.

not be given begrudgingly. The Epistle of Barnabas, a first-century letter included in the Codex Sinaiticus, records, "Thou shalt not hesitate to give, nor murmur when thou givest."[15] Cyril of Alexandria insists that one must not grieve the loss of possessions. He notes that in this text that even "if a man have but one outer garment, he must not count it a thing unendurable to put off with it also his undergarment, if it so befall." Cyril feels that such an attitude is only possible for the mature: "But this is a virtue possible only for a mind entirely turned away from covetousness."[16]

Many in the early church emphasize that giving to the poor is a way of giving to God. For Augustine, God is served when the poor are fed: "For, in the person of the poor, He who experiences no hunger wished Himself to be fed. Therefore, let us not spurn our God who is needy in His poor, so that we in our need may be filled in Him who is rich."[17] Basil the Great, the fourth-century bishop of Caesarea, instructs, "He that hath mercy on the poor, lendeth to God."[18]

The early church eagerly anticipated spiritual rewards for those who practiced generous benefaction. Gregory of Nyssa sees the poor as "stewards of our hope, doorkeepers of the kingdom, who open the door to the righteous and close it again to the unloving and misanthropists."[19] For Augustine, generosity empowers our prayers. He urges, "Let us by our prayers add the wings of piety to our almsdeeds and fasting so that they may fly more readily to God."[20] One should shut up alms in the heart of the poor, and they will pray for you to the Lord.[21] Basil notes that the God who receives "trifling things through a poor man, will give great things in return for them."[22] While our motivation for giving ought to come from within, we can see a clear theme that one who is greedy should not expect generosity from God. Augustine asks, "If a farmer is not justified in seeking a harvest when he knows he has sowed no seed, how much more

---

[15]Ep. Barn. 19, in *ANF* 1:148.
[16]Cyril of Alexandria, *Comm. Luke* 29, 137.
[17]Augustine, *Sermon* 206.2, in FC 38:87-88.
[18]Basil of Caesarea, *Homily* 12.5, in FC 46:190.
[19]Gregory of Nyssa, "On Good Works," 195.
[20]Augustine, *Sermon* 206.2, in FC 38:87.
[21]Augustine, *Sermon* 376A.3, in WSA III/10:350, citing the Vulgate on Sir 29:12.
[22]Basil of Caesarea, *Homily* 12.5, in FC 46:190.

unreasonably does he who has refused to hear the petition of a poor man seek a generous response from God?"[23]

The Parable of the Rich Fool (Luke 12:13-21)

Is it wrong to possess great wealth? Many in the early church thought that wealth could, in fact, be dangerous. For Cyprian, the third-century bishop of Carthage, this text shows that riches are "full of peril, that in them is the root of seducing evils."[24] He cautions that in "proportion as you are rich in this world, you may become poor to God."[25] He even feels that such people "cannot labour in the church" for they "do not see the needy and poor."[26] For Cyril of Alexandria, this text teaches that idolized wealth is "a snare of evil spirits, by which they drag down man's soul to the meshes of hell."[27]

Patristic writers are quick to highlight the rich man's foolishness. Cyprian notes that ironically "God rebukes the rich fool" whose "life already was failing" as he was thinking of the abundance of his food.[28] He warns those who are not mindful of this text, "You are the captive and slave of your money. . . . You keep your money, which, when kept, does not keep you."[29] Ambrose, the fourth-century archbishop of Milan, points out that the rich man foolishly accumulates his wealth "in vain," "when his full barns were broken by the new harvest" and he did not know for whom he gathered his abundant harvest.[30] Cyril of Alexandria says that the rich man foolishly "settles for himself the duration of his life," while he has not been rich toward God.[31]

Some early Lukan interpreters highlight the impact of the rich man's greed on his community. For Chrysostom, the fourth- and fifth-century archbishop of Constantinople, known for his asceticism, "there is nothing more wretched" than such a greedy attitude. He remarks, "In truth he took

---

[23]Augustine, *Sermon* 206.2, in FC 38:87.
[24]Cyprian, *Dom. or.* 20, in *ANF* 5:453.
[25]Cyprian, *Eleem.* 13, in *ANF* 5:479.
[26]Cyprian, *Eleem.* 15, in *ANF* 5:480.
[27]Cyril of Alexandria, *Comm. Luke* 89, 360.
[28]Cyprian, *Treatise* 4, *Dom. or.* 20, in *ANF* 5:453.
[29]Cyprian, *Treatise* 8, *Eleem.* 13, in *ANF* 5:479.
[30]Ambrose, *Exp. Luc.*, 280.
[31]Cyril of Alexandria, *Comm. Luke* 89, 361.

down his barns; for the safe barns are not walls but the stomachs of the poor." Because of the rich man's greed, he was "led away as a prisoner" by the angels.[32] According to Cyril of Alexandria, the rich man is judged because he "purposed to enjoy for himself alone those revenues that were sufficient for a populous city."[33] Cyril points out that those like the rich man, "who with avaricious hand gathers that which is not his," should realize that the powerless, wronged by his actions "can but raise his eyes to Him Who alone is able to be angry for what he has suffered. And He, because He is just and good, accepts his supplication, and pities the tears of the sufferer, and brings punishment on those who have done wrong."[34] For Basil of Caesarea, this man "did not remember that he shared with others a common nature, nor did he think it necessary to distribute from his abundance to those in need."[35] He is warned, "Do not suppose that all this was furnished for your own gullet! Resolve to treat the things in your possession as belonging to others" because "a strict accounting of their disbursement will be demanded from you."[36] For Basil, just as the rich man's wealth was not his own, so also Christians should release our excess for the good of the poor. He urges: "The bread you are holding back is for the hungry, the clothes you keep put away are for the naked, the shoes that are rotting away with disuse are for those who have none, the silver you keep buried in the earth is for the needy. You are thus guilty of injustice toward as many as you might have aided and did not."[37] Instead, we must invest in eternal wealth. For Ambrose, "an inheritance of immortality, not of money, should be sought."[38] Connecting this text to Luke 16:9, he points out that "virtue alone is the companion of the dead, compassion alone follows us, which . . . through the use of worthless money, acquires eternal dwellings for the dead."[39] For Cyril, one who "is rich towards God" is also

---

[32]Chrysostom, *On Wealth and Poverty* 43.
[33]Cyril of Alexandria, *Comm. Luke* 89, 361.
[34]Cyril of Alexandria, *Comm. Luke* 89, 360.
[35]Basil of Caesarea, *Homily* 6, "I Will Tear Down My Barns," trans. M. F. Toal in *On Social Justice: St. Basil the Great* (New York: St. Vladimir's Seminary Press, 2009), Kindle.
[36]Basil of Caesarea, *Homily* 6.
[37]Basil of Caesarea, *Homily* 6.
[38]Ambrose, *Exp. Luc.*, 280.
[39]Ambrose, *Exp. Luc.*, 280.

one for whom "few things are sufficient" and one "whose hand is open to the necessities of the indigent, comforting the sorrows of those in poverty, according to his means, and the utmost of his power," guaranteeing a future bountiful harvest "in the storehouses that are above."[40]

Trust in God's Provision (Luke 12:22-34)

In our Christian culture today, we generally cut some slack for those who are anxious about their finances—including ourselves. Some patristic writers might seem a little harsh in comparison. Tertullian says that God "prohibits all anxiety . . . as an outrage against his liberality." For Tertullian, if God "knows what things man has need of, and yet has failed to supply them, he is in the failure guilty of either malignity or weakness." But, he says, God does graciously supply our needs. To worry about such things, therefore, is to be "defective of faith." For Tertullian, this text teaches us "to be free from the embarrassments of a perplexed and much occupied life."[41] Similarly, Ambrose thinks that "it is unseemly for the soldiers of the Kingdom . . . to worry about food. . . . The King knows how to feed, cherish, and clothe his Household."[42] Cyril of Alexandria adds, "Nor does he permit us at all to doubt, but that most certainly He will . . . bestow upon us in all things a sufficiency," and it is a "wicked thing" to not trust God "when He promises us the necessaries of life."[43]

Are we really to see it as a sinful thing to be stressed out when we can't find jobs, lose our homes, are faced with crushing medical bills, or are drowning in student loans? This seems like a particularly harsh and out-of-touch teaching in light of the economic suffering in our world today. First, God knows what we are thinking and feeling, and it doesn't do us or our relationship with God any good to pretend that we are doing fine when in fact we are not. If we are crippled with anxiety over the future we should bring those fears into the presence of God—not just once but again and again, asking both for God's material provision and that God will walk

---

[40]Cyril of Alexandria, *Comm. Luke* 89, 362.
[41]Tertullian, *Marc.* 4.28, in *ANF* 3:398.
[42]Ambrose, *Exp. Luc.*, 283-84.
[43]Cyril of Alexandria, *Comm. Luke* 90, 364.

with us as we battle our deepest fears about our futures. We can learn some important lessons from the early church on this text, however. In our society, which runs on the pursuit and enjoyment of money, the potential loss of income can feel like the end of the world. One of the most important perspectives the early church provides on this text is an ability to tamp down the felt importance of money in our lives. Cyril of Alexandria tells us that God wants us to "choose the wise and more excellent life." This is why God "makes them abandon superfluous anxiety, and does not permit them to practice a careworn and urgent industry through the wish of gathering what exceeds their necessities." Instead, one should "bestow your earnestness on things of far higher importance. For the life indeed is of more importance than food, and the body than raiment."[44] The heightened levels of need in our world today offer many invitations. Those who are jobless, lacking insurance, at risk of losing their homes, and consumed with worry about how to provide for their families should enlist God as companion and counselor, handing over their urgency to God. Those who are in less dire straits should consider that they may be the means through which God cares for those who are suffering.

The early church has an overwhelming confidence in God's ability and willingness to supply our needs. Cyprian writes,

> For daily bread cannot be wanting to the righteous man, since it is written, "The Lord will not slay the soul of the righteous by hunger"; and again, "I have been young, and now am old, yet I have not seen the righteous forsaken, nor his seed begging their bread" [Prov 10:3; Ps 37:25]. . . . To those who seek God's kingdom and righteousness, He promises that all things shall be added. For since all things are God's, nothing will be wanting to him who possesses God, if God Himself be not wanting to him.[45]

For Cyril of Alexandria such confidence is rooted in God's character: "The Lord is worthy to be trusted; and He clearly promises it to thee, and by little things gives thee full assurance that He will be true also in that which is great."[46] Ambrose points to the lesson from nature. If the birds and

---

[44]Cyril of Alexandria, *Comm. Luke* 90, 364.
[45]Cyprian, *Dom. or.* 21, in *ANF* 5:453.
[46]Cyril of Alexandria, *Comm. Luke* 90, 364.

flowers are "so clad by God's Providence that they lack no use for Grace or
for ornament," how much more has "rational man, if he places all his use-
fulness in God and does not dishonor the Faith with intent to
waver . . . rightly presumed on the favour of God?"[47] If our desire is for
Christ's kingdom, God will take care of the rest. Ambrose declares that
"Grace will not be lacking for the Faithful in the present or in the future, if
only those who desire the heavenly do not seek the earthly."[48] Such assur-
ances may push the limits of our belief, given the troubled times in which
we live. Our Western values of self-sufficiency and individualism fight
against our ability to live into this attitude of dependency. The early church
invites us to levels of trust that challenge the core of our identity.

Many in the early church are quick to point out that God supplies what
we *need* and no more. Here again, their ascetic perspective butts up un-
comfortably against our materialistic one. For Ambrose, greed is "the
cause of our poverty." Birds do not claim ownership over the food God
provides to all of them. In contrast, "we lose what is common when we
claim it as our own." Ambrose asks, "For why do ye value your riches when
God wished also your subsistence to be shared with all other creatures?
The birds of the air claim nothing for themselves, and, therefore, know no
lack of food, because they do not know how to be envious of others." For
Ambrose the example of the birds is "truly a great and fitting example,
which we should follow with faith."[49]

Others go even further. For Clement of Alexandria, the second- and
early-third-century leader of the school of Alexandria, whatever is
beyond eating for sustenance is "of the devil," but "of bare sustenance" he
says, "Your Father knoweth that ye need these."[50] For Tertullian, too,
bread "is the only food necessary for believers"; for "all the other things
the nations seek after."[51] Are we all called to a life of asceticism? In 2000,
Daniel Suelo quit his job, moved to Utah, and has lived ever since in caves,
eating wild berries, roadkill, and what he can find in dumpsters, wanting

---

[47]Ambrose, *Exp. Luc.*, 282.
[48]Ambrose, *Exp. Luc.,* 283-84.
[49]All quotations in this paragraph come from Ambrose, *Exp. Luc.,* 281.
[50]Clement of Alexandria, *Paed.* 2.11, in *ANF* 2:264.
[51]Tertullian, *Or.* 6, in *ANF* 3:683.

to remain free from the control of money.[52] Is this the ideal? It is certainly not for everyone!

Cyril of Alexandria points out that God will give us only what will benefit us. He asks, "And what benefit at all is there in living luxuriously? Or rather, will it not bring with it utter destruction?"[53] Rather, clothing should be "such as necessity requires," "decorous and easily procurable" and with it "such a bare sufficiency of food as merely satisfies the demands of nature."[54] While we may not embrace the full asceticism of the early church's perspective, we should certainly hear the lesson in simplicity that they are attempting to impart and seek to apply it to our lives. Movement into simplicity goes against the grain of our culture and typically takes some time and intentionality.

For Gregory of Nyssa, God's generous provision in nature is a model for Christians to follow. Noting that "God is the original designer of good deeds, nourishing the starving, watering the thirsty, clothing those who are naked,"[55] he says that we must "imitate our Savior and creator—as much as mortal can try to imitate eternal" and not "monopolize all for our own pleasure."[56] For Gregory, "Mercy and good deeds are the works God loves."[57]

It is very difficult for people who are worried about money to give generously. Luke suggests that if we are able to place our confidence in God to provide for our needs, we will be released from such anxiety and will then be able to submit ourselves completely to God's rule, which includes generous benefaction for the poor. Cyprian observes that unlike the rich man who hoarded his goods, the one who acts on Luke 12:33 "becomes perfect and complete who sells all his goods, and distributes them for the use of the poor, and so lays up for himself treasure in heaven." Such a person "is able to follow Him, and to imitate the glory of the Lord's passion"

---

[52]Erin Daley, "These People Live Without Money," *MSN*, July 15, 2019, www.msn.com/en-us/money/personalfinance/these-people-live-without-money/ss-AAEfe75#image=4.

[53]Cyril of Alexandria, *Comm. Luke* 90, 364.

[54]Cyril of Alexandria, *Comm. Luke* 90, 365.

[55]Gregory of Nyssa, "On Good Works," 196.

[56]Gregory of Nyssa, "On Good Works," 197.

[57]Gregory of Nyssa, "On Good Works," 197.

and "accompanies his possessions, which before have been sent to God." If one lacks this attitude toward money, one should pray for it and "know, from the character of the prayer, what he ought to be."[58] Interestingly, Cyril of Alexandria thinks that this command will be difficult for many: "Now the commandment indeed is beautiful, and good, and salutary; but it did not escape His knowledge, that it is impossible for the majority to practice it."[59] He sees Luke 16:9 as a remedy for this: if Christians are unwilling to *completely* dispossess themselves, they can at least give generously to the poor.[60] There will always be people who have more and less than we do. In an age of uncertainty, we need to relax our tight-fisted dependency on our own provision, pray for a growing ability to trust in God's, and regard each other's scarcity with the same concern that we would have for our own.

Counting the Cost (Luke 14:25-33)

In contrast to those promoting the prosperity gospel today, Luke's earliest interpreters remind us that prosperity is not a natural consequence of faithfulness to God; in fact, those who are thinking about committing themselves to Christ's rule should consider that material hardship may be part of the cost they pay to follow him. Tertullian discusses this text in conjunction with Luke 12:22-34. He asks how Christians can declare, "I have no means to live" after committing themselves to Christ. For him, this question "is advanced too late." Like the builder in the present text, they should have counted the cost before responding to Christ: "Deliberation should have been made before." The Christian should not be preoccupied with such material needs. "For what is it you say? 'I shall be in need.' But the Lord calls the needy 'happy.' 'I shall have no food.' But 'think not,' says He, 'about food; and as an example of clothing we have the lilies.'" He reminds his audience, "If you wish to be the Lord's disciple, it is necessary you 'take your cross, and follow the Lord.'" He declares, "Faith fears not famine. . . . It has learnt not to respect life; how much more food?" He

---

[58]Cyprian, *Dom. or.* 20, in ANF 5:453.
[59]Cyril of Alexandria, *Comm. Luke* 111, 452.
[60]Cyril of Alexandria, *Comm. Luke* 111, 452.

realizes the difficulty of what he asks: "How many have fulfilled these conditions? But what with men is difficult, with God is easy."[61] Such discussions might seem out of touch for parents who are going without dinner so that their children can eat. Luke, however, emphasizes God's provision (Lk 12:31) and urges those of us who still have enough to care for those who don't. If we read Luke individualistically, then each person focuses on his or her own need or excess. If we read the Lukan text as a community, however, then another's desperation is *my* problem—and my invitation to do something about it.

Luke's earliest interpreters envision a society where Christians actively meet the needs of others. Cyprian points out that the reward of those who invite the lame, and the blind, and the poor, is a "recompense [that] shall be made thee at the resurrection of the just." These rewards "are [to take place] in the times of the kingdom" when the righteous "shall have a table at hand prepared for them by God, supplying them with all sorts of dishes."[62] A kingdom perspective on our finances assumes that those who metaphorically (or actually) dine at our table and benefit from our paychecks will not just be our family members and friends but all of those in need of our generosity, our compassion, and our acceptance.

THE DISHONEST MANAGER (LUKE 16:1-9)

While some contemporary readers might wonder how they might use "dishonest wealth" to make friends, for the early church it is clear: this story is about almsgiving. For Ambrose, one makes friends "of the mammon of iniquity" by "giving it to the poor."[63] Chrysostom similarly understands that regarding this text, "it is not friendship in this which will vouch for you, but almsgiving."[64] This parable promotes action—caring for the needs of the poor—not just attitude.

For many ancient commentators, wealth is given to us so that we can bestow it on those in need. For Ambrose, just as the manager was "the

---

[61]Tertullian, *Idol.* 12, in *ANF* 3:68.
[62]Cyprian, *Fort.* 7, in *ANF* 5:500.
[63]Ambrose, *Exp. Luc.*, 328.
[64]Chrysostom, *On Wealth and Poverty* 77.

steward of the riches of others,"[65] so are we. Ambrose warns that we cannot assume that wealth is ours to spend as we choose: "For us the riches are Another's . . . and they are neither born with us nor do they die with us."[66] Ambrose sees those[67] who will not share their goods with the poor as "charged with deceit and avarice." He says that "since they knew them to belong to others—for the fruit of the earth was given by the Lord to all for their common use—they should share with the poor."[68] Cyril of Alexandria argues that the wealthy "have been entrusted with worldly wealth by the merciful permission of Almighty God; according nevertheless to His intention they have been appointed stewards for the poor." Not all, however discharge their stewardship rightly. Some "scatter, so to speak, what has been given them of the Lord; for they waste it solely on their pleasures," forgetting the decrees of the Lord.[69]

For Cyril of Alexandria, a discussion of this text provides the perfect opportunity to answer the question raised in Luke 14:33 and Luke 18:25. He asks, "For is it the case, that every one who is rich, and possesses abundant wealth, is determinately cut off from the expectation of God's grace?" Cyril sees an answer and provision of salvation in Luke 16:1-9: "For the Savior pointed out a way of salvation to those who possess earthly wealth, saying, Make unto yourselves friends of the unrighteous mammon, that when ye depart this life they may receive you into their tents."[70] For Cyril, this passage teaches that even the wealthy can be saved as long as they use their resources for kingdom purposes. He adds, "It is, that while they are yet in this world, if they are unwilling to divide all their wealth among the poor, that at least they should gain friends by a part of it. . . . For it is impossible for love to the poor ever to remain unrewarded. Whether therefore a man give away all his wealth, or but a part, he will certainly benefit his soul."[71]

---

[65]Ambrose, *Exp. Luc.*, 328.
[66]Ambrose, *Exp. Luc.*, 328.
[67]For him, "the Jews." Ambrose, *Exp. Luc.*, 328.
[68]Ambrose, *Exp. Luc.*, 328.
[69]Cyril of Alexandria, *Comm. Luke* 106, 440.
[70]Cyril of Alexandria, *Comm. Luke* 29, 135.
[71]Cyril of Alexandria, *Comm. Luke* 106, 441.

Those who keep the wealth that God has given them solely for their own pleasures are judged as greedy and deserving of punishment. Cyril says that such a person forsakes a heavenly reward "by treating with contempt those who are in utter poverty, and refusing even sometimes to admit their words into our ears; while, on the other hand, we luxuriously provide a costly table, either for friends who live in pomp, or for those whose habit it is to praise and flatter."[72] The greedy are warned "lest eternal and never ending poverty should follow upon wealth here, and everlasting torment succeed to the pleasures of the present time."[73] Almsgiving, an act that "becometh the saints,"[74] instead "saves the soul."[75] The early church took seriously Jesus' mandate in Luke to care for the poor. If we interpret simplicity as merely decluttering our homes or cultivating a garden, we have missed the point. It is the use of our resources for those who are in need.

LAZARUS AND THE RICH MAN (LUKE 16:19-31)

This parable was an important one for the ancient Lukan scholars, some of whom write on it at length. Several point out the callousness of the rich man. Jerome, the fourth- and fifth-century scholar, addresses him directly: "Most wretched of men, you see a member of your own body lying there outside your gate, and have you no compassion?"[76] Cyril of Alexandria does likewise, "Thou never once calledst to mind the sick and sorrowful; thou hadst no compassion on Lazarus when thou sawest him thrown down at thy portals. Thou beheldest the man suffering incurable misery, and a prey to intolerable griefs."[77] Chrysostom points out that if the rich man "did not give alms to this man who was continually prostrate at his gate, lying before his eyes, whom he had to see every day once or twice or many times as he went in and out," then to "whom of those he encountered would he ever have been moved to pity?"[78] The rich man's continued neglect of Lazarus

---

[72]Cyril of Alexandria, *Comm. Luke* 109, 443.
[73]Cyril of Alexandria, *Comm. Luke* 111, 452.
[74]Cyril of Alexandria, *Comm. Luke* 106, 441.
[75]Cyril of Alexandria, *Comm. Luke* 109, 444.
[76]Jerome, *Homily* 86, in FC 57:201.
[77]Cyril of Alexandria, *Comm. Luke* 112, 456.
[78]Chrysostom, *On Wealth and Poverty* 21.

compounds his guilt. Chrysostom observes that he "surely ought to have been moved on the third or fourth or the day after that, even if he were more cruel than the wild beasts."[79] Cyril of Alexandria, too, notes, "But the rich man was more cruel than the beasts; for he felt neither sympathy for him nor compassion; but was full of all mercilessness."[80]

Gregory of Nyssa is quick to apply this text to his own day. He complains of those who "indulge in a frenzy of pleasures," who are "gourmands" dining at a "delicate" table, living in "sumptuous dwellings," who like to "squander their goods on enormous houses and superfluous ornaments," while outside "a myriad of Lazaruses sit at the gate, some dragging themselves along painfully, some with their eyes gouged out, others with amputated feet, some quite literally creep, mutilated in all their members." These, "the beloved of Christ, who embody the essential commandment without having gained one mouthful of bread or meat" are instead "satiated with insults and blows." He warns, "Twofold is the sin that reigns in this house of shame: one is the excess of the drunkards, the other the hunger of the poor who have been driven away."[81]

For Chrysostom, this parable teaches that failure to provide alms to the poor is theft. He states, "Not only the theft of others' goods but also the failure to share one's own goods with others is theft and swindle and defraudation."[82] He says,

> God has allowed you to have more: not for you to waste on prostitutes, drink, fancy food, expensive clothes, and all the other kinds of indolence, but for you to distribute to those in need. Just as an official in the imperial treasury, if he neglects to distribute where he is ordered, but spends instead for his own indolence, he pays the penalty and is put to death, so also the rich man is a kind of steward for the money which is owned for distribution to the poor. He is directed to distribute it to his fellow servants who are in want. So if he spends more on himself than his need requires, he will pay the harshest penalty hereafter. For his own goods are not his own, but belong to his fellow servants.[83]

---

[79]Chrysostom, *On Wealth and Poverty* 21.
[80]Cyril of Alexandria, *Comm. Luke* 111, 454.
[81]Gregory of Nyssa, "On Good Works," 198,
[82]Chrysostom, *On Wealth and Poverty* 49.
[83]Chrysostom, *On Wealth and Poverty* 50.

He then urges his hearers, "Therefore let us use our goods sparingly, as belonging to others, so that they may become our own. How shall we use them sparingly, as belonging to others? When we do not spend them beyond our needs, and do not spend for our needs only, but give equal shares into the hands of the poor."[84]

The early Christian writers highlight the rich man's fate. Clement warns that if one engages in the "superfluity" of extravagant dress and a "love of ornament," one's deeds will be like "hay," "good for nothing but to be burned with fire."[85] After describing similar disparities between the excessively wealthy and the poor whom they ignore, Gregory of Nyssa asks, "If God sees these scenes—and I am sure He does—what fatal catastrophe, do you think, does He hold in store for those who hate the poor? Answer me! Or do you not know that it is to this end that the holy gospel shouts out and testifies with scenes of horror and dread? And thus it describes the deep groaning of the man flung into the pit and held captive in the abyss of the wicked."[86] Jerome notes that "torments . . . are the rewards of covetous wealth."[87] For him, the Christian soul "naked follows the naked Christ," and "when it looks with envy upon a rich man, or when it itself revels in wealth and display, may it call to mind Dives;[88] may it ponder well his voice as he cries out and begs for the touch of Lazarus's finger."[89] Cyril of Alexandria, addressing the rich man, observes that if he had "been a partner with Lazarus" then "a portion of his consolation would have been given thee by God. . . . But this thou didst not do, and therefore thou alone art tormented."[90] For Cyril, care for the poor is "better than any kind of well-doing; for it works in our souls a certain divine likeness which molds us, so to speak, after God's image."[91] Chrysostom captures the pastoral warning:

---

[84]Chrysostom, *On Wealth and Poverty* 50.
[85]Clement of Alexandria, *Paed.* 2.11, in *ANF* 2:264.
[86]Gregory of Nyssa, "On Good Works," 199.
[87]Jerome, *Homily* 87, in FC 57:203.
[88]The original Greek text just refers to the rich man as "the rich man." Church tradition gives him a name, Dives, from the Latin word for "rich man."
[89]Jerome, *Homily* 87, in FC 57:208-9.
[90]Cyril of Alexandria, *Comm. Luke* 112, 456.
[91]Cyril of Alexandria, *Comm. Luke* 112, 457.

When you consider that in the most extreme cold, in the middle of the night, when you are sleeping on a bed, the poor man has thrown himself on a pile of straw by the door of the bath-house, wrapping the stalks around him, shivering, stiff with cold, pinched with hunger . . . I am sure that you will condemn yourself for providing for yourself unnecessary luxury while not allowing him even what is necessary.[92]

Ancient commentators look to this parable for a redefinition of wealth and poverty. For Chrysostom, one who is truly wealthy "needs few possessions" and one who is poor "has many desires." He notes, "We ought to consider this the definition of poverty and wealth."[93] One's true state of wealth or poverty is revealed at death, as with Lazarus's and the rich man's reversal. When "everyone puts off the masks of wealth or poverty and departs to the other world" then "all are judged by their deeds alone, some are revealed truly wealthy, others poor, some of high class, others of no account."[94] People in our culture sometimes look at the poor as lazy or unambitious, and assign a moral value of "success" to those who are wealthy. Chrysostom invites us to imagine ourselves at the end of life, stripped of all of our possessions. Who are we without these external things that give us value?

THE RICH RULER (LUKE 18:18-30)

Early Lukan interpreters also have much to say on the rich ruler of Luke 18. Basil of Caesarea and Cyril of Alexandria doubt the ruler's sincerity. For Basil, he is a "tempter who crafted his questions disingenuously."[95] Cyril notes, "Observe, therefore, how he mixes up flattery with fraud and deceit . . . for he supposed that he could in this way deceive Him."[96] Cyril does not think that he asks "with a view to learn; for then his question would have been worthy of all praise."[97] Because Christ could discern the rich man's ill motives, Cyril says, he "proceeds at once to that which would

---

[92]Chrysostom, *On Wealth and Poverty* 26.
[93]Chrysostom, *On Wealth and Poverty* 40.
[94]Chrysostom, *On Wealth and Poverty* 47.
[95]Basil of Caesarea, Homily 7, "To the Rich Ruler," in *On Social Justice: St. Basil the Great,* trans. C. Paul Schroeder (New York: St. Vladimir's Seminary Press, 2009).
[96]Cyril of Alexandria, *Comm. Luke* 122, 487.
[97]Cyril of Alexandria, *Comm. Luke* 123, 489.

grieve him" with the call to dispossession.[98] In contrast, those who sincerely receive the gospel "become superior to wealth and the love of lucre; their mind is established in courage; they set no value on temporal things, but thirst rather after things eternal; they honor a voluntary poverty, and are earnest in love to the brethren."[99]

The issue of whether or not the rich could be saved was a significant discussion in the early church. Clement of Alexandria, although he thinks that the wealthy "ought to have diminished and curtailed wealth, as a perilous and deadly disease,"[100] feels that this text has caused some wealthy people to "despair of themselves, feeling that they are not destined to obtain life."[101] He argues that "salvation is not impossible"[102] for them. Cyril of Alexandria agrees that Christ "does not altogether cut away the hope of the rich, but reserves for them a place and way of salvation. For He did not say that it is impossible for a rich man to enter in, but that he does so with difficulty."[103]

Clement of Alexandria thinks that the story of the rich man who was unwilling to dispossess himself "must not be interpreted in a merely literal sense,"[104] but that this text has "hidden meaning."[105] Clement does not see this text as "a command to fling away the substance that belongs to him and to part with his riches, but to banish from the soul its opinions about riches, its attachment to them, its excessive desire, its morbid excitement over them, its anxious cares, the thorns of our earthly existence which choke the seed of the true life."[106] He argues that "it is no great or enviable thing to be simply without riches"[107]; rather, the essential thing is to "strip the soul itself and the will of their lurking passions."[108]

In the present text, Jesus declares that "it is easier for a camel to go through the eye of a needle than for someone who is rich to enter the

---

[98]Cyril of Alexandria, *Comm. Luke* 123, 490.
[99]Cyril of Alexandria, *Comm. Luke* 123, 490.
[100]Clement of Alexandria, *Quis div.*, LCL 92:271.
[101]Clement of Alexandria, *Quis div.*, LCL 92:273-5.
[102]Clement of Alexandria, *Quis div.*, LCL 92:275.
[103]Cyril of Alexandria, *Comm. Luke* 123, 491.
[104]Clement of Alexandria, *Quis div.*, LCL 92:281.
[105]Clement of Alexandria, *Quis div.*, LCL 92:283.
[106]Clement of Alexandria, *Quis div.*, LCL 92:291-3.
[107]Clement of Alexandria, *Quis div.*, LCL 92:293.
[108]Clement of Alexandria, *Quis div.*, LCL 92:295.

kingdom of God" (18:25). Several ancient commentators struggle with the harshness of this statement. Clement of Alexandria thinks that the church has got it all wrong in interpreting this text literally. For him, the text has "some higher meaning," which is that the wealthy must learn "how and in what manner wealth is to be used."[109] Cyril, in an attempt to tamp down the radical edge of Jesus' statement, interprets the "camel" in Luke 18:25 as a "thick cable,"[110] (in Greek the terms differ by a single letter and were probably pronounced the same way).[111] Ambrose broadens the text's application. He sees the eye of the needle as the narrow way through which the sinner can enter the kingdom of God. This is made possible through the work of Christ, who "piercing the way of death by the Passion of his Own Body, like a needle restored the torn garments of our nature." Ambrose observes of this image that one "can also understand it morally, about every sinner and haughty rich man." He asks,

> Does it not seem to you that the publican, laden with the awareness of his own sins, when he dared not raise his eyes to God, will like a camel through the help of his confession, pass more easily through the eye of a needle than the Pharisee will enter the Kingdom of Heaven, arrogant in prayer, boasting of innocence, overconfident of glory, reproacher of mercy, proclaimer of himself, impeacher of another, who accosted the Lord than beseeched Him? So if anyone trembles at the camel, let him shudder at him who is uglier than the camel in his deeds.[112]

We might wonder how ancient writers who diminish the severity of Jesus' teachings here deal with the disciples' reaction. Clement's attempt to deal with the disciples' shock at Jesus' teachings (Lk 18:26) is fascinating, given his unwillingness to maintain the text's jarring message. For Clement, the disciples aren't asking who among the rich may be saved, but because they understand that Jesus is talking about "passions" instead of actual wealth, they are fearful for their *own* salvation: the disciples "perceived the depth of His words. As far as lack of riches and possessions went they had good

---

[109]Clement of Alexandria, *Quis div.*, LCL 92:327.

[110]Cyril of Alexandria, *Comm. Luke* 123, 490.

[111]François Bovon, *Luke 2: A Commentary on the Gospel of Luke 9:51–19:27*, Hermeneia (Minneapolis: Fortress, 2013), 567.

[112]All quotations in this paragraph are from Ambrose, *Exp. Luc.*, 361.

hopes for salvation, but since they were conscious that they had not yet completely put away their passions" they "began to despair of themselves no less than did the very rich man who clung desperately to his possession."[113]

We must not forget that even the early Lukan interpreters who struggle with the severity of Jesus' teachings in this chapter emphasize the urgency of generosity to the poor. For Clement, the wealthy person knows that he possesses what he owns "for his brothers' sakes rather than his own."[114] For Cyril, as we saw earlier, Luke 16:9 provides the solution to the predicament of wealth. The wealthy

> refuse entirely to abandon what they have, yet it is possible for them in another way to attain unto honor. And the Savior has Himself showed us how and in what way this can happen, saying, *Make to yourselves friends of unrighteous mammon; that when it has failed, they may receive you into eternal tabernacles.* For there is nothing to prevent the rich, if they will, from making the poor partakers and sharers of the abundance which they possess.[115]

Some early Christian writers, however, go much further. For Basil of Caesarea, the ruler who refused Jesus demonstrated that he was "far from fulfilling the commandment" and that he bears "false witness" by claiming to have loved his neighbor as himself.[116] He asks,

> For if what you say is true, that you have kept from your youth the commandment of love and have given to everyone the same as to yourself, then how did you come by this abundance of wealth? Care for the needy requires the expenditure of wealth: when all share alike, disbursing their possessions among themselves, they each receive a small portion for their individual needs. Thus, those who love their neighbor as themselves possess nothing more than their neighbor.[117]

Basil tells him simply, that "the more you abound in wealth, the more you lack in love."[118] Basil mourns that there are "many who fast, pray, sigh, and demonstrate every manner of piety, so long as it costs them nothing,

---

[113]Clement of Alexandria, *Quis. div.*, LCL 92:313.
[114]Clement of Alexandria, *Quis. div.*, LCL 92:303.
[115]Cyril of Alexandria, *Comm. Luke* 123, 491.
[116]Basil of Caesarea, Homily 7.
[117]Basil of Caesarea, Homily 7.
[118]Basil of Caesarea, Homily 7.

yet would not part with a penny to help those in distress."[119] He warns, "The Kingdom of Heaven does not receive such people, for 'it is easier for a camel to go through the eye of a needle than for someone who is rich to enter the Kingdom of God.'"[120] Basil, it appears, feels no need to soften the severity of the Lukan text! Unlike Clement, he feels that "the meaning of our Lord's answer is clear."[121]

For Basil, the rich have "received wealth as a stewardship, and not for their own enjoyment."[122] Instead of worrying that they are disheartened by Jesus' teachings, Basil underscores the text's abrasiveness. He asks: "How many could you have delivered from want with but a single ring from your finger? How many households fallen into destitution might you have raised? In just one of your closets there are enough clothes to cover an entire town shivering with cold. You showed no mercy; it will not be shown to you. You opened not your house; you will be expelled from the Kingdom. You gave not your bread; you will not receive eternal life."[123]

Basil's primary issue is with the "super-wealthy individual" who claims to be a Christian and does not share with the poor.[124] He complains about the "veritable army of servants" it takes to maintain their needs.[125] Bemoaning their "constant accumulation" that does "not quell the craving,"[126] he sees the gross excess of a few as one of the chief evils in his society. The solution is to follow the teachings of Jesus, to "scatter" wealth "in the manner which our Lord directed."[127]

ZACCHAEUS (LUKE 19:1-10)

Ambrose is sensitive to those readers who may be wondering how Zacchaeus can be such a positive character in light of Jesus' harsh saying on wealth in the previous chapter (Lk 18:25). He hopes that readers won't

---

[119]Basil of Caesarea, Homily 7.
[120]Basil of Caesarea, Homily 7.
[121]Basil of Caesarea, Homily 7.
[122]Basil of Caesarea, Homily 7.
[123]Basil of Caesarea, Homily 7.
[124]Basil of Caesarea, Homily 7.
[125]Basil of Caesarea, Homily 7.
[126]Basil of Caesarea, Homily 7.
[127]Basil of Caesarea, Homily 7.

be "too quick to take offence of just distress at Zacchaeus." He says that they "learn that the fault does not pertain to the opportunities, but to those who do not know how to use their opportunities; for just as riches are obstacles for the wicked, so for the good are they aids to virtue." He continues, "Surely Zacchaeus, chosen by Christ, was rich, but by giving away the half of his goods to the poor and restoring fourfold what he had obtained by fraud . . . he received a greater reward than he had bestowed." His wealth is described "that ye may know that not all rich men are covetous."[128] Those who do not share with the poor do not "deserve to receive Christ, Whom Zacchaeus offered half of his goods to obtain."[129]

Cyril of Alexandria does not mince words when describing Zacchaeus's character. In contrast to Ambrose, he sees Zacchaeus as "a man entirely abandoned to covetousness, and whose sole object was the increase of his gains." He and others "shamelessly made open profession of this vice."[130] However, "he was prepared for obedience, and fervent for faith, and ready to change from vice to virtue"[131] and "Zacchaeus continued not among their number, but was counted worthy of mercy at Christ's hands."[132] Cyril rejoices:

> Thou beholdest his repentance . . . the bountifulness of his love for the poor. He . . . at once becomes merciful, and devoted to charity. He promises that he will distribute his wealth to those who are in need, that he will make restoration to those who have been defrauded; and he who was the slave of avarice, makes himself poor, and ceases to care for gains.[133]

Zacchaeus is therefore deemed worthy because he dispossesses himself to care for the poor.

THE GENEROUS WIDOW (LUKE 21:1-4)

Early commentators on this passage highlight the widow's extreme poverty. For Cyprian, the widow "remembered the heavenly precepts,

---

[128]Ambrose, *Exp. Luc.*, 367.
[129]Ambrose, *Exp. Luc.*, 328.
[130]Cyril of Alexandria, *Comm. Luke* 127, 505.
[131]Cyril of Alexandria, *Comm. Luke* 127, 506.
[132]Cyril of Alexandria, *Comm. Luke* 127, 505.
[133]Cyril of Alexandria, *Comm. Luke* 127, 507.

doing good even amidst the difficulties and straits of poverty."[134] For Cyril of Alexandria, she is

> oppressed by hard and unendurable poverty . . . who by scraps scarcely and laboriously gathered a scant and miserable provision, barely sufficient for the day. And finally, she offered two farthings; for it was not possible for her to bestow more, but rather, so to speak, she had stripped herself of all that she had, and was leaving the sacred courts with empty hands. Wonderful deed! She who constantly asked alms of others, lends to God, making even poverty itself fruitful to His honor. She, therefore, vanquishes the rest, and by a just sentence is crowned by God.[135]

The widow's faith in the midst of economic hardship points to the superiority of her sacrifice. For Cyprian, while the rich should "be ashamed of their barrenness and unbelief," this widow, "needy in means, is found rich in works."[136] He notes that Christ "observed and saw, regarding her work not for its abundance, but for its intention, and considering not how much, but from how much, she had given."[137] Ambrose observes of Christ that "with good reason He preferred the widow who contributed the two mites." Her poverty "was rich in the mystery of faith."[138] For Cyril the rich man offers "not so much in proportion to thy means" but the widow offers "a hand bountiful of the little she possessed." Cyril asks, "Did she not therefore, justly carry off the crown? Did not the superiority befall her by a holy judgment? Did she not surpass thy bountifulness, in regard at least of her readiness?" So "even he who possesses very little may also obtain favor by offering his little; nor will he suffer any loss on this account. For He Who is omniscient will praise his readiness, and accept his intention, and make him equal with the rich; or rather, will crown him with more distinguished honor."[139] In a text that reverses the paradigm of honor and shame, the poverty-stricken widow is in the place of distinguished honor, while the wealthy are shamed.

---

[134]Cyprian, *Treatise 8, Eleem.* 15, in *ANF* 5:480.
[135]Cyril of Alexandria, *Comm. Luke* 138, 552.
[136]Cyprian, *Treatise 8, Eleem.* 15, in *ANF* 5:480.
[137]Cyprian, *Treatise 8, Eleem.* 15, in *ANF* 5:480.
[138]Ambrose, *Letters to Laymen* 84, in *FC* 26:469-70.
[139]Cyril of Alexandria, *Comm. Luke* 138, 552.

For Gregory of Nyssa, this narrative encourages everyone to give to those less fortunate. Gregory envisions someone saying "I am poor; me too!" Gregory responds, "So it is! Nevertheless, give. Give what you have. God does not demand what is beyond your means. You give bread, someone else a cup of wine, another an outer garment; in this way, through a collective contribution, the misfortunes of one person are eased."[140] He reminds his audience of the value of their meager gifts, "Do you remember how the widow's coin surpassed the liberality of the wealthy? (Luke 21:1-4). She emptied herself of all that she possessed. The rich, for their part, gave only a portion."[141] As Gregory and many others in the early church recognized, this narrative highlights the difference between the widow's gift, which cost her everything, and the gifts of the wealthy, which cost them nothing.

SUMMARY

We have a lot to learn from Luke's early interpreters about simplicity. The first and most basic point is that they universally assume the need for generosity and almsgiving. Even Cyril of Alexandria, who thinks that Jesus' teachings on wealth are difficult for most to follow, reminds us that God has provided a means for the wealthy to be saved—through generosity. Keeping all of one's wealth for one's own use and pleasure is simply incompatible with the values of the kingdom of God.

Perhaps one reason for the emphasis on radical almsgiving is the lens through which early Christian writers look at wealth. In their opinion, we don't really own our wealth. It is placed in our care by God so that we may bestow it to those who have less than we do. Therefore, when we spend our wealth on ourselves alone, we are essentially stealing from the poor (and thereby from God). The reverse is also true. When we give to the poor, we show ourselves to be good stewards of the resources God has trusted us with, and we are, in essence, giving to God. This attitude could not be further from the attitude that many Christians in America have today. Wealth is seen as earned and deserved. The reward of hard work is a life of

---

[140]Gregory of Nyssa, "On Good Works," 195.
[141]Gregory of Nyssa, "On Good Works," 195.

comfort. Luke's early interpreters suggest that we look again at our solidarity as human beings and that we see another's need as we would see our own.

The early church has a unique perspective on poverty. Poverty and wealth are redefined. The truly wealthy are those who have few needs; the truly poor are those who possess material wealth but are never satisfied with what they have. Because God is the source of all wealth and because God has promised to care for us, ancient Lukan scholars have little room for doubt with respect to God's provision. They hold in tension, on the one hand, a deep trust in God's ability to meet our needs and, on the other, an acknowledgment that our actual needs ought to be modest and that in any case the blessings of the kingdom far outweigh any economic hardship that might accompany our commitment to Christ.

Finally, Luke's earliest interpreters see a right attitude (and action) regarding money as possessing the potential for deep spiritual rewards. For them, it molds us in God's image, it empowers our prayers, and it endears us to God. It also releases us from the kind of fear and hesitation that encumbers our lives and it frees us to participate fully in God's kingdom work

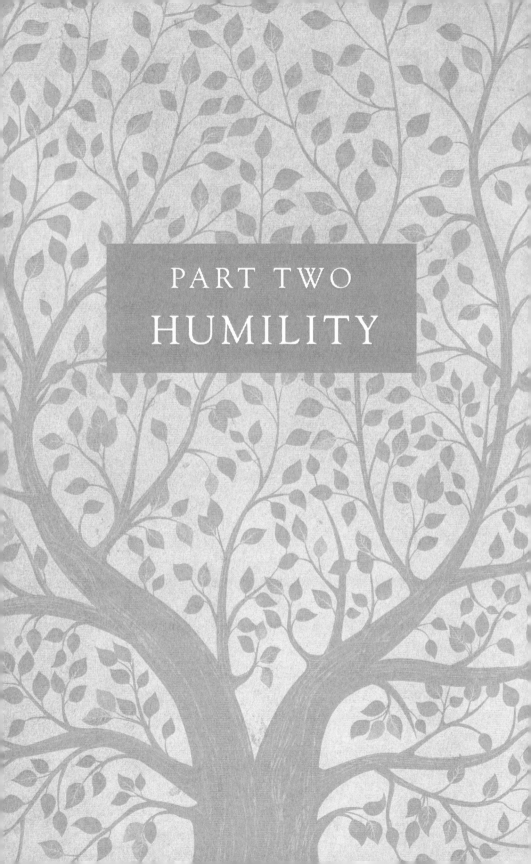

PART TWO

HUMILITY

4

HUMILITY IN THE
GOSPEL NARRATIVE

THOMAS MERTON ONCE WROTE, "My false and private self is the one who wants to exist outside the reach of God's will and God's love—outside of reality and outside of life. And such a self cannot help but be an illusion."[1] We can't hope to have an authentic relationship with God if we operate out of a false self. In Luke's Gospel, the religious leaders' negative depiction is linked not only to their inability to perceive the activity of God through Jesus but also to the tenacity with which they cling to their false selves and to their blindness concerning their own spiritual state. Like them, we often reject God's will and love but can't see this in ourselves because we have convinced ourselves that we are living at the center of God's will. When we live out of a false self, we are reduced to a life of petty competitiveness and anxious attempts to bolster our own honor and importance in society and even with God. Luke's ideal of humility centers around a true sense of self in relationship to God.

THE HUMBLE CENTURION (LUKE 7:1-10)

I didn't really notice how ingrained expectations of reciprocity were in our society until I had kids. With playdates and carpools, in order to keep things fair, everyone takes a turn. Sometimes it can feel like a bit of an exchange—you do this, and then I'll do that. The first-century biblical world also lived with this mentality. As we will see in the next chapter, Seneca complained about the benefaction system of which he was a part.

---

[1]Thomas Merton, *New Seeds of Contemplation* (New York: New Directions, 1961), 34.

A benefaction, or good favor, that was done with the expectation of getting something in return was not really a favor at all. But that's how the system worked.

In this story, we encounter the centurion as a benefactor. He is described as "doing good" for the Jewish people—building their synagogue. Because of this, there is the expectation that Jesus "owes" him something: "He is worthy of having you do this for him" (Lk 7:4). We rarely possess enough awareness to step outside of our societally dictated patterns. The centurion, however, is able to do this. He recognizes Jesus' authority over him, in spite of the fact that the centurion is supposed to be the benefactor in this situation.

The centurion's humility is the focus of this narrative; he is "important," part of Antipas's own militia, but seeks no special treatment.[2] Respecting the separation of Jews and Gentiles required by law,[3] he sends an urgent[4] request (not demand) through the elders.[5] His attitude contrasts with that of the Jewish elders, who, exemplifying the values of the patron-client system Jesus has previously critiqued (Lk 6:35-36),[6] point out that the centurion is a "worthy" benefactor to them (Lk 7:5).[7] Jesus goes with them, in spite of their attitude of "he did this for us, so you owe him." Expressing his humility, the centurion sends a group of "friends," this time with the message that he is not "worthy" to have Jesus come to his house (Lk 7:6).[8] The centurion shows that he has Jesus' own values.[9] He fully believes in

---

[2]At this time under Antipas non-Roman troops were typically stationed in Galilee, so the centurion would have had to have belonged to Antipas's militia (which included non-Jewish troops). François Bovon, *Luke 1: A Commentary on the Gospel of Luke 1:1–9:50*, Hermeneia (Minneapolis: Fortress, 2002), 260.

[3]The centurion is a Godfearer. As such, he would not have been circumcised but would have embraced the law and Jewish worship. Bovon, *Luke 1*, 260-61.

[4]Bovon, *Luke 1*, 261. The adverb expresses the urgency of the request.

[5]Darrell L. Bock, *Luke*, IVP New Testament Commentary (Downers Grove, IL: InterVarsity Press, 1994), 131.

[6]Joel B. Green, *The Gospel of Luke*, New International Commentary on the New Testament (Grand Rapids: Eerdmans, 1997), 287.

[7]Green, *Gospel of Luke*, 284.

[8]The second delegation (of friends) and the centurion's humble remarks are consistent with behaviors of a benefactor. Mikeal C. Parsons, *Luke* (Grand Rapids: Baker Academic, 2015), 120, citing Frederick W. Danker, *Benefactor: Epigraphic Study of a Graeco-Roman and New Testament Semantic Field* (St. Louis: Clayton, 1982), 379n107 and 351-52.

[9]His faith stands in sharp contrast to the typical expectation of the time that miraculous healings could only take place through direct contact. Bovon, *Luke 1*, 262. Also see Luke 5:17; 6:19.

Jesus' power to heal even at a distance—a radical faith to which Luke's own readers could aspire.[10] He humbly submits to Jesus, calling him "Lord."[11] In doing so, the centurion recognizes Jesus' superiority to the benefaction system of which he is also a part.[12] He understands that Jesus' authority is from God (Lk 7:8).[13] Jesus is amazed, and affirms the centurion's awareness of the nature of his mission (Lk 7:9).[14]

THE DISCIPLES ARGUE OVER WHO IS THE GREATEST (LUKE 9:46-48)

The disciples, who were fantasizing about sharing Jesus' glory in Luke 9:28-36, and who are blinded to God's purposes through Jesus in Luke 9:44-45, here *still* fail to understand that Jesus' mission involves humiliation.[15] This passage heightens the irony that *just* as Jesus is trying to teach his disciples that his journey involves humiliation, the disciples are consumed by their desire to figure out which of them has the greatest status as a follower of Jesus.[16] Luke's characterization of the disciples is not flattering: their lack of humility here only adds to their increasingly adversarial position in the text. Their fear in Luke 9:45 was rooted in the denial of faith.[17] Here it is clear that the disciples' prideful inquiry proceeds from the quality of their hearts.[18] Luke's note that Jesus is "aware of their inner thoughts" (Lk 9:47) recalls similar instances when he is aware of the evil intentions of the religious leaders (Lk 2:34; 5:21-22; 6:8; 20:14).[19]

Jesus responds to the disciples' immature competition for status by granting a child a position of honor at his side (Lk 9:47).[20] Whenever I ask my students why Jesus chose a child for this object lesson, I get answers like,

---

[10]Bovon, *Luke 1*, 261.
[11]John Nolland, *Luke*, 3 vols., Word Biblical Commentary 35A-C (Dallas: Word, 1989–1993), 317 (pages are numbered sequentially throughout the three vols.).
[12]Parsons, *Luke,* 120.
[13]Nolland, *Luke*, 315.
[14]Bock, *Luke*, 131, notes that it is rare when someone receives a complete commendation from Jesus.
[15]Nolland, *Luke*, 517.
[16]Bock, *Luke*, 176.
[17]Green, *Gospel of Luke*, 391.
[18]Bovon, *Luke 1*, 394. *Dialogismos*, used in Lk 9:46 for the disciples' "discussion," typically has a negative sense in Luke.
[19]Green, *Gospel of Luke*, 391.
[20]Bock, *Luke*, 176.

"The child represents innocence," or "The child has a pure heart." Because that is what a child represents in our society, we might be tempted to posit that in regard to the first-century world as well. For the disciples, however, a child would have had a completely different association. The child was a threat because the child had no status in society. That a *child* receives the place for which the disciples were competing provides a perfect object lesson in humility. The disciples were, of course, afraid that associating with children would compromise their fragile social standing.[21] Jesus, however, equates receiving a child with receiving God. The disciples should also welcome such social inferiors "in my name" (Lk 9:48) or in keeping with Jesus' own actions and attitudes,[22] as a way of respecting and acting as host to Jesus himself.[23]

For Jesus, true greatness is found in those who have the attitude of humility. The disciples have defined greatness according to their relative worth compared against one another. Let's linger for a moment on that phrase: *relative worth*. How many of us are guilty of judging ourselves in comparison to our peers, either positively or negatively? It would help us to remember that Jesus defines greatness without using comparisons to anyone else—true greatness can only be granted by God to those who refuse to assign human value on the basis of superficial comparisons.[24] This story is ultimately not about the relative greatness of individuals but instead asks who is willing to accept the values of the kingdom and embrace Jesus' teachings on humility.[25]

THE DISCIPLES SEEK EXCLUSIVE RIGHTS TO JESUS' MINISTRY (LUKE 9:49-50)

Imagine that you are taking a class that you love in your major. After starting the required paper at the beginning of the semester and putting your best effort into it all semester long, you receive a grade of B-. You have a friend in the class majoring in something else who is just taking the class as an elective, who gets an A. You want to feel happy for your friend but

---

[21]Nolland, *Luke*, 519.
[22]Green, *Gospel of Luke*, 392.
[23]Nolland, *Luke*, 520-21.
[24]Bock, *Luke*, 178.
[25]Bovon, *Luke 1*, 395.

instead find yourself overwhelmed by a dark cloud of envy and self-doubt. We do sometimes struggle with the success of others, even if we want to feel happy for them. In Luke 9:49-50, we find the disciples having a similar struggle. Just as our envy is often rooted in insecurity, theirs seems to be as well. In Luke 9:1, Jesus sent out the disciples, giving them "power and authority over all demons and to cure diseases." However, in Luke 9:40, we see that the disciples are incapable of casting a demon out of a boy. Shortly after this, the disciples begin to face their shortcomings with fear (Lk 9:45). Still smarting from their own failures, the disciples try to bolster their own worth by limiting access to Jesus' ministry.[26] They want to stop this person who actually *successfully* ministers in Jesus' name (unlike the disciples themselves) because he does not "follow [you] with us" (Lk 9:49). Unfortunately, their behavior proves that they still have not grasped Jesus' mission. Their insecurity has blinded them to the fact that they are all playing for the same team. Jesus suggests that they should be glad that others are furthering the kingdom and that they can't demand exclusive rights to Jesus' ministry.[27] Jesus does not question the man's motives and welcomes his ministry.[28] We should get the point: we don't need to stake out our territory in ministry. Any glory for our actions goes to God, not us. When we feel slighted at another's success, perhaps we need to take a deeper look at our own feelings of insecurity that might be fueling that envy.

SEEKING HONOR AT THE BANQUET TABLE (LUKE 14:1-24)

In this next story, an important Pharisee has invited his fellow elite to dine with him.[29] The Pharisees were watching Jesus closely (Lk 14:1; see also Lk 6:7), likely waiting to pounce at his next offense.[30] In an ironic twist,

---

[26]Bock, *Luke*, 179.

[27]Nolland, *Luke*, 524-25.

[28]We might be tempted to attribute false motives to the exorcist in this story, seeing him using the name of Jesus for his own agenda, as the sons of Sceva do in Acts 19:13-17, but Jesus here does not.

[29]The Pharisees were not organized into a hierarchy, so the description of this "leader of the Pharisees" might instead convey his importance within society. Bovon, *Luke 1*, 340.

[30]*Paratēreō* is used in Lk 6:7 and Lk 20:20 and can imply hostile intent. The Pharisees probably see Jesus as a flagrant lawbreaker. In Luke's narrative, Jesus has already healed three times on the Sabbath (Lk 4:31-37; 6:6-11; 13:10-17).

Jesus, who does not seek honor, gains it at the expense of those who most desire it, fulfilling his own words in Luke 14:11. Dropsy was a condition associated with uncleanness and immorality,[31] perhaps evoking the stigma that AIDS has in our country. Jesus touches this unclean man, compromising his own cleanliness, healing him on the Sabbath and provoking the religious leaders' anger.[32] Jesus then bests the Pharisees by showing them the hypocrisy of their own actions: any of them would lift out a son, or even an ox, from a pit on the Sabbath; how much more should Jesus show compassion on the Sabbath?[33] Jesus' response effectively silences the honor-loving Pharisees, shaming them through their inability to respond to his question.[34]

In much the same way as the social politics in high school cafeterias force students to quickly navigate the social hierarchy of their school in order to avoid public humiliation, meals in the first century also functioned as a public gauge of honor. In Luke 14:7, the guests at the dinner party are taking great care in going about choosing the most honorable seats for themselves (Lk 14:7). To grab an important seat and then to have to take the last seat available would be a crushing humiliation.[35] Jesus uses this scenario to draw a connection between self-promotion and a lack of humility before God (Lk 14:11).[36] Like the host in this story, God will honor those who seek no status and humiliate those who think they are worthy of the best places in the kingdom. This verse alludes to Ezekiel 21:26, implying that self-promotion will be worthless on the day

---

[31]Bovon observes that the disease was thought to be a curse caused by sin. François Bovon, *Luke 2: A Commentary on the Gospel of Luke 9:51–19:27*, Hermeneia (Minneapolis: Fortress, 2013), 342. It was also seen as a consequence of gluttony. David E. Garland, *Luke*, Zondervan Exegetical Commentary on the New Testament (Grand Rapids: Zondervan, 2011), 566. According to Stobaeus, Diogenes compared those with dropsy to money lovers: just as those who are wealthy crave more money, so those with dropsy crave fluids even though they are bloated (*Flor* 3.10.45, cited in Garland, *Luke*, 567).

[32]Medical treatment in Jesus' day would have consisted of puncturing the skin to provide relief; however, this was not permitted on the Sabbath. Bovon, *Luke 2*, 342.

[33]Charles H. Talbert, *Reading Luke-Acts in Its Mediterranean Milieu* (Leiden: Brill, 2003), 197.

[34]David Gowler, *Host, Guest, Enemy, and Friend: Portraits of the Pharisees in Luke and Acts* (New York: P. Lang, 1991), 248.

[35]Plutarch tells the story of a pompous dinner guest who actually chose to leave a banquet when he saw that all of the honorable places had been taken! *Mor.* 615 C-D.

[36]Nolland, *Luke*, 749.

of judgment.[37] The world's honor systems aren't important in the kingdom of God; the only real honor that has meaning comes from God.[38]

Jesus then furthers the lesson on humility, critiquing his host's guest list. The host had invited guests of his own social class (Lk 14:12). Getting an invitation from an important person confirmed that one was a part of that elite group. Reciprocity is assumed: if I invite you to a party today, you'd better invite me to your party next time if you want the invitations to keep coming (Lk 14:12-14).[39] We are no strangers to this mentality in our culture either. In the Lukan story, Jesus proposes a different guest list, including "the poor, the crippled, the lame, and the blind." His suggestion seems ridiculous. Hospitality was an investment meant to bring returns in status and honor. The host has nothing to gain from their presence. Jesus, however, promises that such socially subversive action will bring a spiritual blessing (Lk 14:14). What might this sort of hospitality look like today? I know several colleagues who moved closer to the heart of the Twin Cities to form genuine communities with their neighbors. One quite literally tore down the fences separating her from her neighbors. She had an "open-door" policy with them; their kids were always in her house, making themselves at home, eating her food, feeling as comfortable in her space as they were in their own. She wasn't on a mission; she was just living missionally.

When Jesus finishes critiquing his host, a guest tries to curry favor with Jesus with a comment about the blessedness of those who will dine in the kingdom of God, totally missing Jesus' point about humility. In response, Jesus tells a story about another banquet. There are actually *two* invitations to this banquet (Lk 14:16-17). The first invitation functions as the announcement but is a binding invitation, as there would be no way to keep the leftovers.[40] The second invitation indicates the dinner is now ready, like ringing the dinner bell.[41] By the time the dinner date approaches, the

---

[37]Joseph A. Fitzmyer, *The Gospel According to Luke*, 2 vols., Anchor Bible 28-28A (Garden City, NY: Doubleday, 1985), 1047 (pages are numbered sequentially throughout the two vols.).

[38]Green, *Gospel of Luke*, 552.

[39]Talbert, *Reading Luke*, 197.

[40]Garland, *Luke*, 586.

[41]Bovon, *Luke 2*, 356; Parsons, *Luke*, 227.

guests have come up with a string of excuses (Lk 14:19-20), which would
have been considered rude.[42] The fact that they all, "without exception,"
have rejected the invitation suggests that a "coordinated act of ostracism"
is taking place.[43] Much like young teenagers who decide to shun an un-
popular kid by standing him up at his party, the guests at this party have
decided to embarrass their host by boycotting the banquet together. The
excuses are pathetic: Who buys a field without looking at it first? Are we
supposed to think that another guest married between the first invitation
and the second?[44] The host gets their message and angrily tells his slave to
invite the poor, crippled, blind, and lame (Lk 14:21). When it becomes clear
that even they cannot consume the amount of food prepared for the guests,
the slave is bidden to invite those from the "roads and lanes"—in other
words, beggars, prostitutes, and others who are not permitted to live
within the city walls and interact with the elites.[45] They are "compelled" to
attend, reassured that there will be no expectation of repayment.[46] This
different guest list echoes what is happening in the kingdom. Jesus'
banquet is the opposite of the Pharisee's banquet; the outcasts that the
Pharisee excluded from his banquet are the ones accepting the invitation
to Jesus' banquet.[47]

THE PRODIGAL AND HIS PRIDEFUL
BROTHER (LUKE 15:11-32)

I love both of my children equally and do my best to not privilege one
above the other, but occasionally, when they were younger, one would
cry, "Unfair!" This is the complaint of the prodigal's brother. Jesus tells
this story to defend his ministry to the outcasts, inviting the religious

---

[42]Bovon, *Luke 2*, 370.

[43]Robert C. Tannehill, *Luke*, Abingdon New Testament Commentaries (Nashville: Abingdon, 1996), 234; see also Parsons, *Luke*, 227.

[44]Parsons, *Luke*, 228.

[45]Parsons, *Luke*, 228, citing Richard L. Rohrbaugh, "The Pre-Industrial City in Luke-Acts: Urban Social Relations," in *The Social World of Luke-Acts: Models for Interpretation*, ed. Jerome H. Neyrey (Peabody, MA: Hendrickson, 1991), 144-45.

[46]Parsons, *Luke*, 228.

[47]John A. Darr, *On Character Building: The Reader and the Rhetoric of Characterization in Luke-Acts* (Louisville, KY: Westminster John Knox, 1992), 108.

leaders to celebrate their salvation instead of remaining "outside" like the elder brother.[48]

In this parable, the younger brother asks for his share of the inheritance, an unusual and highly discouraged practice.[49] In spite of the fact that the younger son shames his father through such a request, the father nonetheless honors it.[50] The prodigal then lives disgracefully, squandering any money that might have been used to care for his family.[51] Eventually, realizing that his father's servants live better lives than he, the prodigal "came to himself," deciding to return home. The saying "to come to oneself" was part of the religious and philosophical terminology of the day.[52] Luke's readers would have understood this term to describe the process of personal transformation that takes place when one confronts one's failures and gradually comes to an awareness of one's own identity.[53] The prodigal then says to himself, "I am lost,"[54] realizing that he is unworthy of the privileges of a son[55] and deciding to offer himself to his father as a day laborer.[56] By planning to tell his father, "Father, I have sinned against heaven and before you; I am no longer worthy to be called your son" (Lk 15:18-19), he models the ideal humility of those who turn to God.[57]

---

[48]Gowler, *Host, Guest, Enemy, and Friend*, 252. Jesus directly addresses the Pharisees (Lk 15:3), whom we as readers have come to experience as hypocrites (Lk 11:39-40; 12:1). They reject God's purpose for themselves (Lk 7:30) and are full of greed and wickedness (Lk 11:39-40).

[49]Bovon, *Luke 2*, 425. It was possible but discouraged to disperse one's estate during one's lifetime because the idea of begging from one's children was distasteful. Sirach 33:22 observes, "It is better that your children should ask from you than that you should look to the hand of your children."

[50]Bovon, *Luke 2*, 425. The term *bios* has a primary meaning of "life," and then "means of subsistence," or "resources." The father gives his son what he needs to make a living.

[51]Talbert, *Reading Luke*, 149.

[52]Bovon, *Luke 2*, 426. The term *erchomai* means "to come back." It is used in the Testament of Joseph (3.9) and in Epictetus (*Discourse* 3.1.15), and for early Christians it signified a return to God.

[53]David Holgate, *Prodigality, Liberality and Meanness: The Prodigal Son in Graeco-Roman Perspective*, Journal for the Study of the New Testament Supplements Series 187 (Sheffield: Sheffield Academic, 1999), 200.

[54]Bovon, *Luke 2*, 426. The term *apollymi* is used in the middle voice (*apollymai*) to mean "be lost."

[55]Green, *Gospel of Luke*, 579.

[56]Bovon, *Luke 2*, 425. Also, by taking his inheritance early, the son forfeited any future claim on his father's estate.

[57]Bock, *Luke*, 259.

The father, in turn, also demonstrates humility by acting in an unexpected way. With no regard for his own dignity, the father sprints down the road to throw his arms around the son who shamed him.[58] He cuts short his son's speech, accepting him completely and showing no concern for the dishonor he has brought on himself by accepting back into the family such a rebellious son.[59] He gives a ring, robe, and sandals,[60] all tokens of honor, to the son who shamed him.[61]

The father then shames himself again by going to plead with his son who had humiliated him publicly by refusing to join the celebration (Lk 15:28).[62] The elder son, still operating out of a false self, points to himself as an obedient child and a "slave" (Lk 15:29). The family is not rich; he has been working the modest estate himself.[63] He complains that he is worthy (reminiscent of the Pharisee of Lk 18:9-14), and has never had a kid slaughtered for him.[64] His attitude has separated him so much from his brother and father that he does not know who he is as a part of the family. He refuses to refer to his sibling as "brother," referring to him instead as "your son." The father appeals to him as a member of the family, calling him a son, and asking him to rejoice with "this brother of yours" (Lk 15:32).

The elder son prefers to wait outside alone rather than join his brother and his father in the celebration (Lk 15:28). He is too caught up in his own self-righteousness and the injustice of the situation to celebrate his brother's return.[65] His father wants him to celebrate that he has regained a brother just as he is rejoicing in regaining a son. The father reminds the elder brother, "All that is mine is yours," attempting to ease any fears that he

---

[58]Cf. Sir 19:30: "A man's manner of walking tells you what he is." Talbert, *Reading Luke*, 150.

[59]Gowler, *Host, Guest, Enemy, and Friend*, 255.

[60]Bovon, *Luke 2*, 428. The "first" robe might be the son's robe that was taken out of storage or the first in the sense of "best" robe. The ring recalls the status conveyed when Pharaoh places his ring on Joseph's finger. In ancient Israel, when one would take possession of land, one would walk around with shoes on while surveying the land—the shoes may have a similar connotation in that they belong on one who is "home."

[61]Green, *Gospel of Luke*, 583.

[62]Gowler, *Host, Guest, Enemy, and Friend*, 255.

[63]Bovon, *Luke 2*, 428.

[64]Bock, *Luke*, 260.

[65]Bock, *Luke*, 261.

might have about his inheritance (Lk 15:31).[66] At the end of the narrative, the question remains as to whether he will ever join the family in their celebration, or continue to sulk outside because he has not received the honor he feels he is due.

THE PHARISEE AND THE TAX
COLLECTOR (LUKE 18:9-19)

At this point in the narrative, the Pharisees have been portrayed as prideful so often that they have actually come to represent pride itself.[67] They are self-delusional, fully believing their claims to superiority.[68] Their assurance about their own righteousness is not rooted in genuine self-confidence but in the fragile kind of boasting that maintains its position by criticizing another.[69] Motivated by a desire to be seen as righteous "in the sight of others" (Lk 16:15) and not simply before God,[70] as François Bovon observes: "Their conscience is determined by how they live rather than having their life determined by their conscience."[71]

The Pharisee in this passage prays according to correct Jewish liturgy (Ps 17:3-5).[72] He also fasts beyond the required public fast days,[73] giving up not only food but also drink. He gives more than what is normative. However, with no mention of God's grace, he lists his good deeds as proof of his worthiness to be received by God (Lk 18:11-12), and his thanksgiving prayer, which one would expect to end in praise for God's actions (Lk 18:11),[74] is twisted and praises his own good works instead of God's (Lk 18:11-12).[75]

Feeling the need to put someone else down in order to boast about one's own achievements is like hanging a sign that says "I am terribly insecure"

---

[66]Bovon, *Luke 2*, 425. Just because the younger brother claimed his share of the estate does not mean that the elder brother had received his. He stayed in his father's house, expecting to receive his inheritance, which was twice the amount of the younger brother's, at his father's death.

[67]Gowler, *Host, Guest, Enemy, and Friend*, 266.

[68]Darr, *On Character Building*, 114.

[69]Bovon, *Luke 2*, 544.

[70]Bovon, *Luke 2*, 544.

[71]Bovon, *Luke 2*, 545.

[72]Talbert, *Reading Luke*, 170.

[73]Luke Timothy Johnson, *The Gospel of Luke*, Sacra Pagina 3 (Collegeville, MN: Liturgical Press, 1991), 272.

[74]Bock, *Luke*, 296.

[75]Green, *Gospel of Luke*, 648.

around one's neck. Unfortunately, the Pharisee has every reason to be insecure. His contempt for others proves that he is unfit for the kingdom and
nullifies any claim to righteousness that he might have supposed to have
had.[76] The Pharisee sees his praying neighbor in the same category as
"thieves, rogues, adulterers" (Lk 18:11), "sinners" who are beyond redemp-
tion.[77] His pride blinds him to his self-division. The reader recognizes his
hypocrisy: Jesus has declared the Pharisees to be greedy, hypocritical, and
lacking justice (Lk 11:39, 42).[78]

In contrast, the tax collector stands "far off,"[79] beating his breast in
mourning,[80] with a lowered gaze.[81] His humble prayer echoes the beginning of Psalm 51, which, since it is associated with David's repentance,
suggests that God forgives even the worst crimes. The tax collector throws
himself on God's mercy, willing to be humbled before God and whoever
might be praying in the temple. Through his humility, he receives the justification that the Pharisee was seeking, while ironically, the Pharisee is not
justified at all.[82] Jesus concludes, "All who exalt themselves will be
humbled, but all who humble themselves will be exalted" (Lk 18:14).

JESUS AND THE CHILDREN (LUKE 18:15-17)

In Luke 18:15-17, a child provides the perfect illustration for Jesus' teachings
on humility.[83] The younger the child, the less he or she could contribute to
society, and the lower the child's status. The disciples object that people are

---

[76]Bovon, *Luke 2*, 545. The verb *exoutheneō* means "to hold to be of no account, nothing" or "to
scorn." The same term is used to describe Herod's attitude toward Jesus in Lk 23:11.

[77]Darr, *On Character Building*, 114.

[78]Darr, *On Character Building*, 114.

[79]Bovon notes, "In the Jewish and Christian biblical tradition, keeping a certain distance was
tantamount to preserving the possibility of an encounter or dialogue. In order to be able to enjoy
another person's face, one must remain a certain distance from it." *Luke 2*, 549.

[80]One is reminded of the crowds during the crucifixion (Lk 23:48) and the women who accom-
panied Jesus on the way to the cross (Lk 23:27). Bovon, *Luke 2*, 549.

[81]A lowered gaze was atypical of the customary prayer stance in the temple where one raised one's
eyes to look on God's glory. Bovon, *Luke 2*, 549.

[82]The demonstrative pronoun "this" shows that it is the tax collector and not the other who is
justified. Bovon, *Luke 2*, 550.

[83]Green, *Gospel of Luke*, 650; Jesus does not cite the children as examples because of their innate
"openness and sheer receptivity" (Fitzmyer, *Gospel According to Luke*, 1193). It is not their character that is under debate but their position in society.

bothering Jesus with "infants," pointing to their lowly position (Lk 18:15).[84] In response, Jesus teaches his disciples that receiving children is tied to receiving the kingdom.[85] To receive the children means to grant them the kind of hospitality normally reserved for those of equal or greater status.[86] The disciples' attitude shows that they still don't have the humility required in God's kingdom. They must serve the least in the human realm if they are to ever enter the heavenly one.[87]

CRITIQUE OF THE SCRIBES (LUKE 20:45-47)

Here again we see Jesus condemning the arrogant pride, exploitative greed, and hypocrisy of the scribes. The warning that he gave in Luke 11:37-54 still stands.[88] Powerful and important societal leaders, the scribes enjoy a degree of social status well beyond their merit. With evil motivations, they do not even know how to interpret the law correctly (Lk 20:20, 41-44). They abuse the weak, proving their lack of experiential knowledge of the law by "devouring widows' houses"[89] and their lack of knowledge of God by saying prayers "for the sake of appearance" (Lk 20:47).[90] Interested only in the prestige that accompanies their positions, they have failed in their duties to both humanity and to God. The greater condemnation (Lk 20:47) is reserved for those who ironically have devoted their lives to the pursuit of honor.[91] One of the marks of discipleship is humility and genuine care for others.[92] Jesus warns the disciples to beware, lest they find themselves acting like the religious leaders (Lk 20:46). His warning is not superfluous. The disciples have already been tempted to vie with each other for positions of honor (Lk 9:46-48) and are about to do so again (Lk 22:24-27).

---

[84]Green, *Gospel of Luke*, 651.

[85]Green, *Gospel of Luke*, 651.

[86]Green, *Gospel of Luke*, 651.

[87]Green, *Gospel of Luke*, 652.

[88]Bock, *Luke*, 330.

[89]Exactly what this means is unclear. What is clear is the biblical mandate for the care of widows and the accusation that the scribes are taking advantage of them in some way instead.

[90]Nolland, *Luke*, 976.

[91]Green, *Gospel of Luke*, 728.

[92]Bock, *Luke*, 331.

WHO IS THE GREATEST DISCIPLE? (LUKE 22:24-27)

In Luke 22:24, the disciples ask "which one of them" is the greatest. The importance of the incident is seen in its position in Luke—while they are eating with Jesus at the Last Supper.[93] The disciples have heard similar teaching before (Lk 9:46-48) and have even been warned against imitating the actions of the religious leaders (Lk 12:1; 20:46). In the previous verse they asked "which one of them" would betray Jesus. There Luke suggests that they all will betray Jesus through their constant failure to understand his teachings and example concerning issues of status and honor.[94]

Jesus responds to the disciples' query about who the best disciple is by contrasting the idea of leadership in this world with leadership in the kingdom of God.[95] In contrast to "kings of the Gentiles" (Lk 22:25) or benefactors who "serve" society to gain personal honor and power, Jesus' negative "but not so with you" spurs the disciples on to a higher ideal (Lk 22:26). Jesus identifies himself with the household servant and suggests that his followers should do the same. Jesus confers authority on his disciples and highlights their future role as empowered leaders.[96] However, their honor-seeking behavior must be curbed. They need to embrace Jesus' humiliation, realizing that in the next realm they will share in Jesus' glorification.[97]

JESUS' OWN EXAMPLE OF HUMILITY IN LUKE

Why do we hate hypocrites so much? A recent study suggests that hypocrites are really trying to claim a reputation that is totally undeserved.[98] An honest hypocrite, who admits personal inconsistency, is forgivable, but a true hypocrite, who condemns certain behaviors (and therefore deceptively implies that he or she behaves morally), is noxious to us. Luke often casts the Pharisees in this sort of light. He goes out of his way, however, to

---

[93]Fitzmyer, *Gospel According to Luke*, 1412.
[94]Green, *Gospel of Luke*, 766.
[95]Bock, *Luke*, 351.
[96]Green, *Gospel of Luke*, 770.
[97]Nolland, *Luke*, 1068.
[98]Jillian J. Jordan et al., "Why Do We Hate Hypocrites? Evidence for a Theory of False Signaling," *Psychological Science* 28, no. 3 (January 11, 2017): 356-68, https://ssrn.com/abstract=2897313.

show a total unity between Jesus' teachings and lifestyle. We also see this in Luke's depiction of Jesus' humility.

Jesus refuses praise (Luke 11:27-28). Flattery will get you everywhere with a narcissist. Not so with Jesus. In this story, Jesus deflects a woman's attempt to praise him. While it was customary to praise a mother because of her son, her praise is likely aimed at Jesus as much as or more than Mary.[99] Jesus immediately informs her that her affirmation is misdirected.[100] Attention should not be on him but on God's kingdom.[101] He corrects her perspective out of modesty;[102] he does not reject her praise of Mary but widens the scope of her praise to include a blessing on everyone who is obedient to God (Lk 11:28).[103] Mary is not "blessed" simply because she is the mother of Jesus but because she believes the Word of God (Lk 1:45) and acts on it (Lk 8:21).[104] This woman, who has been impressed by Jesus' words or deeds, must put them into practice herself.

Jesus refuses praise again (Luke 18:18-19). In this text, a ruler asks Jesus a question, beginning his request by addressing Jesus as "Good Teacher" (Lk 18:18).[105] By addressing him in this way, the ruler attempts an exchange of mutual worth with Jesus: he flatters Jesus and expects Jesus to reciprocate. Instead, Jesus questions the ruler's motives and declares that only God is good (Lk 18:19). He makes clear that since only God is worthy

---

[99]Bovon, *Luke 2*, 130. Several Jewish parallel texts seem to be based on Gen 49:25, like the Palestinian Targum of Gen 49:25: "Blessed are the breasts at which you sucked and the womb in which you rested." Targum Neofiti 1, cited in Bovon, *Luke 2*, 130. The woman's praise reflects a well-known custom in Judaism of praising a mother on account of her son. Elizabeth does this also in Lk 1:42. Gerhard Schneider, *Das Evangelium nach Lukas* (Würzburg: Echter-Verlag, 1984), 268.

[100]Green, *Gospel of Luke*, 460. Luke does honor Mary because she hears, believes, and obeys. Walter Grundmann, *Das Evangelium nach Lukas* (Berlin: Evangelische Verlagsanstalt, 1961), 240. However, the point of this narrative is that the woman's praise is inadequate because her intention is to indirectly praise Jesus, while Jesus prefers that honors are granted to all who practice a behavior rather than to an individual.

[101]Talbert, *Reading Luke*, 138.

[102]*Menoun* shows reservation because there needs to be a contrast or correction to what one has just heard. Bovon understands the sense of the verse like this: "The reservation is, first of all, an act of modesty: You honor me; well and good! But let us speak of something else." *Luke 2*, 132.

[103]Schneider, *Das Evangelium nach Lukas*, 269.

[104]Fitzmyer, *Gospel According to Luke*, 927.

[105]The "ruler" is probably a member of the Sanhedrin or one of the Pharisaic leaders. Bovon, *Luke 2*, 566.

of such honor, he is not going to participate in this little exchange.[106] He does, however, ask the ruler to become a disciple, on the condition that he dispossess himself and lead a life of humble service (Lk 18:17), an invitation he rejects.[107]

Jesus shows deference to no one (Luke 20:21). In this verse, the religious leaders correctly observe of Jesus, "You are right in what you say and teach, and you show deference to no one,[108] but teach the way of God in accordance with truth," a remark that points to the truth of Jesus' pronouncement against them in Luke 20:46-47.[109] While they themselves can observe that Jesus pays no regard to the conventions of status and honor in his society, they have sacrificed their own integrity for superficial honor (Lk 20:46-47). On some level, they recognize that Jesus is different.

Jesus as servant (Luke 22:27). Someone who is genuinely humble will show humility consistently. Pope Francis startled many by rejecting the opulent papal apartments and popemobile in favor of a humble guest residence and a Fiat, until it was discovered that as archbishop he was in the habit of cooking his own meals and riding the subway. In this text, Jesus concludes his instruction on humility by pointing to the example of his lifestyle: "I am among you as one who serves" (Lk 22:27). Since the setting for this narrative is a meal, Jesus could have simply pointed to the single example of serving the disciples at the table.[110] However, Jesus points to his entire life and mission as a model of humble servanthood.[111] He calls himself a king (Lk 22:29), but he draws a sharp distinction between the actions of pagan kings, whose example the disciples are not to follow, and his own kingship, whom the disciples are to imitate. The path to Jesus' glory is different from the path to glory of worldly kings: it involves humility and service.

---

[106]Green, *Gospel of Luke*, 655.

[107]Bock, *Luke*, 299.

[108]Jesus teaches "without respect of the person" (*ou lambaneis prosōpon*). The idiom *lambanein prosōpon*, literally, "to receive the face," was a normative expression for showing favoritism. Martin M. Culy, Mikeal C. Parsons, and Joshua J. Stigall, *Luke: A Handbook on the Greek Text* BHGNT (Waco: Baylor University Press, 2010), 629.

[109]Fitzmyer, *Gospel According to Luke*, 1295.

[110]Grundmann, *Das Evangelium nach Lukas*, 401, who with Karl Heinrich Rengstorf, *Das Evangelium nach Lukas* (Göttingen: Vandenhoeck & Ruprecht, 1965), 247, sees this as a fulfillment of Lk 12:37.

[111]Erich Klostermann, *Das Lukasevangelium* (Tübingen: J. C. B. Mohr, Paul Siebeck, 1929), 211.

THE CORRELATION OF JESUS' LIFE AND
TEACHING REGARDING HUMILITY

Luke highlights a unity of Jesus' life and teachings with respect to humility. Luke's intended readers would have understood this significance. Not only would they have recognized the unity of teaching and lifestyle as the mark of a true philosopher-king, but, as we will see in the next chapter, their literary culture provided many examples of the humility of such ideal leaders. Their recognition of these characteristics in Jesus would have primed them to turn to his example as a way of forming humility within their own attitudes and lifestyles. In Luke, Jesus regularly criticizes those whose actions are motivated by pride (Lk 14:7-14; 20:45-47) and praises those who seek no special treatment (Lk 7:1-10). The religious leaders who seem to be entirely lacking humility show little promise for future spiritual growth (Lk 18:14). Jesus teaches about the spiritual dangers of pride (Lk 18:9-19), correcting the self-seeking attitudes of his disciples (Lk 9:46-50; 22:26). Such instruction comes directly from Jesus' own life-style. Jesus rejects the praises of others (Lk 11:27-28; 18:18-19) and often shows disregard for societal customs of honor (Lk 11:37-54; 20:21). Jesus is worthy of all honor (Lk 22:29) but instead models servant leadership for his disciples (Lk 22:27). This humility is a foundational characteristic of those who would be useful in the kingdom of God (Lk 22:26).

SUMMARY

Luke presents humility as a foundational quality for Christian life. It is easy to see the caricature of the prideful in Luke: their lack of self-knowledge blinds them to their spiritual need. They desire flattery and bask in honors that they do not deserve (Lk 20:45-57). They compare themselves with others in attempts to bolster their self-worth at the expense of others (Lk 18:9-14). Lukan readers who wish to participate in the kingdom must avoid the self-division that characterizes these religious leaders. They must also go beyond the behavior of the disciples in Luke, who argue with one another about who can claim the title of best disciple and jealously guard their roles (Lk 9:46, 49-50; 18:15-17). They should aspire to the self-knowledge and humility of the centurion in Luke 7:1-10. The message to the church is clear: those who have a false sense of self risk spiritual ship-wreck (Lk 18:14); those who wish to further Christ's kingdom must cling to Jesus' own model of servant leadership (Lk 22:27).

Luke's intended audience would have likely felt the same degree of disdain for pompous leaders that we see in Luke. Their culture would have provided examples of egomaniacal rulers who sought nothing above their own glory. Luke's authorial audience likely longed for the kind of humble integrity seen in an ideal philosopher king and would have recognized Jesus as such. To that discussion we now turn.

5

HUMILITY THROUGH
FIRST-CENTURY EYES

THE ROMAN EMPEROR CALIGULA claimed for himself the title "The
Greatest and Best Caesar," dressed in silks and jewels, and considered
himself a god, ordering statues of the gods to be brought from Greece and
having their heads cut off and replaced with his own image.[1] He commis-
sioned a golden statue of himself to be placed in one temple, and had it
dressed on a daily basis to match his own garments.[2] Enraged that the
Jews would not honor him, he ordered his statue to be placed in
the Jerusalem temple. (Herod later talked him out of it.) Once he stood
next to a statue of Jupiter, asking someone which seemed greater. When
the man hesitated, Caligula had him flayed with whips.[3] Tall, pale, and
quite hairy, Caligula made it a crime punishable by death for anyone to
mention a goat in his presence.[4] He even had a writer who composed
some witty line with a double meaning burned alive.[5] Going to great
lengths to protect his fragile ego, he demolished all the statues of famous
men.[6] Virgil he referred to as a man of no talent and Titus as a verbose
and careless historian.[7] Caligula delighted in humiliating others. He fa-
mously planned to make his horse consul to emasculate the political

---

[1]Suetonius, *Cal.* 22. Granted, this is not an unbiased view. Suetonius provides a helpful caricature
of pride which can, perhaps, help us to understand the ways in which the (also not unbiased)
portraits of the religious leaders in Luke contribute to ancient Mediterranean understandings of
pride and humility.
[2]Suetonius, *Cal.* 22.
[3]Suetonius, *Cal.* 33.
[4]Suetonius, *Cal.* 50.
[5]Suetonius, *Cal.* 27.
[6]Suetonius, *Cal.* 34.
[7]Suetonius, *Cal.* 34.

ambitions of the senators (all of whom would have given their right arm to be consul). He made the wives of honorable men parade in front of him, inspecting them as if he were buying slaves, choosing from the lot his favorites to sleep with, and then returning to publicly comment on their abilities.[8] He shaved the backs of the heads of the most honorable people to make them a laughingstock and forced senators to run for miles in their togas, to wait on him and to attend to his feet.[9] Such humiliations were designed to keep them in their place. "Remember," he said, "I have the right to do anything to anybody."[10]

How do we understand humility in this kind of a context? The historian Suetonius mocks Caligula relentlessly for his pompous behavior, his desire to be flattered as a god, and the lengths to which he goes to maintain his fragile ego. Certainly, in an honor-shame-based society, being *humiliated*, like Caligula humiliated the Senate, was something to be feared and despised.[11] However, true humility—deliberately living a lifestyle free of conceit and desire for fame—*was* considered to be virtuous behavior, and claiming false honors for oneself was despicable.[12] Luke's intended audience would have understood that people who possess genuine self-knowledge would not be dependent on the flattery of others, would be able to face their own limitations without insecurity, and would possess a right relationship to honors.

Reading Luke within his own literary context, imagining the first reception of the text, gets us closer to understanding the text as it was meant for its intended readers. Reading Luke through first-century eyes allows us to get a little closer to joining an ancient conversation that we still need very much to hear. This is necessary because in our own culture, we struggle with humility and need to hear what Luke has to say about it. In every person there is a pride that emerges as soon as our own resources fail us.[13] We operate out of a false self too much of the time, hiding our

---

[8]Suetonius, *Cal.* 36.
[9]Suetonius, *Cal.* 26.
[10]Suetonius, *Cal.* 29.
[11]See Klaus Wengst, *Humility: Solitary of the Humiliated* (Philadelphia: Fortress, 1988), for examples and further discussion on this topic.
[12]Wengst, *Humility*, 15.
[13]Thomas Merton, *New Seeds of Contemplation* (New York: New Directions, 1961), 180.

fragile egos behind our public personas. As Carl Jung once reportedly said, "Through pride we are ever deceiving ourselves. But deep down . . . a still, small voice says to us, something is out of tune."

A Caricature of Pride

Glorying in undeserved honors. We have a general expectation that if one is honored in our society, that person should be *deserving*. Throughout his acting career, Bill Cosby was granted honorary degrees by a number of universities. After twenty women came forward accusing him of rape, many of these universities rescinded their honors.[14] A similar thing happened in 2007 when protesters appealed to the University of Edinburgh to rescind the honorary degree that they had granted to Zimbabwe's Robert Mugabe.[15] That a murderer should continue to hold such honors was unpalatable.

Similarly, in Luke's day, people were repulsed by those who claimed honors of which they were not worthy. There was no shame in being proud of one's merits if they were actually *deserved*. However, many felt disgusted by prideful attitudes when the coveted honors were *undeserved*. Plutarch, for instance, points out that "a man is puffed up and ruined by those who praise him falsely and beyond his deserts."[16] Even for Aristotle, who would certainly allow a meritorious person to own his or her praise, the person who claims honor without deserving it is a fool.[17] For Aristotle, someone who lacks the merits of which they boast is essentially *dishonest*. He defines a "boaster" as one who is "fond of pretending to have things that men esteem, though he has them not, or not to such extent as he pretends."[18]

---

[14]Susan Adams, "Universities Strip Bill Cosby of Honorary Degrees," *Forbes*, April 27, 2018, www .forbes.com/sites/susanadams/2018/04/27/universities-strip-bill-cosby-of-honorary-degrees /#4b2db96847b0.

[15]"Scottish University Revokes Mugabe Degree," June 6, 2007, https://uk.reuters.com/article/uk -mugabe-degree/scottish-university-revokes-mugabe-degree-idUKL0674486520070606.

[16]Plutarch, *Adul. amic.* 59a.

[17]"By a high-minded man we seem to mean one who claims much and deserves much: for he who claims much without deserving it is a fool; but the possessor of a virtue is never foolish or silly." Aristotle, *Eth. nic.*, in Frederick W. Danker, *Benefactor: Epigraphic Study of a Graeco-Roman and New Testament Semantic Field* (St. Louis: Clayton, 1982), 4.3.3.

[18]Aristotle, *Eth. nic.* 4.7.1-7.

Many in Luke's literary world felt that pride was distasteful when the honors were based on power or position rather than on deeper virtues. Aristotle complains about those who are "arrogant and insolent" because they merely "have . . . good things." They, "thinking themselves superior to everybody else, . . . look down upon others, and yet themselves do whatever happens to please them."[19] We see this same attitude in the religious leaders in Luke. The religious leaders are undeserving but bask in superficial honors (Lk 20:20, 24-26, 39-40, 45-47). In contrast, Jesus, while completely deserving, rejects superficial honors (Lk 11:27-28; 18:18-19).

I remember the first time I tried on my doctoral robe. My mother, who had flown to Texas for my graduation, kept taking pictures of me in it. One still sits on her nightstand in her bedroom. The robe was not just a fancy dress for a ceremony; it signified a lot—persistence through a very long academic journey and the culmination of years of hard work, sacrifice, hopes, and dreams. In Luke's day, it was possible to tell if someone was a philosopher by his clothing.[20] The philosopher's cloak, too, signified a lot: virtue, wisdom, and authority. Unfortunately, as Lucian tells us, it could easily just be put on by anyone pretending to be a philosopher.[21] Epictetus complains about philosophers who glory in their attire and honors without first earning the merit that should accompany their station in life: "Man, take a winter's training first. . . . Practice first not to let men know who you are; keep your philosophy to yourself a little while."[22] Lucian similarly mocks those who desire a philosopher's honors without having undergone the necessary training. He jeers,

> As you yourself wish to become a speaker . . . you need not feel any hesitation or dismay because you have not gone through all the rites of initiation. . . . Bring with you, then, as the principal thing, ignorance. . . . But you need also a very loud voice, a shameless singing delivery, and a gait like mine. They are essential indeed, and sometimes sufficient in themselves. Let your clothing be gaily-coloured. . . . First of all, you must pay especial attention to outward appearance, and to the graceful set of your cloak.[23]

---

[19]Aristotle, *Eth. nic.* 4.3.21.
[20]Dio Chrysostom thus notes that "there is one kind of dress for the philosopher and another for the layman." *Discourses,* trans. H. Lamar Crosby (1951), 67.8.
[21]Lucian, *Perger.* 15.
[22]Epictetus, *Discourses* 4.8.34-36.
[23]Lucian, *Rhet. praec.* 13-16.

Epictetus warns that those who glory in the trappings of philosophy without merit have lost their "plan of life." He tells them instead, "Be content, therefore, in everything to *be* a philosopher, and if you wish also to be taken for one, show to yourself that you are one, and you will be able to accomplish it."[24] Similarly, in Luke 20:45, Jesus mocks the religious leaders who take pride in their long robes. They have just demonstrated their ineptitude with respect to the law (Lk 20:1-44) and they prey on the helpless (Lk 20:47). They are totally undeserving of the garments that adorn them.

Plutarch points out that concern with external trappings of status are the mark of a novice and will disappear in the life of one who truly becomes a philosopher. Then,

> when men are being filled with the really good things, their conceit gives way . . . and, ceasing to feel pride in their philosopher's beard and gown, they transfer their training to their mind, and apply their stinging and bitter criticism most of all to themselves, and are milder in their intercourse with others. They do not arrogate to themselves, as before, the name of philosophy and the repute of studying it, or even give themselves the title of philosopher; in fact, a young man of good parts, on being addressed by this title by another, would be quick to say with a blush: I am no god, I assure you; why think me like the immortals?[25]

We are reminded of a similar saying of Jesus in Luke 18:19. Readers are often quick to jump to a theological defense of Jesus' divinity. Perhaps Luke's intended audience might have seen this as a statement about Jesus' humility.

We can see a similar distaste for outward trappings of status in Jewish literature. Several writers disapprove of the practice of according honor on the basis of external status symbols. Sirach warns, "Do not praise individuals for their good looks or loathe anyone because of appearance alone. . . . Do not boast about wearing fine clothes."[26] Similarly, in the Testament of Job, Job prays for his children, thinking, "Possibly my sons

---

[24]Epictetus, *Ench.* 23.
[25]Plutarch, *Virt. prof.* 81c-d.
[26]Sir 11:2-4.

may have sinned before the Lord through boasting by saying with disdain, 'We are sons of this rich man, and these goods are ours. Why then do we also serve?' For pride is an abomination before God."[27] For these Jewish writers, glorying in such undeserved honors is not only distasteful but sinful.

Jewish literature in particular sees pride as a sin and anticipates that the prideful will suffer an ultimate reversal of fortune. In Proverbs, the proud are "unclean" and God "resists" them.[28] In Psalm 18:27, God saves the humble but humbles the proud. Isaiah looks to the future when the haughtiness of humanity is brought low.[29] For Ezekiel, God will bring low the exalted and exalt the humble.[30] Zephaniah declares that in the day of judgment, God will remove the pride of Israel and leave with her a humble people.[31] The guest in the Letter to Aristeas declares, "God destroys the proud, and exalts the gentle and humble."[32] Sirach declares that "vengeance" lies in wait for the proud "like a lion" and that the Lord will supplant the thrones of rulers and "enthrone the lowly in their place."[33] Philo expects that "men of windy pride, whose intensified arrogance sets them quite beyond the cure" will have God as their "accuser and avenger."[34]

Self-praise. Most of us at least try to avoid openly bragging about ourselves in public. Harris Wittels, a comedian and writer and producer for the television show *Parks and Recreation*, coined the term *humblebrag* to describe what we do instead—finding ways to announce our accomplishments under a thin guise of humility. Twitter examples include, "It always feels a little odd to me when I get recognized randomly in public. I never know what to say. I'm glad it doesn't happen often"; or "9 hrs in room with 7 comedy writers yesterday 4 CBS sitcom about my life. Lots of talented, funny people in this world, who never get props"; or "Totally walked down the wrong escalator at the airport from the flashes of the

---

[27]T. Job 15.6-8.
[28]Prov 16:5; 3:24.
[29]Is 2:11-17.
[30]Ezek 17:24.
[31]Zeph 3:12.
[32]Let. Aris. 263.
[33]Sir 27:28; 10:14-15.
[34]Philo, *Virtues*, 171-74.

cameras . . . Go me."[35] Such thinly veiled boasts are openly mocked on Twitter, largely because they are disingenuous.

In Luke's literary world, many philosophers felt that an ideal leader would avoid self-praise. Epictetus warns, "In your conversation avoid making mention at great length and excessively of your own deeds or dangers."[36] He found it particularly unsavory to boast about one's virtuous acts: "When you have become adjusted to simple living in regard to your bodily wants, do not preen yourself about the accomplishment."[37] We are no strangers to boasting about our virtues either. One person offered this tweet: "Setting up your own charity and event is no joke. Would have thought it to be easier . . . this serious."[38] For Plutarch, this sort of self-praise is "held in the greatest contempt, as it appears to aim at gratifying ambition and an unseasonable appetite for fame."[39] Lucian openly mocks those who engage in self-praise: "He will address you, I say, using very moderate language about himself: 'Prithee, dear fellow, did Pythian Apollo send you to me, entitling me the best of speakers. . . . Because you hear everybody speak of my achievements with astonishment, praise, admiration, and self-abasement, you shall very soon learn what a superhuman you have come to.'"[40] Plutarch suggests that those who praise themselves do so since they think no one else will. Like a starving person forced to "feed unnaturally on their own persons . . . so when those who hunger for praise cannot find others to praise them, they give the appearance of seeking sustenance and succour for their vainglorious appetite from themselves, a graceless spectacle."[41] For Plutarch, this is a shameful practice. He states that "praise of ourselves is for others most distressing. For first we regard self-praisers as shameless, since they should be embarrassed even by praise from others; second as unfair, as

---

[35]Twisted Sifter, "The 50 Funniest 'Humble Brags' on Twitter," May 10, 2011, http://twistedsifter.com/2011/05/funniest-humble-brags-on-twitter/.

[36]Epictetus, *Ench.* 33.14.

[37]Epictetus, *Ench.* 47.

[38]Twisted Sifter, "50 Funniest."

[39]Plutarch, *De Laude* 540a.

[40]Lucian, *Rhet. praec.* 13.

[41]Plutarch, *De Laude* 540a.

they arrogate to themselves what is for others to bestow."[42] Plutarch affirms that a true philosopher will avoid such conduct, except in special circumstances. He says, "It is therefore the mark of a man who is making progress . . . to keep all this to himself and put the seal of silence on it."[43]

Among the darker manifestations of self-praise are those who choose to praise themselves at the expense of another, much as we see the Pharisee doing in Jesus' parable of Luke 18:9-14. In Plutarch's eyes, "when a man intermingles praise of himself with censure of another, and uses another's disgrace to secure glory for himself, he is altogether odious and vulgar, as one who would win applause from the humiliation of another."[44] Most people are sufficiently mature enough to avoid extended self-flattery while openly pointing to another's humiliating defeat. We do sometimes see those who glory in their accomplishments in the presence of another's defeat, however. In one episode of the television show *Everybody Loves Raymond*, Raymond is crushed when his book is rejected by a publisher. Robert, who at first hesitates to announce his promotion, clearly relishes the shift in fortune in their family, the taste of glory made sweeter by his brother's humiliating blow. Plutarch warns against such rivalry, chiding those who "try to rival the honour that belongs to others and set against it their own accomplishments and acts in the hope of dimming the glory of another."[45] When we have a true sense of self and are not motivated by insecurity, we can sit comfortably with our successes and learn from our failures. Until we get there, we would be well served by Epictetus's advice: "Above all, do not talk about people, either blaming, or praising, or comparing them."[46]

Deception of self. Parker Palmer once said that the "true self" is "not the ego self that wants to inflate us." Instead, the true self "is the self planted in us by the God who made us in God's own image—the self that wants nothing more, or less, than for us to be who we were created to be."[47] One

---

[42]Plutarch, *De Laude* 539d.

[43]Plutarch, *Virt. prof.* 81a-b.

[44]Plutarch, *De Laude* 547a.

[45]Plutarch, *De Laude* 540b.

[46]Epictetus, *Ench.* 33.1-3.

[47]Parker J. Palmer, *Let Your Life Speak: Listening for the Voice of Vocation* (San Francisco: Jossey-Bass, 2000), 69.

of the primary dangers of pride is that it often is a symptom of self-deception. Luke's readers would have been familiar with the command "Know thyself"; it was universally known in his literary world. They would have recognized what was really plaguing the religious leaders in Luke's Gospel: the scribes' and Pharisees' inauthenticity was wedded to the construction and maintenance of their false selves. They had become so intoxicated by superficial honors and the public maintenance of their image that they could not see their own hypocrisy. Experts in the intricacies of God's law, they failed to allow that law to form them into a people of justice, mercy, faith, and love. Aristotle depicts the internal division of vain people in a similar way: They are "foolish persons, as well as ignorant of themselves, and make this plain to all the world; For they undertake honourable offices for which they are unfit, and presently stand convicted of incapacity; they dress in fine clothes and put on fine airs and so on; they wish everybody to know of their good fortune; they talk about themselves, as if that were the way to honor."[48] Both Jesus and Aristotle deem such individuals "fools" for their pride that stems from a lack of self-understanding.

Brennan Manning talks about the false self as an "imposter," whose identity is formed externally from achievements and maintained by the "adulation of others."[49] For Epictetus, such a lack of self-knowledge motivates people to invite honors that may not really be theirs. Rebuking such imposters for bragging, he asks, "Why did you pride yourself upon things that were not your own? Why did you call yourself a Stoic?"[50] On the contrary, for Epictetus, those who have self-knowledge are content in themselves and therefore do not have to put such energy into maintaining such false personas.[51]

Plutarch notes that often people suffering from a slight malady welcome a doctor's care, but those who are self-deceived are so blinded to their own errors that they are like the extremely ill who suffer from delusions. They are those who have reached such a state that they "sometimes cannot

---

[48] Aristotle, *Eth. nic.* 4.3.36.

[49] Brennan Manning, *Abba's Child: The Cry of the Heart for Intimate Belonging* (Colorado Springs: NavPress, 1994), 50.

[50] Epictetus, *Discourses* 2.19.19.

[51] Epictetus, *Discourses* 1.21.1-4.

endure even the physicians' visits, but either drive them away or run from them, not realizing even that they are ill, because of the violence of their illness."[52] In Luke, the religious leaders' self-division is similarly severe. Their hearts are hardened, and they regularly respond to Jesus with antagonism. His invitation into the authentic existence that comes from living as one beloved by God is just too threatening to their fragile false selves.

Manning writes of our relationship with imposter, or the false self: "As we come to grips with our own selfishness and stupidity, we make friends with the imposter and accept that we are impoverished and broken and realize that, if we were not, we would be God."[53] Philo similarly notes that "man should know himself and banish from the soul the grievous malady of conceit," pointing to some who "in their braggart pride assumed godship, closing their eyes to the Cause of all that comes into being."[54] Being in the presence of God reminds us of the fact that we are both beloved and deeply flawed. In Philo's words, "None as he approaches the altar should be uplifted or puffed up by arrogance; rather gazing on the greatness of God, let him gain a perception of the weakness which belongs to the creature . . . let him reduce the overweening exaltation of his pride by laying low that pestilent enemy, conceit."[55] Philo warns teachers not to weave elegant theories about the world until they have come to know themselves. Addressing those who are "laden with vanity and gross stupidity and vast pretense," he urges, "For pray do not, O ye senseless ones, spin your airy fables . . . until you have scrutinized and come to know yourselves. After that, we may perhaps believe you when you hold forth on other subjects: but before you establish who you yourselves are, do not think that you will ever become capable of acting as judges or trustworthy witnesses in the other matters."[56] Self-knowledge brings authenticity and is the only basis for authority. Devoid of these qualities, Luke's religious leaders fought to maintain their fragile public image, because, tragically, that was all they had.

---

[52] Plutarch, *Virt. prof.* 82a.
[53] Manning, *Abba's Child*, 41.
[54] Philo, *Spec. Laws* 1.10.
[55] Philo, *Spec. Laws* 1.293-95.
[56] Philo, *Migration* 136, 138.

CHARACTERISTICS OF THE HUMBLE

Deserving but modest. In our culture, we typically don't see a problem with accepting deserved honors. We have awards ceremonies, publicly recognize the accomplishments of our peers, celebrate the heroism of our military, and honor the achievements of our greatest writers and artists. It is important to point out that not all ancient Mediterranean people would have shunned praise either. For instance, Aristotle sees nothing wrong with honor, as long as it is deserved. In fact someone who is truly "high-minded" is one who "behaves as he ought."[57] As with our culture, honors are a tricky thing to manage; getting it right says something about one's character. On the one hand, truly great people are going to receive honors, and they should accept them graciously. To do so is to have a truthful assessment of one's abilities. Aristotle would have had little time for the humblebrags that some of us engage in. He affirms that "honour is what high-minded men are concerned with; for it is honour that they especially claim and deserve."[58] When my daughter was in elementary school, she would sometimes do what we called the "smartypants dance," in response to getting a good report card. I at first looked at this as being a little too cocky. Later, as I began reading more books on the need for adolescent girls in our culture to own their strengths, I wished could go back in time and dance with her. Some of us have just as difficult a time with acknowledging our accomplishments as others do with overestimating theirs or basing their estimations on superficial qualities. Neither extreme, however, supports the true self because neither is rooted in reality.

Xenophon pictures Cyrus as someone who has a right relationship to honor. He is an ideal king who is a model of virtue and very deserving. Cyrus undergoes all kinds of dangers and enjoys the praise that he rightly

---

[57]He continues, "Without going about to prove it, that honour is what high-minded men are concerned with." Aristotle does observe, however, that "high-mindedness, then, seems to be the crowning grace, as it were, of the virtues; it makes them greater, and cannot exist without them." He further claims, "But the high-minded man, as he deserves the greatest things, must be a perfectly good or excellent man; for the better man always deserves the greater things, and the best possible man the greatest possible things," *Eth. nic.* 4.3.9-16.

[58]Aristotle, *Eth. nic.* 4.3.9-11.

deserves for his virtue and heroic actions.[59] In fact, it is the very position of esteem in which his subjects hold him that inspires him to greater acts of virtue.[60] Even though he enjoys the praise of his subjects, however, Cyrus is modest. Xenophon tells us, "But as he advanced in stature and in years to the time of attaining a youth's estate, he then came to use fewer words, his voice was more subdued, and he became so bashful that he actually blushed whenever he met his elders."[61] Unlike those whose fragile sense of self is threatened by the accomplishments of others, Xenophon tells us of Cyrus that "the king was delighted to see him laugh at one and praise another without the least bit of jealousy."[62]

Deflecting praise in favor of virtuous actions. Just as we walk a tightrope to figure out how to live out of the truth of who we are and have a right relationship to praise without appearing too braggadocios, so ancient Greeks and Romans fought to achieve that balance as well. Aristotle, who clearly thought that the virtuous are correct to seek the honor they deserve, also observes that the truly great-souled have no real *need* for honor. For, "at great honour from good men he will be moderately pleased . . . seeing that not even honour affects him as if it were a very important thing."[63] Others go even further. While it is no crime to accept genuine praise, particularly from those who are honorable people themselves, Epictetus also says that a truly virtuous person focuses more on doing good than being honored. He asks the imaginary virtuous person, "Do you wish to do good or to be praised?" replying, "Immediately you get the answer, 'What do I care for praise from the mob?' And that is an excellent answer."[64] A virtuous person will also not take praise too seriously: "Signs of one who is making progress are: He . . . praises no one . . . says nothing about himself as though he were somebody or knew

[59]Xenophon, *Cyr.* 1.2.1.

[60]Xenophon, *Cyr.* 1.6.25.

[61]Xenophon, *Cyr.* 1.4.4.

[62]Xenophon, *Cyr.* 1.4.15.

[63]Aristotle, *Eth. nic.* 4.3.17, 18. Nonetheless, a "fondness for honor" is virtuous. Aristotle notes, "But sometimes a man is called ambitious or fond of honour in praise, as being . . . fond of noble things; and sometimes a man is called unambitious or not fond of honour in praise, as being moderate and temperate," *Eth. nic.* 4.4.4.

[64]Epictetus, *Discourses* 3.23.8.

something. . . . And if anyone compliments him, he smiles to himself at the person complimenting; while if anyone censures him, he makes no defense."[65] Epictetus commends one modest philosopher who "although he was a man of the very highest worth, he never praised himself, but used to blush even if someone else praised him."[66]

Plutarch also thought that a truly virtuous person would show modesty when praised and be more concerned with virtue than praise. He advises, "For you should blush when praised, not be unblushing; you should restrain those who mention some great merit of yours,"[67] and he instructs, "But if a friend has to tell what he has done, he reports it modestly and says nothing about himself."[68] Again, having a right relationship to honors is a bit like walking a tightrope: lean too far in one direction and you might end up looking like a pompous fool. Lean too far in the other and you violate the truth about what is actually deserved. Plutarch is fully aware of what the excesses look like. A virtuous person is not an applause junkie: "It is rather to be expected, therefore, that those whose strivings are toward virtue and honour will avail themselves of the occasion and subject, and give least thought to the shouting and applause that may be called forth by their manner of speaking."[69] The focus of attention should always be on the content of the message and not the fanfare it might produce. It is "expected that the lover of honour and wisdom . . . should keep his pride in himself to himself and be silent, feeling no need of eulogists and auditors."[70]

One kind of praise Plutarch *does* admire is praise for virtuous actions— particularly when that praise may be shared by all people who act in like manner: "See whether the praise is for the action or for the man. It is for the action if . . . they, too, cherish the same desires and aspirations themselves and praise not us alone but all persons for like conduct."[71]

---

[65]Epictetus, *Ench.* 48.2.
[66]Epictetus, *Frag.* 21.
[67]Plutarch, *De Laude* 547b.
[68]Plutarch, *Adul. amic.* 64b.
[69]Plutarch, *Virt. prof.* 80e.
[70]Plutarch, *Virt. prof.* 80e-f.
[71]Plutarch, *Adul. amic.* 55f.

We are reminded of Jesus' attitude in Luke 11:27-28. When the woman attempts superficial praise ("Blessed is the womb that bore you and the breasts that nursed you!"), he deflects her praise in favor of all who obey God's word. Plutarch gives instructions for deflecting superficial praise that sound a lot like what Jesus does here:

> With the fair-minded it is not amiss to use another device, that of amending the praise: when praised as eloquent, rich, or powerful, to request the other not to mention such points but rather to consider whether one is of worthy character, commits no injuries, and leads a useful life. He that does this does not introduce the praise, but transfers it; and he leaves the impression of not delighting in encomiasts but of being displeased with them for praise that is unbecoming and bestowed for the wrong reasons, using his better points to draw attention from the worse, not from a desire for praise, but to show how to praise aright.[72]

Plutarch gives further advice on what to do when confronted by a flatterer: "When the praise runs on the contrary to extravagance, as with the invidious flattery used by many, it permits one to say: 'No god am I; why likenest thou me to the immortals? If you know me truly, commend my probity, temperance, reasonableness, or humanity.'"[73] Luke's auditors might well see Luke 18:19 in the same light. For Plutarch, true praise is the praise of virtuous actions and is intended to glorify not an individual but all who practice such behavior. He notes, finally, superficial praise: "Such praise is best shown for what it is when true praise is set beside it."[74]

A true sense of self. Thomas Merton wrote, "We have the choice of two identities: the external mask which seems to be real . . . and the hidden, inner person who seems to us to be nothing, but who can give himself eternally to the truth in whom he subsists."[75] The external mask is the false self, with a fragile ego and deep insecurities masked by an external "successful" persona. The true self lives authentically, unmoved by flatterers and critics alike and refusing to hide from personal failures and

---

[72]Plutarch, *De Laude* 543a-b.
[73]Plutarch, *De Laude* 543d.
[74]Plutarch, *De Laude* 545f.
[75]Merton, *New Seeds of Contemplation*, 295.

limitations. The speed with which we rush to our own defense when criticized betrays a fragile ego hiding behind our public persona. Epictetus once said, "If someone brings you word that So-and-so is speaking ill of you, do not defend yourself against what has been said, but answer, 'Yes, indeed, for he did not know the rest of the faults that attach to me; if he had, these would not have been the only ones he mentioned.'"[76] Self-knowledge evicts the imposter of the false self, making flattery unnecessary. Plutarch urges his readers to "eradicate from ourselves self-love and conceit": "But if, in obedience to the god, we learn that the precept, 'Know thyself,' is invaluable to each of us, and if at the same time we carefully review our own nature and upbringing and education, how in countless ways they fall short of true excellence . . . we shall not very readily let the flatterers walk over us."[77] Embracing our true selves means that we won't shy away from self-examination. Plutarch counsels, "And if we keep repeating to ourselves Plato's question, 'Can it be that I am like that?' . . . we shall no longer make much use of 'righteous indignation' toward others when we observe that we ourselves stand in need of much indulgence."[78]

Finally, there is a natural progression toward wisdom and humility in those who are willing to face their own limitations. Mark Twain was once reported to have said, "When I was a boy of 14, my father was so ignorant I could hardly stand to have the old man around. But when I got to be 21, I was astonished at how much the old man had learned in seven years."[79] Plutarch once similarly observed that "the multitudes who came to Athens to school were, at the outset, wise; later they became lovers of wisdom, later still orators, and, as time went on, just ordinary persons, and the more they laid hold of reason the more they laid aside their self-opinion and conceit."[80]

For some Jewish writers, true self-knowledge is rooted in the understanding that we are creatures. In the first chapters of Genesis, people seem

---

[76]Epictetus, *Ench.* 33.9.

[77]Plutarch, *Adul. amic.* 65f.

[78]Plutarch, *On the Control of Anger* 463e.

[79]The *Reader's Digest* in 1937 attributed this quote to Mark Twain. His authorship has been disputed.

[80]Plutarch, *Virt. prof.* 81f.

to struggle with the reality of their humanity. From the eating of the forbidden fruit in Eden to the erection of the Tower of Babel, people seem quite unwilling to accept the humility of their human condition. The frailty of humanity invites humility. Sirach asks, "How can dust and ashes be proud? Even in life the human body decays. A long illness baffles the physician; the king of today will die tomorrow. . . . Pride was not created for human beings."[81] Pride also comes from taking credit for what we have received from God. Pseudo-Phocylides accordingly states, "Do not pride yourself on wisdom nor on strength nor on riches. The only God is wise and mighty and at the same time rich in blessings."[82] For Philo also, if we understand ourselves as creatures in relationship to the greatness of God, there will be no place for pride. He observes that "the arrogant man is always filled with the spirit of unreason, holding himself, as Pindar says, to be neither man nor demigod, but wholly divine, and claiming to overstep the limits of human nature."[83]

Humility, with integrity. Merton tells us, "In great saints you find that perfect humility and perfect integrity coincide."[84] The union of word and deed—in other words, integrity—was the mark of a true teacher in the ancient Mediterranean world. Those who teach against hubris also exhibit modesty in their personal lives. Epictetus recalls Socrates's modesty: "Listen, what does Socrates say? 'Nor would it be seemly for me, O men of Athens, at my time of life to appear before you like some lad, and weave a cunning discourse.'"[85] Epictetus points out that Socrates was so modest that he used to make introductions to other philosophers in spite of who he was:

> And for that reason who ever heard Socrates saying, "I know something and teach it"? But he used to send one person here and another there.[86] Therefore men used to go to him to have him introduce them to philosophers, and he

---

[81]Sir 10:9-10, 18.

[82]Ps.-Phoc 53-54.

[83]Philo, *Virtues* 172.

[84]Merton, *New Seeds of Contemplation*, 99.

[85]Epictetus, *Discourses* 3.23.25.

[86]This refers to Socrates's practice of introducing people to renowned philosophers, rather than being insulted that he was not taken for a famous philosopher.

used to take them around and introduce them. But no, your idea of him, no doubt, is that, as he was taking them along, he used to say, "Come around today and hear me deliver a discourse in the house of Quadratus!"[87]

Philo roots Moses' teachings against pride in his lifestyle. Moses sought to set the people "out of the reach of pride and arrogance,"[88] teaching them "to abstain from all sins, but especially from pride."[89] Philo points out that Moses himself sought no powerful position among the people but took his place as their leader only at the command of God. When called by God, he "held back with prayers and supplications, until, when He many times repeated the command," he obeyed.[90] For Philo, this sense of integrity marks Moses as an ideal leader.

When the expected integrity between word and deed was lacking, people were quick to notice. Plutarch remarks, "In theory . . . it is agreed that to speak to others of one's own importance or power is offensive, but in practice not many even of those who condemn such conduct avoid the odium of it."[91] Plutarch points to the hypocrisy of others. Euripides, he says, speaks out against false praise. "Yet he brags most intolerably, interweaving with the calamities and concerns of his tragedies the irrelevant theme of his own praise. Pindar does the like. . . . . He never wearies of extolling his own powers, which indeed deserve all praise—who denies it?—; but even the winners of the crown at the games are proclaimed victors by others, who thus remove the odium of self-praise."[92]

The ancient litmus test for an ideal teacher was the perfect union of word and deed. We see that in Luke's portrait of the humble Jesus. Jesus chastens the religious leaders and his disciples against pride, while he himself rejects flatterers and empty praise. Luke's intended audience would have recognized Jesus as a person of integrity who could therefore speak with authority about humility, his words solidified through his own personal example.

---

[87]Epictetus, *Discourses* 3.23.22-23.
[88]Philo, *Virtues* 161-63.
[89]Philo, *Virtues* 161-63.
[90]Philo, *Virtues* 63.
[91]Plutarch, *De Laude* 539a-c.
[92]Plutarch, *De Laude* 539a-c.

SUMMARY

While Luke's literary world does not yield a uniform view of humility, many ancient writers show disdain for those who seek undeserved honors, who feed off of flattery, or who brag about their own accomplishments. Luke's authorial audience would have been well primed to feel revulsion at religious leaders in his Gospel who seek unjustified honors and bask in unmerited praise. Those who engaged in self-praise would have been apt subjects for mockery in Luke's cultural world and for Luke's intended readers.

Luke's literary world does, however, yield examples of moralists who feel that it is right to shun even deserved honors and who blush when others offer praise.[93] These people are far more concerned with the subject of their teachings than the honors that might come their way for presenting them.[94] Luke's intended audience might see Jesus' rejections of praise (Lk 11:27-28; 18:19) in a similar light, understanding them as an expression of his humility and a refusal of superficial flattery.

The religious leaders in Luke seem to suffer from a false sense of self. This is evidenced by their love of external honors and insecurity about receiving criticism (Lk 20:40, 45-47). Luke's intended readers might wonder at the religious leaders' potential for repentance, given how blind they are to their own reflection (Lk 18:9-14).

Luke's target audience might also see the disciples the way Epictetus sees philosophers with little training.[95] The disciples argue with one another about who is the greatest (Lk 9:46) because they have not yet come to understand that the importance of their task lies in the significance of their message about the kingdom and not their greatness within it. Luke's intended readers might hold some hope for them, however. With a little maturity, they might eventually blush at their former ambitions.[96]

Finally, Luke's intended readers would be primed to recognize the unity of Jesus' life and teachings as a mark of a true teacher. They would have

---

[93]Epictetus, *Frag.* 21; Plutarch, *De Laude* 547b.
[94]Plutarch, *Virt. prof.* 80e.
[95]Epictetus, *Discourses* 4.8.34-36.
[96]Epictetus, *Ench.* 48.2.

appreciated his deflection of superficial honors (Lk 11:27-28; 18:19) as a sign of spiritual adulthood and a true sense of self. They would have appreciated that Jesus' rebukes against pride and appeals to humility emerge directly from his own example of modesty (Lk 22:27).

Reading Luke through the lens of his literary world allows us to understand a bit more about the religious leaders' desperate attempts for glory and the disciples' strivings for recognition. We can anticipate the ways in which Luke's authorial audience would have recoiled against the braggadocios attitudes of the Pharisees and their contrasting responses to Jesus' humble integrity that marks him as a true philosopher-king. Reading Luke through the eyes of the early church broadens the horizons of our understanding even further. The Fathers and Mothers of the church, who value humility above all other virtues, invite us to look with them at the predicament of the honor-seeking disciples and to consider the ways in which we too may be struggling for significance. They warn us of the peril of prideful self-sufficiency and urge us to follow after Jesus' humble example. We turn to that discussion next.

6

LEARNING HUMILITY
WITH THE CHURCH

WE DON'T REALLY VALUE HUMILITY. We seem to think of it as an *optional* virtue—we recognize a certain degree of integrity in people who exhibit humility but don't really see a lack of humility as that much of a problem. For many contemporary Christians fighting for cultural and political significance, humility is a particularly undesirable quality. It smacks of weakness and timidity—a hindrance to those seeking to establish a basis of authority in society. The church fathers and mothers had a very different perspective on humility! Because they recognized humility as *the* very foundation for Christian life and all other Christian virtues, they quickly recognized the spiritual bankruptcy of one who entirely lacked it. They knew that humility is not simply one virtue among many but the essential defining characteristic of a Christ follower. John Chrysostom, for instance, says that humility is the "mother, and root, and nurse, and foundation and bond of all good things."[1] For John Cassian, it is the "mistress of all virtues."[2] Thomas Aquinas talked about humility as the very "foundation of the spiritual edifice" because it removes the pride that prevents people from submitting to the grace of God.[3] Humility is the quality *that makes possible* all other spiritual virtues and the defining mark of Jesus' own life. Without humility, it is impossible to be a follower of Jesus. Jesus' call to humility will fall on deaf ears unless we can find others who have gone before us who truly recognize humility as the very foundation of Christian life, who

---

[1]Chrysostom, *Hom. Act.* 13.42.
[2]John Cassian, *Conf.* 15.7.
[3]Thomas Aquinas, *Summa theologiae* II-II, q. 161, art. 5, ad. 2.

can take us by the hand and show us what the humility of Jesus looks like enfleshed in the examples of their own lives. For this, we turn to the early church.

THE HUMILITY OF THE CENTURION (LUKE 7:1-10)

In Luke's story, the Jewish elders present their request to Jesus as his *obligation*: "He is worthy of having you do this for him, for . . . it is he who built our synagogue" (Lk 7:4-5). Slaves to the honor codes of their day, they behave in what seem to us as embarrassingly manipulative ways. Cyril of Alexandria winces at the religious leaders' audacity. Pointing out their lack of faith in the other Gospels (Mt 12:24; Jn 9:24), he wonders how they dare to come with such a request.[4] Ambrose of Milan is quick to point out that the centurion did not initiate this expectation for an obligatory healing. The centurion sends his friends to mitigate the Jewish elders' transparent attempt to maneuver Jesus into a healing "lest his presence seem to have embarrassed the Lord's modesty, and by service to have provoked service."[5] For Ambrose, the centurion's humility gives him the ability to engage in a mature social negotiation, treating Jesus with the respect that he deserves.

While contemporary scholars focus on the humility of the centurion, for Ambrose, the real example of humility is Christ's. He asks, "How great is the sign of Divine humility, that the Lord of Heaven by no means disdained to visit the centurion's servant!" Jesus went to heal the man himself "lest He seem to have despised the humble rank of the centurion's servant." Jesus heals that the centurion "may know both the power of Divinity and the grace of humility." For Ambrose, however, the ultimate purpose of Jesus' visit is to provide the church with an example of humility: "Surely He did not act because He could not cure in His absence, but in order to give you a form of humility for imitation, whereby He taught the need to defer to the small and the great alike."[6] We should get the point: the mentality that "he did this for us, you owe him" among the Jewish

---

[4]Cyril of Alexandria, *Comm. Luke* 35, 151.
[5]Ambrose, *Exp. Luc.*, 178.
[6]Ambrose, *Exp. Luc.*, 177.

elders stands in stark contrast to the grace-filled social exchange between the centurion and Jesus. Both the centurion and Jesus exhibit a mature sense of self that makes genuine interaction possible. This is what social exchanges should look like in the kingdom of God.

WHO IS THE GREATEST? (LUKE 9:46-48)

Like some of us, the disciples had fragile egos. Newly minted as Jesus' ambassadors of the kingdom, and possibly feeling crippled by their immediate failures, they sought to validate their self-worth by comparing themselves with each other. Dismayed by this evidence of the disciples' spiritual immaturity, early Christian writers are quick to use their negative example for the church's instruction. Cyril points out that it was "utter foolishness" to not recognize that all of them "were to be accepted on equal terms."[7] When we evaluate our kingdom worth by comparing ourselves with each other instead of realizing that we are all playing for the same team and are all accepted on equal terms as God's servants, we rob ourselves of the joy that comes from knowing that God has gifted us to do exactly what God has called us to do and deprive ourselves of the ability to take pleasure in the successful ministries of other people. Comparison of ourselves with others either diminishes our own kingdom value or another's and is not based on the truth. As Cyril asks, "For what is there more delusive than vainglory? . . . It is a weakness, therefore, despised even among us, and numbered among the great evils."[8] Instead, humility is the "ornament of a soul."[9]

Lest readers think that they are above this kind of temptation, Cyril points out that it also besets the righteous. In this attack, Satan "humbles to base lusts even a well-confirmed mind" for "in those in whom there is something noble, and the praise of an excellent life, he excites the passion of vainglory, exciting them by little and little to an abominable haughtiness."[10] For Cyprian, their question is a "risk" and "snare of death."[11] Particularly at risk are those who are just beginning to see some progress in their Christian journey. Cyril

---

[7]Cyril of Alexandria, *Comm. Luke* 54, 238.

[8]Cyril of Alexandria, *Comm. Luke* 54, 239.

[9]Cyril of Alexandria, *Comm. Luke* 54, 238.

[10]Cyril of Alexandria, *Comm. Luke* 54, 236-37.

[11]Cyprian, *Zel. liv.* 10, in *ANF* 5:493-94.

tells us of the need to nip this prideful tendency in the bud while we still can. He warns, "For when passions are but beginning in us . . . they are easily overcome. But when they have increased, and grown strong, they are hard to put off, and bear themselves with no little audacity."[12] If the disciples were to continue in their trajectory, they could easily end up like the pompous religious leaders of Luke's Gospel who are entirely blinded to kingdom values (Lk 7:4-5; 18:9-18; 20:46).

Why does Jesus use a child as an object lesson to get his point about humility across? As discussed earlier, the child exemplifies a lack of status. Early commentators point this out as well. For Origen, children are naturally humble, "for neither haughtiness, nor conceit in respect of noble birth, nor wealth, or any of those things which are thought to be good, but are not, comes to a little child."[13] Ambrose, noting that here the "Lord teaches that sincerity must be without arrogance," points out that a child "claims nothing for himself"[14] and does not "strive after honour and ambition."[15] For Cyril, the child "covets not rank, and knows not what is meant by one man being higher in station than another; he has even no unwillingness to be regarded as the least, nor sets himself above any other person whatsoever."[16] It is this same attitude that the disciples (and we) most need.

So what do we do if we are prone to base our self-worth on comparisons with others? First, we should know that these comparisons are not of God. Cyril points to the source of the disciples' question: it is "Satan" who "caused the prideful question to rise in the disciples' midst."[17] This kind of pride is "a malady invented by the wickedness of the devil."[18] Second, the ancient commentators use this narrative to show that Christ has the ability to eradicate this kind of attitude from us. In Luke's narrative, it is Jesus' swift instruction on humility that saves the disciples from sure destruction. Cyprian notes that through his swift action, Jesus "cut off all envy by His reply. He plucked

---

[12]Cyril of Alexandria, *Comm. Luke* 54, 237.

[13]Origen, *Fr. Matt.* 13.16, in *ANF* 9:484.

[14]Ambrose, *Exp. Luc.*, 245.

[15]Ambrose, *Exp. Luc.*, 354.

[16]Cyril of Alexandria, *Comm. Luke* 54, 237.

[17]Cyril of Alexandria, *Comm. Luke* 54, 236.

[18]Cyril of Alexandria, *Comm. Luke* 54, 239.

out and tore away every cause and matter of gnawing envy."[19] Cyril similarly sees that, although Satan intended destruction by introducing the prideful question, Christ struck down "the tare, the work of the wicked sower; and before it grew up high."[20] Readers should not fail to receive the message: The teaching of Christ in Luke's narrative provides an abiding remedy for pride.

Christ not only provides instruction in humility but also perfectly exemplifies it. If we want to participate in kingdom life without the kind of soul-robbing comparisons that we see the disciples display here, we should imitate Christ. Cyril again points to Jesus' example:

> For He said, Learn of Me: for I am meek, and lowly in heart. And if He who transcends all, and is crowned with such surpassing glories, is lowly in heart, how must it not bring upon such as we are, yea, even upon our very selves, the blame of utter madness, if we do not bear ourselves humbly towards the poor, and learn of what our nature is, but love to vaunt ourselves ambitiously above our measure.[21]

For Cyprian and for Cyril, the ultimate humiliation of the crucifixion makes Jesus our best model of humility. Since Jesus was "led as a sheep to the slaughter," Cyprian asks, "dares any one now . . . lift up himself and be haughty, forgetful, as well of the deeds which He did?" Cyril argues, "But if 'the servant is not greater than his Lord,' let those who follow the Lord humbly and peacefully and silently tread in His steps, since the lower one is, the more exalted he may become."[22]

JOCKEYING FOR HONORS AT A BANQUET (LUKE 14:7-11)

We are all too familiar with contemporary politicians and rank-climbing preachers who seek to attach themselves to a more prominent political figure in order to gain power and notoriety for themselves. Celebrity worship is nothing new. Plutarch once remarked that just like a young ivy will entwine itself around a tall tree in order to gain height, so an obscure person will seek a connection with one of greater status to be "under the shelter of his power

---

[19]Cyprian, *Zel. liv.* 10, in *ANF* 5:493-94.
[20]Cyril of Alexandria, *Comm. Luke* 54, 237.
[21]Cyril of Alexandria, *Comm. Luke* 54, 237.
[22]Cyprian, *Epistle* 6.4, in *ANF* 5:284-85.

and grow great with him."[23] We catch a glimpse of these kinds of behaviors at the banquet described in Luke 14.

Early Lukan interpreters show dismay at the self-seeking grasping of power in this text. For Ambrose, Jesus uses this occasion to teach humility using the "humanity of persuasion" instead of the "harshness of coercion."[24] For him, Jesus' gentle correction will chasten pride. Cyril, for one, is disgusted with the guests' behavior. They hurry about "inconsiderately" after honors that are not "suitable" and are "foolish, rude, and arrogant," saying to themselves, "I wish to be illustrious and renowned."[25] Cyril points out the obvious: such a person is not following Christ. Whoever "thinks great things of himself" and "prides himself on an empty loftiness, is rejected and accursed. He follows a course the contrary of Christ's Who said: Learn of Me, for I am meek and lowly in heart."[26]

Cyril can see that this grasping at importance is rooted in a basic lack of self-knowledge. If the guests at the party possessed an awareness of who they really were, they would not need to seek superficial significance. It is foolish to think of riches, wealth, and honor as an actual indicator of our importance. These things "come to us from without, and are not really ours." Rather, if anyone had adequate self-knowledge "to regard his state with understanding eyes, he would then become like Abraham, who mistook not his nature and called himself dust and ashes." The path to actual greatness begins with an awareness of who we are before God. For the one who knows oneself enough to understand that he is nothing, "this very nothingness becomes a great and admirable and honorable before God, by knowing himself."[27]

For some, prideful attitudes are rooted in deeply set assumptions about the innate superiority of certain kinds of people: people of a certain race, economic level, gender, nationality, religion, and so on. Lactantius points out that there can be no reason for pride since no one can claim intrinsic superiority over another. He asks, "Some one will say . . . Is there not some difference between individuals?" He replies, "There is none; nor is there

---

[23]Plutarch, *Mor.* 805 E-F.
[24]Ambrose, *Exp. Luc.,* 311.
[25]Cyril of Alexandria, *Comm. Luke* 102, 410-11.
[26]Cyril of Alexandria, *Comm. Luke* 102, 411.
[27]Cyril of Alexandria, *Comm. Luke* 102, 412.

any other cause why we mutually bestow upon each other the name of brethren, except that we believe ourselves to be equal." Only "in the sight of God we are distinguished by virtue."[28] Cyril also points to virtue as the only thing that might distinguish people in the sight of God: if any "wish to be set above others," such a person should "surpass the many by having the testimony of glorious virtues."[29] For Cyril this is not advocating a spiritual competitiveness but is itself rooted in humility.

Sometimes those seeking to climb ladders of status and power do so because they feel that the influence that comes with such positions will afford opportunities to serve God. They (and we) might do well to consider the testimony of early Christian writers on Luke 14:11. God is pleased with those who exhibit humility of character. For Lactantius, Luke 14:11 "teaches that he who shall simply place himself on a level with other men, and carry himself with humility, is esteemed excellent and illustrious in the sight of God."[30] An even higher "rank of dignity in the judgment of God" will be granted to those who consider others as better than themselves. For Cyril, such a humble person is "is crowned by God with honor and praise"[31] and is "worthy of emulation."[32] Benedict envisions this kind of a person climbing a ladder quite different from the one that most of us have in mind. He envisions a metaphorical ladder that we ascend through humility and descend through pride. Through his ladder of humility, Benedict highlights the paradox that humility leads to greatness: true humility causes one to mount the ladder in lowliness and good works. Pride and exaltation cause one to move downward on the ladder.[33]

THE PRODIGAL SON (LUKE 15:11-32)

In the story of the prodigal son, the son comes to an awareness of his limitations and comes to terms with his identity, a process that leads him to humility. If we are unwilling to face the darker aspects of our character, we will put a great deal of energy into maintaining a false self before others. Such a

[28]Lactantius, *Inst.* 5.16, in *ANF* 7:151.
[29]Cyril of Alexandria, *Comm. Luke* 102, 411.
[30]Lactantius, *Inst.* 5.16, in *ANF* 7:151.
[31]Cyril of Alexandria, *Comm. Luke* 102, 412.
[32]Cyril of Alexandria, *Comm. Luke* 102, 411.
[33]Benedict, *The Holy Rule of St. Benedict,* trans. Boniface Verheyen (Grand Rapids, MI: Christian Classics Ethereal Library, 1949), 7.

false self projects the self we would like to be but doesn't correspond to our actual nature. As Thomas Merton once said, "Every one of us is shadowed by an illusory person: a false self. This is the man that I want myself to be but who cannot exist, because God does not know anything about him. And to be unknown of God is altogether too much privacy."[34] A false self shows up when we have bought into the idealized portrait of our spiritual selves that doesn't quite match the reality. This self values prayer without praying, idealizes connection with God without spending time in God's presence, affirms the values of God's kingdom without living into them. Luke's early interpreters knew that in order to continue to respond to God, the god of the false self had to first be torn down. Without a true sense of self, there simply would not be a self with which to authentically respond to God.

In Luke's story, the prodigal comes to his senses and to himself, authentically responding to his father's love. For Ambrose, the story of the prodigal illustrates what can happen when we depart from our true selves and from Christ. He writes, "'Leaving his home and country, he went abroad into a distant country.' For what is farther than to depart from oneself, not from a place? . . . Surely whoso separates himself from Christ is an exile from his country, a citizen of the world."[35] For Ambrose, the journey to a distant country is a journey away from the true self. It is a departure "from wisdom" and from God.[36] Ambrose later observes that a return to God is also a return to self: "Well did he return to himself who departed from himself. Indeed, whoso returns to the Lord returns to himself, and whoso departs from Christ disinherits himself."[37]

The prodigal's willingness to confront his choices and his character saves him. Ambrose notes that he is "raised by the merit of his own humility."[38] Other early Lukan interpreters observe this also. Cassian, too, points out the prodigal's "humble penitence."[39] Macarius Chrysocephalus observes that his "humility and his accusation became the cause of justification and glory."[40]

---

[34]Thomas Merton, *New Seeds of Contemplation* (New York: New Directions, 1961), 34.
[35]Ambrose, *Exp. Luc.*, 318.
[36]Ambrose, *Exp. Luc.*, 318.
[37]Ambrose, *Exp. Luc.*, 319.
[38]Ambrose, *Exp. Luc.*, 323.
[39]John Cassian, *Conf.* 2.11.7, in *NPNF*[2] 11:417.
[40]Macarius Chrysocephalus, *Oration on Luke 15* 4, in *ANF* 2:583.

In response to the prodigal's humble repentance, the father gives new honor to his son. Peter Chrysologus observes that it is a "the ring of honor"[41] that is placed on the prodigal's finger. He notes, "The father's devotion is not content to restore only his innocence. It also brings back his former honor."[42] Similarly, Athanasius, noting how the father has clothed the prodigal, observes, "By all these things, he begets him new in the image of the glory of Christ."[43]

The prodigal is not the only character who struggles with identity in this story. While the elder brother is obedient to his father, he is so preoccupied with his own merit and the injustice of his father's acceptance of his brother that he struggles to relate authentically to his family. For Cyril of Alexandria, the point to remember is that "if any are called unto repentance, even if they be men highly blameable," one must "rejoice rather, and not give way to an unloving vexation on their account." Cyril admits that "we also sometimes experience something of this sort" when those who are "humbled unto every kind of wickedness" repent. When we complain, he says, we do so from "an empty narrowness of mind," not conforming to God's purposes.[44]

One of the more fascinating elements of the church's reception of this story is how some ancient commentators *practice* humility themselves in the way in which they appropriate the text. While this type of identification with the prodigal is in no way universal,[45] for some patristic writers the hermeneutical process provides opportunity for them to humble themselves in repentance. In a letter to Theodosius, Jerome refers to *himself* as the prodigal son and requests prayer that he may abandon his vices.[46] For

---

[41]Peter Chrysologus, *Sermon 5*, in FC 17:49-50.

[42]Peter Chrysologus, *Sermon 3*, in FC 17:38.

[43]Athanasius, *Ep. fest.* 7, in St. Athanasius, *The Resurrection Letters*, paraphrased and introduced by Jack N. Sparks (Nashville: Thomas Nelson, 1979), 123.

[44]Cyril of Alexandria, *Comm. Luke* 107, 433-34.

[45]Tertullian, unwilling to identify such a figure as a Christian, sees the prodigal squandering the general wisdom he had from God. The prodigal squandered his substance, "having been cast by his moral habits far from the Lord." He was "from the first prodigal, because *not* from the first a Christian." *Pud.* 9, in ANF 4:83. Chrysostom does not sugarcoat the prodigal's sin either, noting that he plunged into "no ordinary vice, but went to the very extremity, so to say, of evil," illustrating how "great is the power of repentance." *Theod. laps.* 7, in NPNF[1] 9:96.

[46]Jerome, *Letter 2, To Theodosius and the Rest of the Anchorites*, in NPNF[2] 6:4. Jerome sees the characters in the parable as "either Jews and Christians, or saints and penitents." *Against Jovinianus* 2.31, in NPNF[2] 6:412.

Jerome, the narrative of the prodigal is an analogy of a sinner receiving again Christ's robe and a kiss of reconciliation and hearing from him "let thy garments be always white."[47] He observes that when one repents, "gladly does Christ embrace the prodigal Son when he returns to Him."[48] This message of grace includes himself as well. Augustine similarly likens the prodigal to himself as one who was "far from Thy face, through my darkened affections."[49] Sometimes the greatest gifts Luke's earliest commentators can give us is a bit of their spirit with which they approach the text. Perhaps we need them to remind us that the journey of the prodigal is the story of *our* journey home—for those of us who sometimes forget who we really are and where we really belong.

The Pharisee and the Tax Collector (Luke 18:9-19)

For the early church, just the mention of pride or humility would also immediately bring a story to mind: the Pharisee and the publican (i.e., tax collector). This narrative was used so widely in the early church as a paradigm of pride and humility that a mere reference to the story functioned synonymously for this virtue and vice.[50] For instance, the desert fathers and mothers tell a tale about a man seeking advice on which ascetic practice to take on next. After the man has suggested going to the desert, seeking anonymity in a foreign place, or confinement with fasting in his cell, the desert father Ammonas says to him, "It is not right for you to do any of these three things. Rather, sit in your cell and eat a little every day, keeping the word of the publican always in your heart, and you may be saved."[51] Another saying attributed to both a desert father and elsewhere a desert mother warns, "Imitate the publican, and you will not be condemned with the Pharisee. Choose the meekness of Moses and you will find your heart which is a rock changed into a spring of water."[52] The pattern of using the "Pharisee and publican"

---

[47]Jerome, *Letter* 122.3, to Rusticus, in *NPNF*[2] 6:228.

[48]Jerome, *Letter* 16, to Pope Damasus, in *NPNF*[2] 6:20.

[49]Augustine, *Conf.* 1.18.28, in *NPNF*[1] 1:53.

[50]Jane Foulcher, *Reclaiming Humility: Four Studies in the Monastic Tradition.* Cistercian Studies Series 255 (Cistercian Publications, 2015), 124n107.

[51]*The Sayings of the Desert Fathers*, trans. Benedicta Ward (Kalamazoo, MI: Cistercian Publications, 1975), 26 (Ammonas 4).

[52]*The Desert Fathers: Sayings of the Early Christian Monks*, trans. Benedicta Ward (New York: Penguin, 2003), 161 (Hyperichius, 15.50); 233 (Syncletica 11).

as synonyms for pride and humility continues as late as Benedict.[53] Benedict begins his chapter on humility with an appeal to Scripture and citation of Luke 14:11 and Luke 18:14, noting that a true monastic should always prayerfully repeat what the "publican in the gospel" said, with his eyes lowered: "Lord, I am a sinner. I am not worthy to raise my eyes to heaven."[54] Benedict warns that one should not "desire to be called holy before one is; but to be holy first, that one may be truly so called."[55]

For early Christian writers, the story of the Pharisee and the tax collector provided a warning about the destructive effect of pride on the spiritual life. Athanasius points out that the Pharisee's pride was so detrimental to his piety that it nullified any merit that might have resulted from his fasting: The "boast of fasting did no good to the Pharisee, although he fasted twice in the week, only because he exalted himself against the publican."[56] Jerome notes that the "self-righteous Pharisee perished in his pride, while the humble publican was saved by his confession."[57] For Jerome, the "publican with his humble confession of his faults went back justified far more than the Pharisee with his arrogant boasting of his virtues."[58] Augustine, in a letter to Casulanus, observes that fasting would be profitable in one with humility, but not in one with such pride as the Pharisee demonstrated.[59] For Cyril of Alexandria, the Pharisee nullified his good acts. He asks, "What profit is there in fasting twice in the week if it serves only as a pretext for ignorance and vanity and makes you proud, haughty and selfish?"[60] Cyril declares that in such an act "thou has mingled dung with thy perfume."[61] For Basil of Caesarea, the Pharisee "made his justice void by being guilty of pride." Basil notes that the Pharisee "was rendered inferior to a humble man and a sinner." He warns his reader, "Be on your guard, therefore, and bear in mind this example of

---

[53]Who of course is dependent on the line of tradition that stretches through the desert fathers and mothers, Cassian, and the Rule of the Master.
[54]Rule of Benedict 7.
[55]Rule of Benedict 4.62.
[56]Athanasius, *Festal Letters* 1.4, in *NPNF*[2] 4:507.
[57]Jerome, *Letter* 122.3, to Rusticus, in *NPNF*[2] 6:228.
[58]Jerome, *Letter* 77.4, in *NPNF*[2] 6:159.
[59]Augustine, *Letter* 36.4.7, in *NPNF*[1] 1:265-70.
[60]Cyril of Alexandria, *Comm. Luke* 120, 481.
[61]Cyril of Alexandria, *Comm. Luke* 120, 481.

grievous loss sustained through arrogance. . . . Never place yourself above anyone, not even great sinners. Humility often saves a sinner who has committed grievous transgressions."[62]

We are so familiar with this parable that we automatically identify with the most positive character in the story—the publican—and feel revulsion for the Pharisee. Chrysostom can be helpful to contemporary readers because he doesn't minimize the publican's sin and thereby allows the story to maintain more of its intended shock effect. His reading also captures more of the destructive effects of the Pharisee's pride. Chrysostom affirms that what the Pharisee "said what was true, 'I am not as this Publican.'"[63] Instead, through his pride, the "Pharisee *came to be* inferior to the Publican."[64] Chrysostom sees the righteousness of the Pharisee (with all of his fastings and tithes) as a foil against which to see the contrition of the (truly) unrighteous publican and highlights the power of humility. For Chrysostom this parable teaches "how great is the gain of humbleness of mind, and how great the damage of pride." He observes that the Pharisee's pride shipwrecked the vessel of his virtue while it was in the mouth of the harbor. Chrysostom instructs, "For humbleness of mind is the foundation of the love of wisdom which pertains to us. Even if thou shouldest have built a superstructure of things innumerable; even if almsgiving, even if prayers, even if fastings, even if all virtue; unless this have first been laid as a foundation, all will be built upon it to no purpose and in vain; and it will fall down easily, like that building which had been placed on the sand,"[65] "The publican was accepted only from his humility, the Pharisee perished by his boastfulness."[66] Chrysostom, observing that the Pharisee "destroyed all his merit," expresses his concern that his readers "render your virtue vain by this boasting of yourselves."[67] He reminds them that the publican became "righteous" through his humility.[68]

The Pharisee's grandiose posturing and self-flattery are indicative of his bankrupt emotional and spiritual state. He seems to genuinely believe in

---

[62]Basil of Caesarea, *Of Humility in Ascetical Works*, trans. M. Monica Wagner, FC 9:481-82.
[63]John Chrysostom, *Hom. Heb.* 21.7, in *NPNF*[1] 14:464.
[64]John Chrysostom, *Hom. Mat.* 3.6, in *NPNF*[1] 10:17.
[65]John Chrysostom, *Hom. Phil* 1.18, in *NPNF*[1] 9:2.
[66]John Chrysostom, *Hom. 1 Tim.* 17, in *NPNF*[1] 13:467.
[67]John Chrysostom, *Hom. 1 Tim.* 2, in *NPNF*[1] 13:483.
[68]John Chrysostom, *Hom. Mat.* 3.6, in *NPNF*[1] 10:17.

his merits and desires recognition for them—even from God. The tragedy of the story is that he does not see himself correctly. Early Lukan interpreters, too, recognized that the Pharisee's pride was rooted in a basic lack of self-awareness. No one who possessed adequate self-knowledge could boast in the presence of God. Origen remarks that every person ought to be "conscious of human infirmity in comparison with the greatness of God."[69] For Ambrose, true humility is rooted in a "knowledge of self," a quality the tax collector possessed but the Pharisee lacked.[70] For Augustine, remembering that one is human supplies the necessary humility for repentance: "How useful and necessary a medicine is repentance! People who remember that they are only human will readily understand this. It is written, 'God resists the proud, but gives grace to the humble.'"[71] For Jerome, those who like the Pharisee are prideful exhibit little knowledge of the human condition when they say, "I will ascend above the stars; I will place my throne in heaven, and I will be like the Most High."[72] They stand in contrast to David, who declares, "My wounds stink and are corrupt because of my foolishness."[73] Jerome reminds his readers that the psalmist sings, "Every man is a liar."[74]

Political leaders who engage in self-praise are often fodder for political cartoons and late-night talk shows. Luke's caricature of the self-congratulatory Pharisee supplied his readers with a similarly pathetic image. We have already seen the distaste that Luke's readers would have probably felt for those who boasted about their accomplishments. The early church shows a similar revulsion for this sort of attitude. Cyril remarks that the Pharisee is "boastful, and without sense; for he praises himself, although the sacred Scripture cries aloud, Let a neighbor praise thee, and not thy own mouth: a stranger and not thine own lips." Cyril points out that not many are willing "to listen to the words of flatterers: yea, and even if men extol them, they often are covered with shame, and drop their eyes to the ground, and beg silence of

---

[69]Origen, *Cels.* 3.64, in *ANF* 4:489.

[70]Ambrose, *On the Duties of the Clergy* 17.90, in *NPNF²* 10:57.

[71]Augustine, *Sermon* 351.1, in *WSA* III/10:118.

[72]Jerome, *Pelag.* 3.14, in *NPNF²* 6:479-80.

[73]Jerome, *Pelag.* 3.14, in *NPNF²* 6:479-80.

[74]Jerome, *Pelag.* 3.14, in *NPNF²* 6:479-80.

those that praise them," but this Pharisee is "shameless." Cyril shows that the Pharisee's standard of comparison is low. He "extols himself because he is better than extortioners, and the unjust, and adulterers," but "being better than those who are bad" does not make him worthy of admiration.

We recognize that using someone else's misfortune as an opportunity to boast about oneself is particularly distasteful. As we saw in the last chapter, boasting at another's expense was generally despised in Luke's literary world. Cyril shows a similar revulsion for the Pharisee's attitude. Besides, "the infirmity of others is not a fit subject for praise for those who are in health." This sort of attitude provokes God to anger: "Moderate thyself, O Pharisee: put a door to thy tongue and a lock. Thou speakest to God Who knoweth all things. . . . Lower thy pride, for arrogance is both accursed and hated by God."[75]

It is easy for us to look at ancient and contemporary examples of pride and imagine that we would never stoop to such attitudes. Luke's early interpreters capitalize on the pastoral implications of this parable. Clement of Alexandria warns his reader, "Woe unto them that are wise in their own eyes, and prudent in their own sight."[76] For Tertullian, this story teaches that prayer must be done "with modesty and humility, with not even our hands too loftily elevated, but elevated temperately and becomingly; and not even our countenance over-boldly uplifted."[77] Chrysostom warns that to boast of one's own merits is to "provoke the Lord" and "arm the enemy" and "invite him to steal them away."[78] However, Chrysostom also observes the potential for righteousness through humility: "If, being sinners, when we account ourselves to be what we are, we become righteous, indeed the Publican did; how much more, when being righteous we account ourselves to be sinners."[79] Cyril urges his reader to pray without ceasing but to "be careful to do so aright" because God "rejects empty haughtiness and a proud look." When one is tempted by pride

---

[75]All quotations in the preceding two paragraphs are from Cyril of Alexandria, *Comm. Luke* 120, 480-81.

[76]Clement of Alexandria, *Paed.* 3.12, in *ANF* 2:293.

[77]Tertullian, *Or.* 17, in *ANF* 3:686.

[78]John Chrysostom, *Hom. Matt.* 3.7, in *NPNF*[1] 10:18.

[79]John Chrysostom, *Hom. Matt.* 3.6, in *NPNF*[1] 10:17.

let him remember Christ, who says to the holy apostles, When ye have done all those things, those namely which have been commanded you, say, We are unprofitable servants, we have done that which was our duty to do. For we owe unto God over all, as from the yoke of necessity, the service of slaves, and ready obedience in all things.[80]

BEWARE OF SCRIBES (LUKE 20:46)

Idi Amin, the third president of Uganda, apparently liked to be addressed by his full title: "His Excellency, President for Life, Field Marshal Al Hadji Doctor Idi Amin Dada, VC, DSO, MC, Lord of All the Beasts of the Earth and Fishes of the Seas and Conqueror of the British Empire in Africa in General and Uganda in Particular."[81] His rule, characterized by human rights abuses, murder, and corruption, rendered him supremely undeserving of his ludicrous title. Luke's audience could have easily supplied their own examples of unjust Roman emperors who gloried in the fawning of their subjects. In the Lukan text at hand, the teachers of the law take pride in superficial honors while simultaneously demonstrating that they are unworthy of such honors. Cyril observes of these scribes, "It was their determination not to depart from their inbred love of praise, nor to abandon their accursed lust of lucre." He asks, "For what was their custom? To walk in the streets beautifully attired, dragging with them a pompous dignity, to catch thereby the praises of those who saw them."[82] The scribes' pride is grounded in a lack of self-knowledge: "They falsely assumed to themselves the reputation of piety" and assumed "a gravity of manners not founded on reality."[83] Instead, Christ commanded his worshipers "to be humble, and not lovers of boasting; not to pay any regard to the desire for vainglory, but rather to seek the honor that cometh from above."[84]

DISPUTE OVER GREATNESS (LUKE 22:24-27)

At the Last Supper, right after Jesus has predicted his passion, the disciples argue about who should have the title of greatest disciple. Cyril wonders

---

[80]Cyril of Alexandria, *Comm. Luke* 120, 482.
[81]Colm O'Regan, "The Rise of Inflated Job Titles," BBC News, July 17, 2012, www.bbc.co.uk/news /magazine-18855099.
[82]Cyril of Alexandria, *Comm. Luke* 137, 546.
[83]Cyril of Alexandria, *Comm. Luke* 137, 546.
[84]Cyril of Alexandria, *Comm. Luke* 137, 546-47.

perhaps if this conflict did not arise because those who held the second rank among them were not willing to give way to those who held the first. Cyril says that it was "from an unprofitable love of glory, the root of which is pride, that this vain and senseless ambition had, so to speak, shot up." He points out that Christ immediately deals with their pride, and "like a vigorous physician cut away, by an earnest and deep-reaching commandment, the passion which had sprung up among them."[85] Unfortunately the disciples are just about out of time: Jesus is about to be crucified. They will need to await the arrival of the Spirit, who will lead them to a deeper understanding of the kingdom of God.

For Cyril, this narrative "was recorded for our benefit, that that which happened to the holy apostles may prove a reason for humility in us." There should be no jostling for superiority in the kingdom of God. We should be of "modest mind, and possess such humbleness of feeling as to abandon out of love to the brethren all idea of preeminence." Cyril exhorts his readers to therefore regard "your companions, that in honor they are better than you." To have such an attitude is "highly worthy of the saints." It "makes our piety unto God more worthy of honor." It "tears the net of the devil's malice" and "rescues us from the pitfalls of depravity." Finally, "It perfects us in the likeness of Christ the Savior of us all."[86]

Christ himself provides the pattern for humility for the church: "For listen how He sets Himself before us as the pattern of a humble mind, and of a will not set on vainglory; for Learn, He says, of Me, Who am meek and lowly in heart."[87] Cyril points to the example of Christ washing the disciples' feet, and then asks,

> And when Christ thus speaks, who can be so obdurate and unyielding as not to cast away all vaingloriousness and banish from his mind the love of empty honor? For He Who is ministered unto by the whole creation of rational services of the universe; He Who is the equal of God the Father in His throne and kingdom; taking a servant's place, washed the holy apostles' feet. . . . He, therefore, Who is ministered unto became a minister; and the Lord of glory made Himself poor, leaving us an example, as it is written.

---

[85]Cyril of Alexandria, *Comm. Luke* 143, 572.
[86]Cyril of Alexandria, *Comm. Luke* 143, 572-73.
[87]Cyril of Alexandria, *Comm. Luke* 143, 573.

Cyril finally admonishes, "Let us, therefore, avoid the love of vainglory. . . . For so to act makes us like unto Him . . . let our exaltation consist in humility, and our glory in not loving glory."[88]

SUMMARY

The early church placed a strong value on humility. Humility was not just one of many Christian virtues but the characteristic hallmark of the mature Christian and an essential quality on which all other virtues depend. They saw true humility rooted in reality and in an accurate self-assessment. Having a right sense of oneself as a created being before God ought to bring one to humility.

Luke's earliest interpreters understood how potentially lethal pride was for the Christian life. They see demonic temptation striking those who begin to feel that they are having some success in their spiritual lives.[89] For them, the fall of the Pharisee in Luke 18 is enough to remind Christians to not think too highly of their accomplishments.[90]

Although some patristic readers see humility in the Greek philosophers,[91] humility expressed as imitation of Christ's servanthood and self-emptying is, of course, a uniquely Christian theology. For the patristic writers, Christ is the perfect example of humility, as one who humbled himself to experience the human condition and suffered on our behalf. They urge any who would take themselves too seriously to remember Christ's humility, and set that example before them as a pattern for emulation.[92]

Finally, the contemporary Western church has all but forgotten how to recognize humility. Evangelicals in North America today seem to fail to recognize it as the mark of a true Christian or to realize how essential it is for the Christian life. Reading Luke with the early church has the potential to reintroduce us to this forgotten virtue.

---

[88]Cyril of Alexandria, *Comm. Luke* 143, 573.

[89]John Chrysostom, *Hom. Matt.* 3.7, in *NPNF¹* 10:18.

[90]John Chrysostom, *Homily Concerning Lowliness of Mind*; and *Commentary on Philippians 1.18*, trans. R. Blackburn, M.A. in *NPNF*, 9:00.

[91]Clement of Alexandria, *Strom.* 22, in *ANF* 2:376; Origen, *Cels.* 3.63, in *ANF* 4:489.

[92]Cyril of Alexandria, *Comm. Luke* 143, 573.

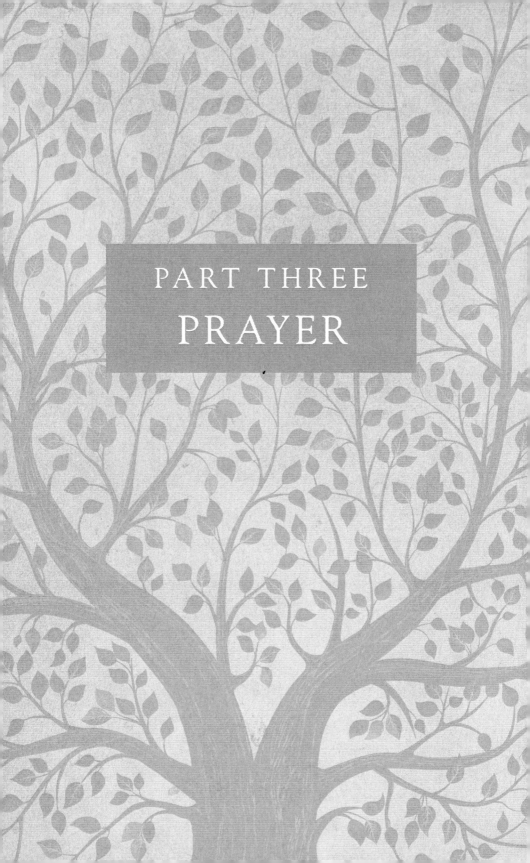

PART THREE
PRAYER

7

PRAYER IN THE GOSPEL NARRATIVE

DOES PRAYER WORK? Is it actually effective in the sense of changing circumstances, or is it something we engage in primarily to get closer to God? For Jesus in Luke's Gospel, prayer is effective: it actually makes a difference in concrete circumstances. We are called to pray not just as our spiritual duty or to grow closer to God, although these motivations are important. We pray because God has chosen to work in response to prayer.

Luke is the go-to Gospel for a theology of prayer. Luke includes more about Jesus' own prayer habits and Jesus' teachings on prayer than any other Gospel, transforming the stories about Jesus' life into narratives about the power of prayer. Luke sets Jesus up as an example of ideal prayer because he wants us to understand how essential prayer is for the life of faith and our participation in God's kingdom. God accomplishes the work of the kingdom in Luke by acting in response to Jesus' prayers. God does the same with the early church in the book of Acts. The point should be clear: prayer aligns us with God's values and opens the door for our inclusion in God's kingdom work.

JESUS' BAPTISM PRAYER (LUKE 3:21-22)

For Luke, this isn't just a story about Jesus' baptism; it is a story about the power of prayer. Jesus' baptism prayer launches his ministry, initiating his anointing, commissioning, and empowerment for ministry. Mark's Gospel doesn't have this emphasis. To Mark's Gospel, Luke adds Jesus' prayer, the physical descent of the dove, and the presence of the crowd. For Luke, it is more a story about what happens when Jesus prays than about

Jesus' baptism. Luke replaces the phrases about Jesus coming up out of the water in Matthew and Mark with "and was praying," making the prayer and not the baptism itself the point of focus.

Immediately, we see Jesus' prayers inviting God to act. Jesus' prayer initiates a divine anointing and ratification of his ministry. Here Luke begins to cement a connection between prayer and the work of God. This text introduces a pattern for both Luke and Acts that highlights the strong connection between prayer and revelation, commission and empowerment (Lk 1:19-20 and Lk 2:37-38; see also Acts 4:23-31; 9:10-19; 10; 13:1-3; 22:7-21).[1] Here and elsewhere, Jesus' prayer brings forth divine revelation[2] (Lk 1:9-11; 2:37-38; Acts 9:11-12; 10:2-6; 10:9-16) in the form of visions and auditions.[3] God speaks from heaven, anointing Jesus for ministry, which Luke's audience would recognize as appropriate for a kingly figure.[4] Jesus clearly sees it this way in Luke 4:18-19.[5] Jesus' quotation of the Isaiah passage in Luke 4:18 also points to his empowerment for ministry given through the Spirit at his baptism.[6]

Jesus' prayer initiates the arrival of the Spirit.[7] The Spirit descends on Jesus "in bodily form" (Lk 3:22),[8] granted for the fulfillment of Jesus' mission[9] but given to him permanently.[10] The descent of the Spirit then begins a chain of events.[11] Luke 4 begins with the description that Jesus is "full of the Holy Spirit." In Luke 4:14, Jesus, "filled with the power of the

---

[1]Joel B. Green, *The Gospel of Luke*, New International Commentary on the New Testament (Grand Rapids: Eerdmans, 1997), 185.

[2]Robert C. Tannehill, *Luke*, Abingdon New Testament Commentaries (Nashville: Abingdon, 1996), 56.

[3]Charles H. Talbert, *Reading Luke: A Literary and Theological Commentary on the Third Gospel* (New York: Crossroad, 1982), 40.

[4]I. Howard Marshall, *The Gospel of Luke: A Commentary on the Greek Text*, New International Greek Testament Commentary (Grand Rapids: Eerdmans, 1978), 154.

[5]Green, *Gospel of Luke*, 186.

[6]Talbert, *Reading Luke*, 41.

[7]Eduard Schweizer, *The Good News According to Luke*, trans. David E. Green (Atlanta: John Knox Press, 1984), 79.

[8]François Bovon, *Luke 1: A Commentary on the Gospel of Luke 1:1–9:50*, Hermeneia (Minneapolis: Fortress, 2002), 128.

[9]Bovon, *Luke 1*, 129.

[10]Tannehill, *Luke*, 85.

[11]Robert C. Tannehill, *The Narrative Unity of Luke-Acts: A Literary Interpretation*, vol. 1, *The Gospel According to Luke* (Philadelphia: Fortress, 1986), 57.

Spirit," returns to Galilee and begins teaching in the synagogues. In Luke 4:18, Jesus announces, "The Spirit of the Lord is upon me" and interprets his ministry as a fulfillment of the Scriptures. The anointing paves the way for Jesus' ministry, enables him to understand his calling, and empowers him to do his task.[12]

Luke draws a vital connection between Jesus' faithfulness in prayer and the inauguration of and empowerment for his earthly ministry. If we want to be used by God for God's kingdom work, the preliminary step for us also is to be faithful in prayer. We often offer up lackluster prayers, resigned to whatever fate throws our way, as if we didn't really expect our prayers to matter. This mentality is not supported by Luke's theology.

Jesus Withdraws for Private Prayer (Luke 5:16)

Faithfulness in prayer matters. Luke emphasizes that Jesus habitually withdrew to commune with God alone in prayer. His statement changes the point of Mark 1:35, which describes a single occasion of prayer: "In the morning, while it was still very dark, he got up and went out to a deserted place, and there he prayed." Luke, however, generalizes this reference: the imperfect tense "he would withdraw" highlights the habitual nature of Jesus' prayer life. The wilderness is not a place for crowds to gather, as in Mark, but becomes a place for the deepening of Jesus' own prayer life.[13]

In addition to Luke 5:16, Luke records many other instances of Jesus' pattern of solitary prayer. In Luke 22:39, Jesus goes to the Mount of Olives, "as was his custom," to pray. He goes off to a deserted place at daybreak (Lk 4:42), he prays alone regularly (Lk 9:18), and he even spends entire nights in prayer (Lk 6:12). Jesus practices what he preaches, illustrating the necessity for prayer through his own dependence on it.[14] Luke pushes us to follow Jesus' example.

We are people who often need a concrete plan of action if we want to be faithful to our best desires (and the invitations of God). Dallas Willard said that we must make "plans" for righteousness—setting ourselves up to

---

[12]Green, *Gospel of Luke*, 186.
[13]Bovon, *Luke 1*, 177.
[14]Green notes that this passage "holds in tandem word and deed." *Gospel of Luke*, 238.

succeed and not fail with spiritual disciplines in spite of the inertia of our human nature.[15] Jesus seemed to have some specific spots (Mount of Olives) and possibly times (daybreak) for regular prayer. If we still need to develop a habit of faithful prayer, simple things like having a designated spot and time can aid our best intentions.

JESUS PRAYS BEFORE CHOOSING HIS DISCIPLES (LUKE 6:12-16)

Prayer aligns us with the will of God. In this narrative, we see that that Jesus' choice of the disciples was also God's by taking a glimpse at Jesus' activity the night before. Before choosing the disciples, Jesus "spent the night in prayer to God"[16] (Lk 6:12) conforming his will to the will of his Father. The Markan parallel only reports that Jesus went up the mountain. In Luke, however, Jesus climbs the mountain *to pray*.[17] The choice to appoint disciples, the number of disciples chosen, and the choice of the particular people all fall within God's design because Jesus has first sought God's will in prayer.[18] The unique expression "in prayer with God" expresses not only Jesus' supplication but also "his silence, the listening, and the answer of God."[19] Jesus' prayer through the night is not a statement about his asceticism but emphasizes his complete focus on the will of God and significance of this event.[20] Many Christians today treat prayer as a one-sided activity where we express our desires to God. Not only is the self-oriented approach misdirected but the manner of prayer is as well. The model we have of prayer here and in Acts 1:14 involves an orientation around God's purposes and extended periods of communal waiting in the

---

[15]Dallas Willard, *Looking Like Jesus: Divine Resources for a Changed Life Are Always Available*, August 20, 1990, www.dwillard.org/articles/individual/looking-like-jesusdivine-resources-for-a-changed-life-are-always-available.

[16]The periphrastic present infinitive illustrates the continual nature of Jesus' prayer.

[17]Bovon provides further insight. Highlighting a parallel in Pseudo-Philo between Moses' act of climbing a mountain to pray after witnessing the apostasy of Israel after the first revelation of God's law, Bovon emphasizes Jesus' initiative. Abandoning expectations for the scribes and Pharisees to embrace God's kingdom (Lk 6:11), Jesus suggests new leadership for Israel who might lead them (indirectly) and others to embrace God's plan of salvation. *Luke 1*, 208.

[18]Green, *Gospel of Luke*, 258.

[19]Bovon, *Luke 1*, 209.

[20]Bovon, *Luke 1*, 208-9.

presence of God. The early church recognized this, as we will see in chapter 9. We should further note the result of Jesus' prayer at the end of the narrative: the crowds were able to discern power coming from him (Lk 4:19).[21]

PRAYER REVEALS JESUS' IDENTITY (LUKE 9:18; 9:28-36)

It shouldn't be a surprise that among the Synoptics, Luke alone sets the transfiguration narrative in a context of prayer.[22] At this point in Luke's story, just the mention of prayer is enough to capture our attention because so far in the Lukan story, prayer has been regularly linked to important divine revelations.[23] Now again, directly prior to revelation, Jesus ascends a mountain to pray (Lk 9:28).

The transfiguration account is connected with Jesus' revelation of himself to the disciples in Luke 9:18-27 by the words "after these sayings" (Lk 9:28). In each story, prayer leads to a further revelation of Jesus' identity.[24] In Luke 9:18, after Jesus has been at prayer, he asks the disciples who he is. The correlation of Jesus' prayer with Peter's response, "the Messiah of God," shows that understanding of Jesus' identity comes through God and is granted through prayer.[25] Jesus' identity is also revealed through his transformed appearance, by the presence of Moses and Elijah, through the emphasis on the presence of God, and by God's public affirmation.

We might wonder if it is significant that Moses and Elijah specifically are present. The echoes from the exodus story—the setting on a mountain, Moses, the change of countenance, the cloud, and the topic of Moses' and Elijah's conversation—suggest that the story is about Jesus' own "exodus."[26] Moses and Elijah, who appear to speak with Jesus about his mission, are also appropriate characters here because both are legendary for their

---

[21]Green, *Gospel of Luke*, 258.

[22]Barbara E. Reid, "Prayer and the Face of the Transfigured Jesus," in *The Lord's Prayer and Other Prayer Texts from the Greco-Roman Era*, ed. James H. Charlesworth, Mark Harding, and Mark Kiley (Valley Forge, PA: Trinity Press International, 1994), 40.

[23]Green, *Gospel of Luke*, 268.

[24]Talbert, *Reading Luke*, 103.

[25]Green, *Gospel of Luke*, 368.

[26]When read in light of Jesus' "mission statement" in Lk 4:18-19, and in light of the enveloping revelation of Jesus' glory, Jesus is seen as the supreme liberator. Green, *Gospel of Luke*, 378-79.

habits of prayer (1 Kings 17:21-22; 18:36-37; 19:9)[27] and both experienced divine revelation while in prayer.[28]

While Jesus is at prayer, the appearance of his face is changed and his clothes become a dazzling white (Lk 9:29). Jesus' shining white garment speaks to his status: Jesus is divine.[29] Readers familiar with the exodus narrative and other elements of Jewish tradition would know that one's face indicates the condition of one's heart and one's relationship to God.[30] Therefore, as a direct result of Jesus' prayer, the disciples are enabled to see his inner self made transparent to them, which should have answered any lingering questions about Jesus' identity.

While this experience further strengthens Jesus for his ministry, the disciples are "weighed down with sleep" (Lk 9:32). This foreshadows the Gethsemane prayer narrative, where the disciples are so overcome with grief that they crumple in sleep (Lk 22:45). Prayer and sleep seem to bring opposite results: through prayer, Jesus receives understanding and strength for his mission; overcome with sleep, the disciples fail to understand or accept Jesus' mission. In spite of their foolishness, God speaks to the disciples, providing further proof of Jesus' identity (Lk 9:35).

The strength and understanding that Jesus receives through prayer should be seen as a foil for the disciples' inability to understand and provides a lesson for Luke's readers about the importance of prayer. We should also not miss Luke's emphasis that the mission of God is being fulfilled through God's response to Jesus' prayers.

THE LORD'S PRAYER (LUKE 11:1-4)

Luke could scarcely do more to emphasize the fact that Jesus is the supreme model of his prayer teaching. After the disciples watch Jesus at prayer, they

---

[27]Barbara E. Reid, *The Transfiguration: A Source- and Redaction-Critical Study of Luke 9:28-36* (Paris: J. Gabalda et Cie E'diteurs, 1993), 119.

[28]Moses conversed with God on the mountain and then gave the people God's instructions (Ex 19). Elijah also experienced a revelation of God after speaking with God on the mountain (1 Kings 19:9-18). Reid, *The Transfiguration*, 122.

[29]Clothing was a sign of status and identity. Bovon, *Luke 1*, 375. White may carry eschatological connotations (Rev 3:4; 7:9). Here Jesus' clothing proves his heavenly status and subjection of death. Reid, *The Transfiguration*, 115.

[30]Green, *Gospel of Luke*, 380.

ask him to teach them to pray (Lk 11:1). The repetition of the verb "to pray" for both Jesus and the disciples and Jesus' acknowledgment of the disciples' prayer life further emphasize the connection between Jesus' example and the disciples' practice.[31]

First of all, we should note that prayer essentially is not about us but about God and God's kingdom work. We don't bring a wish list to our personal genie. Instead, prayer is essentially about aligning oneself with God's will, getting on board with the kingdom work that God is doing, and asking for grace and help in participating in that mission. The Lord's Prayer in Luke has a specific focus: we should pray for the swift arrival of God's reign and for the courage and strength to participate in God's kingdom purposes in the meantime.[32] The narrow focus of this prayer makes an important point for Jesus' followers: our desires should also be this single-minded.[33]

It is assumed that this kind of prayer takes place within the context of an intimate, ongoing, and personal relationship with God. Sometimes my students are jarred by the brutal honesty with which some of the prophets and psalmists in the Hebrew Bible address God. They might fail to see the larger context of trust and relationship in which some of these frustrations are expressed. Here, too, prayer takes place within an overall context of trust between beloved and loving Parent. Jesus addresses his prayer to his *abba*, or "Father," which was his own intimate way of addressing God and the term he provides for his disciples to use as well.[34] In this way, Jesus points to the personalized love of God, a theme that is critical to Luke and characteristic of Jesus' teaching throughout his Gospel.[35]

One reason why a lot of us struggle to be faithful in prayer is that although we would never say it, we struggle to trust that God will answer our requests. We have all experienced disappointment in prayer, and prayed,

---

[31]Green, *Gospel of Luke*, 440; Lk 11:2 should be translated, "Whenever you pray."

[32]Talbert, *Reading Luke*, 129.

[33]Talbert, *Reading Luke*, 129; Marshall, *Gospel of Luke*, 455.

[34]François Bovon, *Luke 2: A Commentary on the Gospel of Luke 9:51–19:27*, Hermeneia (Minneapolis: Fortress, 2013), 85.

[35]Bovon, *Luke 2*, 85. Bovon rightly observes that "the reality of God, who is called Father by virtue of the historical and cultural imperatives that the Bible has not escaped, also includes all that a mother is for her children and all that a woman can offer."

maybe fervently, for people who never got healed, for things that we felt that we needed that we never received, for relationships that fell apart anyway. In the end, we resigned ourselves to God's will and rose from our knees without quite articulating our fears that we had wasted our time, or worse, been intentionally ignored by God. The prophets and psalmists articulate well the heartbreaking silences that many of us experience at times with God. We all experience the realities of living in a fallen world, and often our commitment to Christ intensifies our pain rather than relieving it. What Luke does for us here is enlarge our perspective. When Jesus prays, "not my will but yours be done" in Luke 22:42, his view encompasses more than his own suffering, or even his own death, but the broader work of God's kingdom and how it is being accomplished through him. This is instructive for us as well. We tend to think of God being there *for us*—for our own happiness and comfort. In the Lord's Prayer, it is we who are there *for God*, asking to be used by God in the work that God is accomplishing on earth.

It is probably no accident that Jesus begins with trust as the foundation for prayer. Here, the request for God's name to be "hallowed" means that we can trust God because God acts in ways that are consistent with God's good nature. The term echoes Ezekiel 36:22-28, where God vindicates the holiness of the divine name that the nations have profaned.[36] The verb is passive, which may mean that God is the subject of the prayer: God should act in ways that cause humanity to honor God.[37] God is the only one who can ultimately hallow God's name.[38] God does this by fulfilling God's own will through the plan for salvation.[39] The request fits well with the following parable's teaching of God's trustworthiness to answer prayer. God's graciousness is a focal point in this request, a theme that is common in Luke's theology.[40] The echo of the Ezekiel passage, however, also points to human responsibility: believers are not to behave in a way that shames

---

[36]Joseph A. Fitzmyer, *The Gospel According to Luke*, 2 vols., Anchor Bible 28-28A (Garden City, NY: Doubleday, 1985), 898 (pages are numbered sequentially throughout the two vols.); Green, *Gospel of Luke*, 441.

[37]Marshall, *Gospel of Luke*, 457.

[38]Bovon, *Luke 2*, 86.

[39]Bovon, *Luke 2*, 86.

[40]Green, *Gospel of Luke*, 440.

God.[41] The term reveals something about and makes a request of God but also involves us as worshipers in the act of actually hallowing the God who has been and will be exalted in history.[42]

What follows is a dangerous prayer: the request for the present and future kingdom that is at the very heart of the Lord's Prayer. This is a prayer that enlarges our perspective beyond our sometimes limited horizons. We are to pray for the fullness of God's future reign but also for God's purposes to be accomplished in the present through the Spirit. This request assumes our participation in the kingdom and necessitates a lifestyle in imitation of Jesus. We need to grasp just how powerful this request is. When we offer ourselves up to God with insistent sincerity, asking God to transform our lives and use us for the kingdom, we should know that God will answer such requests in accordance with God's own good nature. We should be confident that God will indeed act on our willingness to embrace God's rule—this verse and the entire context of the Lord's Prayer in Luke affirms it. Such a prayer puts us at God's disposal and concretizes our response to Jesus' summons to follow him, even to death if necessary (Lk 9:23). We should *expect* the transformative, empowering work of the Spirit, conforming us to Jesus' image and strengthening us for the task of engaging the world with kingdom values. This prayer is not the prayer of missionaries and pastors alone—this prayer is at the heart of what it means to be a Christian. We have got it all wrong in our North American culture that sees Christianity as a means to happiness, personal fulfillment, and even prosperity. God does not exist to supply our every desire; we exist to fulfill God's.

The prayer for "daily bread" is a prayer for God's faithful sustenance each day.[43] By this point it should be clear that this is a prayer for what we actually need, not what we want. The provision of bread is miraculous—just as miraculous as the provision of loaves in Luke 9:10-17.[44] One might wonder, however, if the "daily bread" offered here is actual food or spiritual

---

[41]Green, *Gospel of Luke*, 442.
[42]Bovon, *Luke 2*, 86.
[43]Bovon, *Luke 2*, 88. Present imperative, translated "each day."
[44]Bovon, *Luke 2*, 88, reminds us that the God of Israel "has been nourishing his people ever since he created them."

sustenance.[45] As we will see in chapter 9, the early church had a tendency to read John's spiritual "bread" into this request, reading this as a prayer for faith that is supplied by the Word of God or by the Eucharist.[46] An exception is Cyril of Alexandria, who sees the request for material bread as one that should cause no shame.[47] One need not exclude the other. Perhaps here material provision is intertwined with spiritual blessing.[48]

We can also trust that God acts definitively on our request for forgiveness.[49] Luke's use of "sin" has the idea of a multitude of transgressions, like those listed in Luke 10:25-28, which place us very much in need of divine grace.[50] God's forgiveness, however, is assured. It is rooted in God's graciousness and in Jesus' very mission as one who brings good news, proclaims release to the captives, and lets the oppressed go free (Lk 4:18).[51] How often do we carry our guilt around with us as if this were not the case? This verse points to our role as well. The present ("we forgive") implies both an act of forgiveness as a part of the prayer itself and an ongoing willingness to extend grace to others because of the grace that we ourselves have received.[52]

The request, "Do not bring us to the time of trial," should be interpreted, "Do not let us yield to temptation."[53] It does not mean "Help us to avoid difficult things." Jesus and his disciples obviously are not excused from that! Instead, Jesus tells his disciples to pray that, as they are going through trials, they might remain in God's care[54] so that their trials will produce

---

[45]There are two possible etymologies of the term for bread, leading either to an understanding of bread as "bread for the following day"—that is, actual food, but expressed by a concept rich in eschatological connotations—or "necessary bread," bread that is necessary for the sustenance of either our physical or spiritual lives. See the discussion in Bovon, *Luke 2*, 90.

[46]Bovon, *Luke 2*, 89. Justin sees it as food of the Eucharist (*First Apology* 65-67); Clement (*Paed.*, 1.6.47.2) and Origen (*Or.* 22-30) see it as the bread of the Logos.

[47]Cyril of Alexandria, *Comm. Luke* 75, 312; Bovon, *Luke 2*, 95.

[48]Bovon reminds us of the connection between the spiritual and material in the provision of manna: it sustained their lives and fed their spirits. *Luke 2*, 90.

[49]Walter Grundmann, *Das Evangelium nach Lukas* (Berlin: Evangelische Verlagsanstalt, 1961), 233. The aorist imperative is used, not the present imperative (which we might expect if continual acts of forgiveness were indicated).

[50]Bovon, *Luke 2*, 91.

[51]Grundmann, *Das Evangelium nach Lukas*, 203.

[52]Bovon, *Luke 2*, 92.

[53]Grundmann, *Das Evangelium nach Lukas*, 233; Talbert, *Reading Luke*, 130; Marshall, *Gospel of Luke*, 462.

[54]Grundmann, *Das Evangelium nach Lukas*, 233.

perseverance and faith.[55] Luke's own audience would have understood the realities of being willing to take up their crosses to follow Jesus. Like them, we should not expect to be excused from difficult experiences in life and we should request God's strength and sustenance to meet these challenges with courage and faith.

THE FRIEND AT MIDNIGHT (LUKE 11:5-13)

The parable about the friend at midnight (Lk 11:5-8) further illustrates the fact that God can be trusted to answer prayer. God is portrayed as infinitely gracious and trustworthy, who will grant far more than what is requested. Such an understanding of God should inspire our boldness. The friend comes at midnight, when the entire household is asleep for the night, likely on one mat in a single room.[56] In spite of the fact that answering the door will rouse the entire family, it is unthinkable that the owner of the house would fail to answer the request. The parable begins with a question that anticipates a negative answer: Can you imagine trying to borrow bread for a guest and being refused—even if you went in the middle of the night?[57] Of course not. No inconvenience is too great to warrant a refusal of hospitality.

First, the petitioner is a friend.[58] The language of friendship permeates this parable. Jesus uses the word *friend* four times. Luke's audience understood how shocking it would be if one who claimed to be a friend remained in bed when his friend was in need.[59] According to the ideals of friendship in the Greco-Roman world, a true friend would not be selfish with material possessions either.[60] Familiar with the expression "Friends

---

[55]Bovon, *Luke 2*, 93.

[56]Joachim Jeremias, *The Parables of Jesus* (New York: Charles Scribner's Sons, 1963), 158.

[57]Kenneth Ewing Bailey, *Poet and Peasant: A Literary Cultural Approach to the Parables in Luke* (Grand Rapids: Eerdmans, 1976), 119.

[58]If the friend is truly a friend, as he is, he would under any difficulties fulfill the request. Karl Heinrich Rengstorf, *Das Evangelium nach Lukas* (Göttingen: Vandenhoeck & Ruprecht, 1965), 147.

[59]For Seneca, only the rudest of people would remain in bed, ignoring the requests of one who awakened them. Seneca asks, "How many patrons are there who drive away their clients by staying in bed when they call, or ignoring their presence, or being rude" (Seneca, *Brev. Vit.* 14.4, trans. Jo-Ann Shelton, *As the Romans Did: A Sourcebook in Roman Social History*, 2nd ed. [Oxford: Oxford University Press, 1998], 14-15) in Mikeal C. Parsons, *Luke*. Paideia (Grand Rapids: Baker, 2015), 186.

[60]Green, *Gospel of Luke*, 448.

have all things in common," from the time of Aristotle, Luke's authorial audience would have understood the obligation to grant practical hospitality when a friend was in need.[61]

This parable illustrates that we will receive abundantly from our gracious God. In the story, the one who comes at midnight receives far more than he has requested from his friend. According to the codes of ancient Mediterranean hospitality, it would have been an insult for one to offer just the amount that was needed. One loaf would have been more than enough for one guest.[62] The abundance of food reflected the honor with which the host received the guest.[63] Bread was not an unreasonable request either. It was the simplest part of the meal, used as a fork to sop up food from a common dish.[64] Presumably, the one who comes at midnight also needs to borrow the dish that will be eaten with the bread. He has asked for the most basic ingredient, with the implication that he will go to another house for the main dish. At the end of the story the householder will "give him whatever he needs," implying a gift of the entire meal—far more than what was requested. We should get the point: when we offer ourselves up to God, asking God to use us for God's own kingdom purposes, we should expect that we will receive far more than we have even requested.

The homeowner in this story was simply doing his duty to provide hospitality.[65] He would have seen his friend asking not for himself but to honor a guest. The guest would be seen as the guest of the community, not just the individual,[66] and the entire community would be responsible for providing him hospitality. If the homeowner refused his friend, he would be shirking his duties to provide hospitality to the guest of the community.[67] Because he will not risk being shamed for such a lack of hospitality, the friend is assured of a positive response.[68]

---

[61] Aristotle, *Eth. nic.* 9.8.2.

[62] Bailey, *Poet and Peasant*, 122.

[63] Bailey, *Poet and Peasant*, 122-33; Charles M. Fuhrman, "A Redactional Study of Prayer in the Gospel of Luke" (PhD diss., Southern Baptist Theological Seminary, 1981), 239.

[64] Bailey, *Poet and Peasant*, 123.

[65] Grundmann believes that since hospitality was a holy obligation ("heilige Pflichtist"), it would have been unthinkable for such a request to be refused. *Das Evangelium nach Lukas*, 234.

[66] Bailey, *Poet and Peasant*, 122.

[67] Bailey, *Poet and Peasant*, 123.

[68] Bailey, *Poet and Peasant*, 132.

The argument of the parable is "How much more?" If a person, even at great inconvenience to himself and his family, will respond to his friend with great generosity, how much more so will God respond with abundance to those who come with requests for the kingdom?[69] The point of the story is not the unreasonable nature of the request but how unthinkable it would be for the request to be denied.[70] Therefore, God can be trusted to give the Holy Spirit to those who ask.

Luke 11:9-10 adds assurance that God can be trusted to answer prayer: God will answer the one who knocks, just as the homeowner got up at midnight to supply the needs of his friend. The next two verses repeat the "how much more" argument: No one could imagine a person who would deliberately deceive his child and give her a gift that looked like food but could harm her. If people care for their friends and families, how much more will God care for God's people? God's graciousness is evident also in granting the best gift possible: the gift of the Spirit.[71] This analogy echoes the promise of the Hebrew Bible: those who seek God will not be disappointed (Deut 4:29; Is 55:6; 65:1; Jer 29:13).[72]

Here, Jesus teaches that the Spirit will be given in answer to prayer. For Luke, seeking the kingdom and seeking the Holy Spirit may both be ways of seeking the ultimate good.[73] The Spirit indicates the presence of the kingdom.[74] It is the "already" of the kingdom, a foretaste of the eschatological kingdom.[75] Jesus modeled prayer for the Holy Spirit at his baptism, where the Spirit descends as a result of Jesus' prayer. Jesus then taught that the Holy Spirit would be given to those who ask (Lk 11:13). Now the disciples are instructed to pray persistently with the promise that they will be given the Holy Spirit. We should not underestimate the power of this prayer. The Spirit is the driving force behind Jesus' mission and ministry

---

[69]"Only if we understand v. 7, not as describing a refusal of the request, but rather the utter impossibility of such a refusal, that the parable truly depicts the custom of oriental hospitality, and its real point becomes clear." Jeremias, *Parables of Jesus*, 158.

[70]Jeremias, *Parables of Jesus*, 159.

[71]Green, *Gospel of Luke*, 450.

[72]Marshall, *Gospel of Luke*, 467.

[73]James C. Dunn, "Spirit and Kingdom," *Expository Times* 82 (1970): 38.

[74]Talbert, *Reading Luke*, 131.

[75]Dunn, "Spirit and Kingdom," 38.

in Luke and the ministries of the apostles in Acts. The same Spirit is available to us through prayer and is the effective means of transforming and empowering us for God's kingdom work. We should fully anticipate that God will transform our lives for God's own kingdom purposes if we sincerely and insistently ask for it.

THE WIDOW AND THE UNJUST JUDGE (LUKE 18:1-8)

Not guilty. On July 6, 2016, in a routine traffic stop, a police officer shot Philando Castile seven times in front of his girlfriend and her four-year-old daughter while Castile, who had informed the officer that he had a firearm, was retrieving his ID as he had been instructed to do. Eleven months later, the officer was acquitted of all charges.[76] We cry out for justice, but nothing ever seems to change.

Luke's audience felt this same kind of hopelessness. He tells Jesus' next parable because they need to "pray always and not to lose heart" (Lk 18:1). In a parable that provides commentary on the request "your kingdom come" (Lk 11:2),[77] Jesus illustrates his point that ceaseless prayer is essential in times of trial. The disciples are likely facing discouragement as they face the reality of a kingdom that is promised but not yet fully realized.[78] Jesus has just told them that the kingdom is not yet fully present, in spite of the presence of the Holy Spirit (Lk 17:20-37).

This parable includes two connected themes: the faithfulness of God and the persistence of the widow, who is faithful even in a context of injustice.[79] The widow models ideal prayer, evoking images of Anna, who never left the temple but prayed "night and day" (Lk 2:37), and echoing the Hebrew tradition that singles out widows for God's benefaction. Like her, Jesus' disciples are to pray continually, even in the face of injustice.[80] The widow is an example of tremendous boldness: with no male to support her

---

[76]Mitch Smith, "Minnesota Officer Acquitted in Killing of Philando Castile," *New York Times*, June 16, 2017, www.nytimes.com/2017/06/16/us/police-shooting-trial-philando-castile.html.

[77]Hans Conzelmann, *The Theology of St. Luke*, trans. Geoffrey Buswel (New York: Harper & Row, 1960), 123.

[78]Talbert, *Reading Luke*, 166. The *inclusio* of Lk 18:1 and Lk 18:7-8 also gives the text an eschatological flavor. Green, *Gospel of Luke*, 637.

[79]Green, *Gospel of Luke*, 637.

[80]Green, *Gospel of Luke*, 638.

and no other resources, she still is not helpless and receives justice because of her persistence.[81]

The analogy between the judge and God should not be pushed too far. The unjust judge has "no fear of God and no respect for anyone" (Lk 18:2), a stock description of a corrupt leader and a general indicator of evil.[82] The reader has already learned that God is a gracious benefactor (Lk 11:5-8). The comparison is one of difference: if an evil judge will hear the requests of a persistent widow, how much more will a generous God hear the requests of God's children?

This parable highlights the importance of bold persistence in prayer. In the news recently, an 82-year-old woman, Willie Murphy, beat up an intruder using a table and a bottle of shampoo.[83] Just as surprisingly, our present text suggests that the powerful judge is afraid that a seemingly helpless widow will "give me a black eye" (Lk 18:5). The language is borrowed from boxing, although it is difficult to imagine a judge's fear of a widow's physical violence.[84] It may be an exaggerated image to emphasize the persistence of the widow's appeals, which threaten him far more than the possibility of abuse.[85] The term, which means "to strike under," is also sometimes used in a figurative sense, meaning "to blacken a reputation" or "wear out completely."[86] The judge might not care about anyone else but certainly cares about his own honor. A judge in the ancient Mediterranean world was obligated to give priority to a widow's case.[87] The widow's repeated coming could cause the judge to lose face in the community.[88] If

---

[81]Green, *Gospel of Luke*, 640.

[82]Green, *Gospel of Luke*, 639; Fitzmyer, *Gospel According to Luke*, 1178. Josephus describes King Jehoiakim in a similar fashion. *Ant.* 10.5.2.

[83]Elizabeth Wolfe and Douglas S. Wood, "This Powerlifting 82-Year-Old Made an Intruder Regret Breaking into Her Home," CNN, November 26, 2019, www.cnn.com/2019/11/24/us/82-year-old -bodybuilder-grandma-intruder-trnd/index.html.

[84]Although such an incredulous situation may highlight the extreme persistence of the widow. Green, *Gospel of Luke*, 641.

[85]Erich Klostermann, *Das Lukasevangelium* (Tübingen: J. C. B. Mohr, Paul Siebeck, 1929), 178; Grundmann, *Das Evangelium nach Lukas*, 347.

[86]Fitzmyer, *Gospel According to Luke*, 1179.

[87]Marshall, *Gospel of Luke*, 672.

[88]Fuhrman, "A Redactional Study," 257. We know that the judge has no fear of God and no respect for anyone (Lk 18:4), yet the usage of this kind of expression may indicate the general wickedness of the judge rather than function as an analogy to be pushed to its extreme.

even a judge will grant justice to preserve his professional reputation, how much more will God respond to the requests of God's children in a way that brings honor to God's holy name?[89]

So what do we do when evil seems to reign unabated? The characterization of the widow as persistent in prayer, even in the face of injustice, provides a model for the church awaiting the fullness of the kingdom. Jesus here teaches the lesson that he exemplifies elsewhere (Lk 22:39-46): persistent prayer enables one to endure the hardship and injustice that will be a part of this world until the fullness of the kingdom arrives. We won't be able to sustain our efforts to bring about God's kingdom in our own strength alone. We will sigh in resignation and find some source of distraction to help us to forget that the world is not as it is supposed to be. But we are called to action and to pray for the kind of spiritual courage and tenacity that will enable us to get up a thousand times after we are shoved down, insisting on justice over injustice, compassion over hatred, equality over bigotry, good over evil.

THE PHARISEE AND THE TAX COLLECTOR (LUKE 18:9-14)

Attitudes matter in prayer. Jesus tells this parable "to some who trusted in themselves that they were righteous and regarded others with contempt" (Lk 18:9). Outwardly impressive, this Pharisee also prays according to correct Jewish liturgy (Ps 17:3-5).[90] However, this parable provides a correction for some who felt that any kind of prayer was acceptable before God. The way in which one prays reveals one's relationship with God:[91] for the Pharisee, prayer is opportunity for condescension and reveals that the source of his trust and confidence is himself (cf. 2 Cor 1:9).[92]

The tax collector's prayer reveals his attitudes as well. The tax collector throws himself on God's mercy, realizing his impossible condition: he

---

[89]Bovon sees it as a potential undermining of the judge's honor and grants the widow's wish in order to "spare himself a personal humiliation" or threaten his status ("What the widow could do to him would probably damage his professional reputation"). *Luke 2*, 534.

[90]Talbert, *Reading Luke*, 170.

[91]Luke Timothy Johnson, *The Gospel of Luke*, Sacra Pagina 3 (Collegeville, MN: Liturgical Press, 1991), 274.

[92]Jeremias, *Parables of Jesus*, 140.

would have to pay back all those whom he had cheated. If he turns his back on his lifestyle, he faces possible destitution.[93] He provides an unexpected example of one who might have faith when the kingdom is fully realized (Lk 18:8). He receives righteousness as a gift from God, ironically the same status the Pharisee strove to obtain.[94]

JESUS' PRAYER IN GETHSEMANE (LUKE 22:39-46)

In the Gethsemane narrative, Jesus' own struggle in prayer is a teaching tool.[95] The structure of this section strengthens Jesus' admonition to pray:[96] the need for prayer in this situation is repeated six times, with Jesus' prayer framed by the *inclusio* "pray that you may not come into the time of trial" (Lk 22:40, 46).[97] Jesus' prayers for the will of God in Gethsemane mimic the example that he previously set for the disciples in Luke 11:2-4.[98] Jesus models faithfulness to the divine will, even when that obedience is contrary to his own being.[99] Jesus' obedience to the divine will has roots in Isaiah's passages about the suffering servant, who is obedient to God even in the midst of tremendous suffering and humiliation.[100] Jesus' submission is even reflected in his posture.[101] He kneels, while the usual posture for prayer in the ancient world was standing while looking up to heaven.

Luke focuses on Jesus' obedience rather than his emotions, removing Mark's "I am deeply grieved, even to death" (Mk 14:34) and emphasizing Jesus' stoic resolve to do the will of God.[102] Rather than falling to the

---

[93]If he gave up his lifestyle, he would have no livelihood and would have to make restitution plus one-fifth. Talbert, *Reading Luke*, 170.

[94]Fitzmyer, *Gospel According to Luke*, 1184.

[95]Klostermann, *Das Lukasevangelium*, 215.

[96]Grundmann, *Das Evangelium nach Lukas*, 411.

[97]A chiastic structure spans the entire text: Lk 22:40b and Lk 22:46 contain Jesus' instruction; Lk 22:41 and Lk 22:45 have Jesus' movement; Lk 22:42 and Lk 22:44 have Jesus' prayer and situation, respectively, with the central Lk 22:43 containing the heavenly response. François Bovon, *Luke 3: A Commentary on the Gospel of Luke 19:28–24:53*, Hermeneia (Minneapolis: Fortress, 2012), 194.

[98]Rengstorf, *Das Evangelium nach Lukas*, 250.

[99]Stephen F. Plymale, *The Prayer Texts of Luke-Acts*, (New York: Peter Lang, 1991), 61.

[100]Green, *Gospel of Luke*, 778.

[101]Green, *Gospel of Luke*, 779.

[102]Jerome Neyrey, *The Passion According to Luke* (New York: Paulist, 1985), 49-54.

ground in grief, as in Mark, the Lukan Jesus kneels in prayer.[103] In Luke, the attention is on Jesus, not the disciples. Jesus appears focused on his mission and does not repeatedly go to disciples in order to arouse them, as he does in Mark (Mk 14:37, 40).[104] Luke paints a picture of a single-minded Jesus, totally fixed on the will of God, calmly kneeling for prayer and rising afterward to continue his mission.[105]

Luke highlights Jesus' struggle in prayer as the turning point of the entire passion narrative, since it is here that Jesus obtains the strength to embrace his mission and God's will.[106] After an angel appears to strengthen him,[107] Jesus is described as praying more earnestly "in his anguish" (Lk 22:44).[108] The *inclusio* framing Jesus' prayer (Lk 22:40; 22:46) indicates that the content of Jesus' prayer was that he not enter into the temptation to follow his own will instead of God's will.[109] By highlighting the victorious struggle in prayer, Luke sets up Jesus as an example for the kind of prayer that gives one the courage and fortitude to resolutely insist on God's will, even in the face of persecution and death.

In the previous chapter, Jesus warned the disciples to be "on guard . . . praying that you may have the strength to escape all these things that will take place, and to stand before the Son of Man" (Lk 21:34-36). The disciples illustrate what happens when Jesus' words or example are not heeded. Unable to pray for strength, the disciples cannot recognize God's

---

[103]Neyrey, *Passion According to Luke*, 53.

[104]Neyrey, *Passion According to Luke*, 54.

[105]Neyrey, *Passion According to Luke*, 54.

[106]Green, *Gospel of Luke*, 777.

[107]Lk 22:43-44 does not appear in several ancient manuscripts including the Bodmer papyrus, Alexandrinus, and Vanticanus. The verses appear in Codex Sinaiticus, Codex Bezae, and 0171, an uncial from about 300. Modern scholarship is divided on the issue. The verses are well supported by Luke's tendency to anticipate a divine response to prayer, but this, of course, could be used in support of either argument.

[108]Neyrey notes that the word for "anguish" here can be interpreted in two ways: debilitating fear or victorious combat. *Passion According to Luke*, 58. Grundmann sees a more positive connotation of "fear," however. He sees the agony not as a fear of suffering and death so much as it is a fear surrounding the victory of his life. He knows that the fate of the world hangs on his action. *Das Evangelium nach Lukas*, 412. Rengstorf agrees that Jesus' struggle in prayer has less to do with the peace of his soul than whether the victory will take place. *Das Evangelium nach Lukas*, 251.

[109]Marion Soards, *The Passion According to Luke*, Journal for the Study of the New Testament Supplements Series 14 (Sheffield: JSOT Press, 1987), 97.

will and are not prepared to accept it.[110] Jesus finally goes back to them, rebuking them.[111] The disciples' sleep is directly connected to their "exhaustion of moral strength."[112] The persistent widow of Luke 18:1-8 shows us how to pray in the face of evil. Failure to pray during temptation allows overwhelming forces of grief to overtake us, blinds us to the will of God, and contributes to our ultimate failure to follow God when our discipleship is challenged.[113] Luke uses the contrast between Jesus and the disciples as a teaching tool for us: the way to remain faithful to God in the midst of trials is through prayer.[114]

THE CORRELATION BETWEEN JESUS' PRACTICE AND TEACHINGS ABOUT PRAYER

Jesus' instructions on prayer are rooted in his own practice, a model and inspiration for us. The portraits of Jesus at prayer before and during the key moments in his life affirm his teachings about the power of prayer and the abundant benefaction of God. Jesus' prayer at his baptism invokes the presence of the Spirit, resulting in a divine ratification and empowering of his ministry (Lk 4:14) and affirming his teaching that God will give us the Spirit in abundance if we request it (Lk 11:5-8, 13). Jesus' prayer for God's will prior to his choice of the disciples (Lk 6:12) and its resulting display of power (Lk 6:19) support his teachings on prayer for God's reign (Lk 11:2). Jesus' prayer prior to the transfiguration invokes the presence of God, as well as Moses and Elijah, who converse with him about his mission (Lk 9:30-35), affirming his teachings about the efficacy of prayer (Lk 11:9-13). Jesus' prayer in Gethsemane, which invokes the presence of an angel sent to strengthen his resolve (Lk 22:43), points to the power of prayer for spiritual strength.

SUMMARY

Prayer precedes revelation, invites the activity of God, and is the driving force behind Jesus' mission in Luke's Gospel. Luke presents Jesus as a

---

[110]Tannehill, *Gospel According to Luke*, 271.
[111]Green, *Gospel of Luke*, 781.
[112]Tannehill, *Gospel According to Luke*, 271.
[113]The disciples' sleep is a symbol of sadness. Grundmann, *Das Evangelium nach Lukas*, 412.
[114]Green, *Gospel of Luke*, 778.

model of prayer, who teaches out of his own lifestyle of prayer. The message to the church is obvious: if prayer fuels the entire work of God in Luke's Gospel, how can we fail to imitate Jesus' example of prayer?

For Luke, the focus of prayer is on God's kingdom. Jesus' disciples are to pray for God's rule and reign, a prayer that includes them in God's kingdom purposes as well. Prayer is less about presenting a list of personal wishes to God and more about coming to understand what God is doing and asking for the strength and courage to participate in that work. Luke does, however, present a God who intimately knows and cares for us, inviting us to a lifestyle of practical dependency on God for our daily needs.

Luke focuses not only on the outward act of prayer but on the attitudes and motivations involved in prayer as well. The story about the friend at midnight bolsters confidence in prayer that is rooted in the character of our gracious and generous God. We should boldly and persistently bring our requests before God, expecting God to act in ways that are in keeping with God's holy nature (Lk 11:5-13).

Finally, Luke shows us the power of prayer. Prayer has the ability to transform us into people who desire and participate in the work of God's kingdom. The Gethsemane passage points to Jesus as a model of one successfully praying for spiritual strength (Lk 22:39-46). Prayer empowers Jesus for ministry and gives him the courage and fortitude to endure his passion. Luke's readership should understand that prayer is critical to the success of their own faithful witness to Christ as well.

Luke's intended readers would have understood the necessity and power of prayer from their cultural world as well. Luke's literary culture is full of examples of ideal kings and philosophers who were strengthened and sustained by prayer. Such connection with the gods allowed them to internalize the divine law and effectively lead their people to virtue by setting before them a powerful model to copy. Familiar with these models, Luke's readership would have been primed to respond to Luke's narrative with an expectation to be spiritually formed as people of prayer through their imitation of Jesus. To these stories from Luke's cultural world we now turn.

8

PRAYER THROUGH FIRST-CENTURY EYES

LUKE'S TARGET AUDIENCE WOULD have heard the Lukan narrative against the background of their own cultural knowledge about prayer. They would have been familiar with the ideal for leaders who were effective rulers and teachers because of the divine guidance in their own lives. Reading stories about those ideal leaders alongside Luke's portrait of Jesus as a model and teacher of prayer can help us to understand a bit more of the reading experience of Luke's intended audience, inviting us also to become the kind of readers who can live out Luke's instructions on prayer.

PRAYER IN LUKE'S LITERARY WORLD

There was no separation of church and state for Luke's intended audience. In the ancient Mediterranean world, one of a king's chief duties was to intercede for the people. In ancient Athens the king had the responsibility for officiating at all public sacrifices.[1] Roman emperors, of course, held the office of *pontifex maximus*, the highest-ranking priest in Rome. Their cultic duties were exemplary actions for lesser officials and for ordinary people to imitate.[2] Ancient Mediterranean heroes are constantly portrayed

---

[1] Walter Burkert, *Greek Religion, Archaic and Classical*, trans. John Raffan (Oxford: Basil Blackwell, 1985), 95.

[2] Gordon notes that "sacrifices by emperors also became paradigms or exemplars of public sacrifice throughout the empire, ideal and grandiloquent versions of the proper means of communication with the other world." Richard Gordon, "The Veil of Power," in *Pagan Priests: Religion and Power in the Ancient World*, ed. Mary Beard and John North (London: Duckworth, 1990), 208.

as praying or sacrificing.[3] Luke's intended readers would have recognized prayer as a key virtue of an ideal leader. In Luke, Jesus also prays before the critical events in his life, and his life and ministry are sustained by continual communion with God (Lk 5:16; 6:12). Within the framework of Luke's literary world, this would have made Luke's target audience recognize Jesus as an ideal kind of leader.

While many leaders engaged in sacrificing and prayer as part of their official responsibilities, for some heroes in Luke's literary world, prayer extends beyond civic duty. After his father commends him on his ability to pray, Xenophon's Cyrus responds, "I feel toward the gods as if they were my friends."[4] Xenophon notes that Socrates "offered sacrifices constantly, and made no secret of it, now in his home, now at the altars of the state temples, and he made use of divination with as little secrecy. Indeed it had become notorious that Socrates claimed to be guided by 'the deity.'"[5]

Plutarch's hero Numa, who was "inclined to the practice of every virtue," "devoted his hours of privacy and leisure, not to enjoyments and money-making, but to the service of the gods, and the rational contemplation of their nature and power."[6] In fact, Numa spent so much time in contemplation that a legend arose about his company with the gods. Plutarch notes that Numa decided to live a secluded life in the country "and to wander there alone, passing his days in groves of the gods, sacred meadows, and solitudes."[7] Explaining the legend of Numa's marriage to a goddess, Numa concedes, "There is some reason in supposing that Deity . . . should be willing to consort with men of superlative goodness."[8] Even after assuming all the responsibilities of kingship, Numa "passed most of his time,

---

[3]A survey of Greco-Roman prayer texts quickly brings one to the conclusion that prayer was inextricably linked with sacrifice in the ancient world. Burkert, *Greek Religion*, 73. Prayer sometimes occurred without sacrifice but within the context of an ongoing exchange of gifts and blessings between supplicant and deity. Simon Pulleyn, *Prayer in Greek Religion* (Oxford: Clarendon, 1997), 15.

[4]Xenophon, *Cyr.* 1.6.4.

[5]Xenophon, *Mem.* 1.1.2.

[6]Plutarch, *Num.* 3.6.

[7]Plutarch, *Num.* 4.1.

[8]Plutarch, *Num.* 4.3.

performing sacred functions, or teaching the priests, or engaged in the quiet contemplation of divine things."[9]

We should note a couple of important points about these examples. First, Luke's intended readers would have known that the kind of leader who communed with the gods could be trusted. Because of their friendship with the gods, these leaders were not limited to their own abilities and understandings but were guided by the gods in their instruction or rulership. This was one of the defining characteristics of the idealized philosopher-king. Luke's audience would get the point about Jesus too: he can be trusted since he is guided by God. Second, we should note the emphasis on continual prayer: Socrates's sacrificing is "constant"; Numa passes "most of his time" in communion with the gods. Why do these ancient heroes matter for us? In our contemporary, fast-paced society, we aren't accustomed to waiting in prayer or spending our leisure communing with God. We get impatient waiting for a couple of minutes for our soup to cook in the microwave or for the stoplight to change. One of the vivid memories of my childhood is of my father praying as he worked in the yard—which was pretty often. Sometimes he would sing hymns as he turned over the earth. Other times he was so obviously lost in prayer and contemplation that my mother would have to call his name a few times before he even heard her. Prayer for him was never hurried, and scheduled prayer didn't fit his personality—but he loved getting lost in his thoughts for hours in the presence of God, and our yard was his sanctuary.

We find a long list of people who pray continually in the Hebrew Bible and Jewish traditions, as we might expect. In Deuteronomy, Moses prays before the Lord forty days and forty nights that God would not destroy the Israelites (Deut 9:25). Hannah prays continually before God (1 Sam 1:12). Samuel goes as far as to say that it would be sinful for him to cease praying for the Israelites (1 Sam 12:23). Even under threat of death, Daniel continues his habit of regular prayer three times a day (Dan 6:10). Josephus's Moses also engages in continual prayer. On one occasion, when the Israelites "were in sore distress and again vented their wrath on Moses," instead of

---

[9]Plutarch, *Num.* 14.1.

allowing himself to become flustered by their demands, he, "shunning for a while the onset of the crowd, had recourse to prayer, beseeching God."[10] These examples are important to us because they help provide the context for understanding Jesus' invitation into prayer in Luke. If we simply read Luke through the lens of our own limited experiences, we might assume that prayer is something that we can check off of our "to do" lists in five minutes or less per day. While this is probably better than nothing, in Scripture, prayer is an extended communion between intimate partners, not a speech between strangers. We need to cultivate the lost art of spending our hours of leisure attentive to the presence of God.

We might notice another pattern as we look at Luke's portrait of Jesus against the backdrop of the literary culture of his day. Ideal heroes often pray before the significant events in their lives. Sometimes this is easy to understand: military leaders habitually offered prayers or sacrifices before a battle so that they might receive direction and favor from the gods.[11] Prayer does seem to be more mindful for some, however. Socrates declares that "we should always appeal to the gods when we set about speaking or reflecting."[12] He and his friends continually invoke the aid of the gods before beginning a philosophical dialogue.[13] When Plato's Socrates asks Timaeus to invoke the gods before the monumental task of discussing the nature of the world, Timaeus replies, "All men who possess even a small share of good sense call upon God always at the outset of every under-taking, be it small or great."[14] In Luke also, Jesus prays before the significant events in his life, his prayers inviting the work of God and driving forward God's mission. Jesus' prayer on these occasions is the extended, contem-plative, discerning-the-will-of-God type of prayer. Before choosing his disciples, for instance, he spends the entire night in prayer (Lk 6:12). Often those of us who are involved in ministry frequently open classes or meetings in prayer. If we aren't mindful, these prayers can often function

---

[10]Josephus, Ant. 3.34.7.

[11]Xenophon refers to this practice in Oec. 5.19: "And you observe, I suppose, that men engaged in war try to propitiate the gods before taking action."

[12]Plato, Epistle 8.352.e.

[13]Plato, Critias 108d. See also Plato, Leg. 10.887c, 10.893b.

[14]Plato, Tim. 27c.

as a sort of zipper to open and close meetings, much as the pledge to the flag signals the beginning of the school day for school children in America.

In Jewish literature, we again see this pattern of turning to God before the significant events of life. Josephus says it is "usual" for soldiers to "to place their hopes of victory in God and to make supplication to Him" before battle.[15] We also find examples of people committing their spirits to God before death, as Jesus does on the cross (Lk 23:46). Adam asks Eve to do this for him in the Apocalypse of Moses,[16] and at her own death, Eve prays, "God of all, receive my spirit."[17] Josephus's Moses prays similarly before his "departure."[18] These sorts of prayers don't just mark important transitions in life, they point to a life shaped and directed by God. Even prayers preceding death can be seen in this way—as a very appropriate communion within the context of a lifelong intimate relationship, marking the transition from this life to the next.

PRAYER FOR DISCERNMENT

Why does Jesus have to pray? After all, if he is God, doesn't he already *know* what God wills? In Luke, while the incarnated Jesus does seem to have insight into future events at times (Lk 22:18, 22, 32), these insights might also come through prayer, and Jesus himself must pray to discern the will of God. In Luke, Jesus prays for God's will before he chooses his disciples (Lk 6:12) and wrestles for the will of God in Gethsemane as he anticipates his passion (Lk 22:42).

Luke's intended audience would have been familiar with the expectation for ideal heroes to seek divine wisdom through prayer. Xenophon refers to leaders who before warfare "with sacrifices and omens seek to know what they ought to do and what they ought not to do."[19] Cyrus's father tells him, "Mere human wisdom does not know how to choose what is best. . . . But the gods, my son, the eternal gods, know all things . . . and if men consult them, they reveal . . . what they ought to do and what they

---

[15]Josephus, *Ant.* 12.300.
[16]Apoc. Mos. 31.4.
[17]Apoc. Mos. 42.8.
[18]Josephus, *Ant.* 4.316.
[19]Xenophon, *Oec.* 5.19.

ought not to do."[20] Cyrus listens to his father's words. He continually bases his actions on the omens that follow his prayers and sacrifices.[21] At the end of his life, Cyrus thanks the gods for showing him through signs and wonders "what I ought to do and what I ought not to do."[22]

For others, the request for divine will comes in the form of asking to be brought into accordance with divine wisdom in order to fulfill their calling to lead a virtuous life. Timaeus asks that God "will grant to us that medicine which of all medicines is the most perfect and most good, even knowledge,"[23] and asks that God might "bring into tune him that is out of tune."[24] Timaeus is asking to be made an ideal philosopher who understands and speaks with the mind of God. Plato similarly sees ideal prayer as a prayer for this kind of wisdom. He states, "What a man ought to pray and press for is not that everything should follow his own desire, while his desire in no way follows his own reason; but it is the winning of wisdom that everyone of us, States and individuals alike, ought to pray for and strive after."[25] We should note the orientation toward the gods and the ultimate good. Plato's hero, Socrates, similarly asks for divine wisdom and aid in fulfilling his role as a philosopher. Socrates teaches, "In so far as we are powerless of ourselves to foresee what is expedient for the future, the gods lend us their aid, revealing the issues by divination to inquirers, and teaching them how to obtain the best results."[26] Xenophon then says of Socrates, "I have described him as he was: so religious that he did nothing without counsel from the gods."[27] Socrates taught others to do the same. Xenophon says he "denounced for their foolishness" all who depended more on human wisdom than divine and that "he himself despised all human opinions in comparison with counsel given by the gods."[28] Note here also the unity of Socrates' life and teaching.

---

[20]Xenophon, *Cyr.* 1.6.46.
[21]Xenophon, *Cyr.* 2.4.18; 3.3.20, 21, 34.
[22]Xenophon, *Cyr.* 8.7.3.
[23]Plato, *Critias* 106b.
[24]Plato, *Critias* 106b.
[25]Plato, *Leg.* 3.687d-e.
[26]Xenophon, *Mem.* 4.3.12.
[27]Xenophon, *Mem.* 4.8.11.
[28]Xenophon, *Mem.* 1.3.5.

Why is all this important for us to know? We tend to be quite self-oriented in our prayer habits. While Jesus tells us to ask for the "daily bread" that we need, we sometimes approach prayer in the way that a child might write a wish list for Santa Claus. We forget that we are here to please God and do God's will, not the reverse. Luke, steeped in the literary tradition of his day, sees prayer fundamentally within the context of the kingdom of God: we pray for God's kingdom purposes to be realized, for the discernment to know God's will, and for the spiritual strength that we need to accomplish it. Luke's intended audience, familiar with ideals for prayer, likely would have had the cultural context to value the kind of prayer that prioritizes the divine agenda. Joining Luke's authorial audience can have the same effect for us.

Plutarch's ideal kings seek divine will to establish their respective political states as well. Lycurgus tells his people that he must consult the god at Delphi, then "he would do whatsoever the god thought best."[29] After being persuaded that accepting kingship will provide an opportunity for him to serve the gods and sway the people toward piety, Plutarch's Numa declares that "his authority must first be ratified by Heaven."[30] Then he prays aloud and waits to learn the will of the gods. Only after Numa receives favorable omens (birds appear) does he put on his royal robes.[31] After he assumes the throne, Numa continues to seek the divine will, in keeping with his nature and vocation. For Plutarch, Numa seems to have understood that his kingship included "the duty of expounding and interpreting the divine will."[32] Luke's authorial audience would have appreciated Luke's parallel themes. In Luke, of course, Jesus' ministry is ratified by God. The Holy Spirit alights on him (like a dove) before he begins his ministry (Lk 3:22). Jesus seeks divine aid before the key moments of his ministry (Lk 6:12; 9:18, 29) and Jesus regularly and ultimately submits his will to God (Lk 22:39-46).

Seeking divine will and wisdom through prayer is also a theme in the Hebrew Bible and later Jewish literature. In the story of Samson, Manoah

---

[29]Plutarch, *Lyc.* 29.2.
[30]Plutarch, *Num.* 6.2.
[31]Plutarch, *Num.* 6.3.
[32]Plutarch, *Num.* 9.4.

prays that God will send a divine messenger with instructions concerning the care of his child (Judg 13:8). Solomon prays for God's wisdom and righteousness that he might be able to judge the people with God's judgment (Ps 72:1; Wis 7:7; 9:1, 4). In a prayer for wisdom found in 4 Ezra, Ezra prays for the presence of God's Spirit: "If, then, I have found favour before thee, send into me the Holy Spirit, that I may write all that has happened in the world since the beginning."[33] Josephus, too, sees prayer as a means to ascertain the divine will. Before a battle, Moses "inquired of God whether He authorized him to fight."[34] And in Josephus's account of the conquest of the Promised Land, Joshua prays to discern the divine will after a defeat.[35] For Philo, prayers for divine wisdom are appropriate prayers for "the man of worth."[36] Luke's literary culture would have enabled Luke's readers to appreciate his dependency on prayer and insistence on divine will. We tend to be a bit too self-reliant in our contemporary Western culture. Reading Luke within Luke's literary culture can teach us to recognize the value of prayer and raise our expectations for its transformative effects.

Many of us have grown frustrated through our inability to discern God's will. We typically pray for guidance when we are faced with two alternatives but might still not know what to do, feeling that in the end we are left to exercise our own wisdom. We might wonder whether our inclinations are truly following God's promptings or if our imaginations are leading us astray. Sometimes we question whether those who claim to be "led" to a certain action that is very much in their own interests are truly hearing from God. We still have much to learn about prayer, both in terms of understanding a biblical theology of prayer and our practical experience of it. The discernment in question here prioritizes God's interests over our own and assumes an overall relationship of both speaking and extended periods of listening. I do think that God has the ability to break through

---

[33] 4 Ezra 14.22.
[34] Josephus, *Ant.* 4.88.
[35] Josephus notes, "And the response came from God that he should arise and purge the army of the pollution that had been wrought therein . . . they would for ever be assured of victory over their enemies." *Ant.* 5.42.
[36] Philo, *Sobr.* 68.

our deafness. I have had dreams in the past where God's direction was unmistakable. Sometimes the reason why we are not hearing anything specific, however, is because we have not cultivated the habit of listening.

Prayer for Spiritual Strength

Overcome with grief, the disciples in Gethsemane fall asleep instead of praying. Immediately afterward, their courage fails them and they abandon Jesus when he needs them the most. Luke contrasts them with Jesus, who through prayer gains the spiritual strength he needs to remain faithful to God and God's mission. His point is clear: if we want to have the courage to remain with Jesus when things get difficult, we need to be people of prayer. Such a thought would have not been alien to Luke's intended audience. Many ancient heroes pray for the personal strength that they need to fulfill their duties. Socrates believes in seeking divine aid in order to live up to his calling to be a true philosopher. Clearly acknowledging a divine hand in his gifts, he prays that his insight and beauty will grow: "Be kind and gracious to me; do not in anger take from me the art of love which thou didst give me, and deprive me not of sight, but grant unto me to be even more than now esteemed by the beautiful."[37] He describes the tasks of an ideal philosopher and states that that hypothetical person "is likely to be such as you and I might pray that we ourselves may become."[38] Socrates also asks that others be given divine aid in living up to their philosophical calling. Socrates asks that Phaedrus "may no longer hesitate, as he does now, between two ways, but may direct his life with all singleness of purpose toward love and philosophical discourses."[39] We might be reminded of Jesus' prayer for Peter that his faith might not fail (Lk 22:32).

We also see Plutarch's heroes consulting the gods to aid them in the task of leading their citizens to virtue. Plutarch's ideal king Lycurgus, after determining to revolutionize a city, goes to Delphi to sacrifice and consult the oracle. The priestess mediates his request, calling him "beloved of the gods, and rather god than man," and declaring that the gods would help

---

[37]Plato, *Phaedr.* 257a.
[38]Plato, *Phaedr.* 278b.
[39]Plato, *Phaedr.* 257b.

him to create good laws and the best constitution in the world.[40] Similarly, Numa "called in the gods to aid and assist him" in the task of moving his citizens toward peace and piety,[41] a task that he sees as his service to the gods.[42] Luke's intended audience would understand that effective strength for such lofty tasks must come from a divine source.

Jewish heroes also pray for strength. In the book of Jubilees, Abraham prays, "Deliver me from the hands of evil spirits who have dominion over the thoughts of men's hearts, and let them not lead me astray from Thee, my God."[43] Sirach prays, "Who will set a guard over my mouth, and an effective seal upon my lips, so that I may not fall because of them, and my tongue may not destroy me?" (Sir 22:27). He also prays, "Let neither gluttony nor lust overcome me, and do not give me over to shameless passion" (Sir 23:6). Likewise, in the Psalms of Solomon, Solomon prays, "Rule me, O God, (keeping me back) from wicked sin. . . . Protect my tongue and lips with words of truth; anger and unreasoning wrath put far from me."[44]

We know that we should pray for spiritual strength. The difficulty comes when we wait until those difficult times are upon us before praying and then are surprised when we flounder. Like the disciples in Gethsemane, because of the superficiality of our prayer lives, we aren't prepared for unexpected challenges to our faith. The kind of habitual prayer that regularly seeks and submits to God's will in an overall context of intimacy and trust provides the necessary foundation for the radical prayers of trust that God invites in Luke 11:2, 13, and that Jesus models in Luke 22:39-46.

ATTITUDES AND MOTIVATIONS FOR PRAYER

Many people in the ancient world assumed that the piety of the supplicant had a direct impact on the effectiveness of prayer. In Xenophon, Cyrus's father agrees that "only those who had made themselves what they ought

---

[40]Plutarch, *Lyc.* 5.3.
[41]Plutarch, *Num.* 7.3.
[42]Plutarch, *Num.* 6.2.
[43]Jub. 12.20.
[44]Pss. Sol. 16.7, 10.

to be had a right to ask for corresponding blessings from the gods."[45] Similarly, the guest in Aristeas notes that "the prayers of the deserving are fulfilled."[46]

While the acceptance of a tax collector over a Pharisee might have evoked surprise for Luke's readers, they may also have expected the Pharisee's piety to run a little deeper. Plato believed that only the prayers of the pious are received, but his view of pious prayer included proper motivations and attitudes.[47] Thus, in *Laws*, Plato declares that prayer may be "a perilous practice for him who is devoid of reason."[48] Plato's Socrates mocked the kind of piety that regarded prayer and sacrifice as an act of commerce or exchange of favors between the gods and men. For example, Plato's Glaucon suggests to Socrates that an unjust man might perform magnificent sacrifices, but Socrates disagrees that these sacrifices force the gods to respond with favor.[49]

For Socrates, the most acceptable prayers are not those offered as a part of a business transaction with the gods but offered in true piety with the greatest regard for the accompanying attitudes and motivations.[50] On one occasion, Socrates spends an entire day thinking before offering a prayer.[51] For him, the goal of prayer is to become like God.[52] Plato highlights the depth of Socrates's piety by showing the content of and motives behind his prayers. Plato writes prayers for many characters, but those he ascribes to Socrates are far superior in literary value and with regard to the ideas expressed in the prayers.[53] The prayers of Socrates "show us a man whose wishes conform to wisdom and who is becoming like the divine, the goals of prayer which Plato stressed."[54] Socrates asks for inner beauty, prays for the harmony of his inner and outer lives, and asks to become a

---

[45]Xenophon, *Cyr.* 1.6.5.
[46]Let. Aris. 192.
[47]B. Darrell Jackson, "The Prayers of Socrates," *Phronesis* 16, no. 1, 1971.
[48]Plato, *Leg.* 3.688b.
[49]Plato, *Resp.* 364c.
[50]For other examples, see Jackson, "Prayers of Socrates."
[51]Plato, *Symp.* 220d.
[52]Plato, *Symp.* 220d.
[53]Jackson, "Prayers of Socrates," 23.
[54]Jackson, "Prayers of Socrates," 36-37.

philosopher.[55] His prayers reflect his deepest motivations and desires and concern the core of who he is and hopes to become.

In contrast to those who thought that lavish sacrifices might coerce the gods to respond favorably to prayer, according to Xenophon, Socrates offered humble sacrifices and taught that "the gods could not well delight more in great offerings than in small—for in that case must the gifts of the wicked often have found more favour in their sight than the gifts of the upright."[56] When Socrates prayed he asked simply for good gifts, feeling that "the gods know best what things are good."[57] His sacrifices were humble, "according to his means," but he said that "the greater the piety of the giver, the greater (he thought) was the delight of the gods in the gift."[58]

Jewish authors also highlight a distinction between outward piety and the attitude of the heart. In Jeremiah, after witnessing the unrepentant attitude of the Israelites, God tells Jeremiah not to pray for the people because God will not hear their prayers or accept their sacrifices (Jer 14:11-12). Just as God does not always accept the pious actions of the insincere, sometimes, for the sincere, pious actions are unnecessary. When the Israelites fail to purify themselves before eating the Passover, Hezekiah prays for God to be merciful to every heart that sincerely seeks God but is not ceremonially purified (2 Chron 30:19). In this case as in Luke, the graciousness of God overrides the need for ritual purity. In the Prayer of Azariah, God accepts the prayers of the repentant, regardless of the sins committed. Azariah notes that a "contrite heart and a humble spirit" are necessary for God to accept the people's prayers.[59] We might be reminded here of the attitude of the tax collector. In the Prayer of Manasseh, Manasseh exemplifies this attitude when he prays, "I am not worthy to behold and see the height of heaven by reason of the multitude of mine iniquities. . . . I humbly beseech thee, forgive me, O Lord, forgive me."[60]

---

[55]Jackson, "Prayers of Socrates," 27. Plato, *Phaedr.* 279b-c.
[56]Plato, *Resp.* 1.3.3.
[57]Xenophon, *Mem.* 1.3.2.
[58]Xenophon, *Mem.* 1.3.3.
[59]Pr. Azar. 16.
[60]Pr. Man. 9, 13.

In Luke, God rejects duplicitous prayers and accepts the humble (Lk 18:9-14). God accepts the faithful, not those who have the most honorable religious positions (Lk 18:14) or those who give the largest gifts (Lk 21:1-4). There is no sacrifice and no magic formula that can coerce God to answer prayer. We cannot name what we want from God and claim it. Instead, we must throw ourselves on God's mercy (Lk 18:13), believing that God will answer us in keeping with God's holy nature and goodness (Lk 11:13).

THE GRACIOUSNESS OF GOD

Luke paints a portrait of a gracious God who can be trusted to provide for us. Ancient Mediterranean heroes also recognize the gracious character of the gods. In a prayer thanking the deity for a lifetime of blessings, Xenophon's Cyrus refers to the gods' "fostering care."[61] Cyrus "prayed the gods above all things graciously to lead them."[62] At the outset of a journey, Cyrus prays for the gods to "conduct them on with grace and favour."[63] Plato also affirms the nature of the gods as good.[64] Socrates points to the gods' generosity, when in a conversation with Euthydemus, he asks if it has ever "occurred to you to reflect on the care the gods have taken to furnish man with what he needs?"[65] He lists various blessings of life, to which Euthydemus responds, "Truly these things too show loving-kindness."[66] In a discussion with an agnostic, Socrates argues that the gods do indeed interact with people with grace and favor. He illustrates the graciousness of divine gifts by pointing to the wonder of the human body and soul. He then asks, "Do you, then, having received the two most precious gifts, yet think that the gods take no care of you? What are they to do, to make you believe that they are heedful of you?"[67] Socrates implores him, "Try the gods by serving them. . . . Then you will know that such is the greatness and such the nature of the deity that he sees all things and

---

[61]Xenophon, *Cyr.* 8.7.3.
[62]Xenophon, *Cyr.* 4.2.12.
[63]Xenophon, *Cyr.* 2.1.1.
[64]Plato, *Resp.* 379b.
[65]Xenophon, *Mem.* 4.3.3.
[66]Xenophon, *Mem.* 4.3.5.
[67]Xenophon, *Mem.* 1.4.14.

hears all things alike, and is present in all places and heedful of all things."[68]
Socrates' words might also make us wonder—what does God need to do
to convince us of God's care for us? When I look back over my life and
consider the many ways in which God has protected me and provided for
me, why do I still allow the circumstances around me to fill me with fear
and anxiety? Jesus, too, invites us into a deep place of trust in God's
goodness (Lk 12:22-34).

Trust in God's goodness and mercy is rooted in Jewish literature. In
2 Kings, we see that God can be trusted since God acts in accordance with
God's holy name. Hezekiah prays for deliverance that all might know that
God is the only God (2 Kings 19:14-19). Such a prayer both affirms the
power of God and exhorts God to act in a manner in keeping with God's
nature. David, too, asks that God bless humanity in order to create a great
people and honor God's own name (1 Chron 17:18-27). Azariah asks that
God act in a manner that will bring God glory: "Deliver us also according
to thy marvelous works and give glory to thy name, O Lord."[69] Baruch
similarly asks God what "wilt thou do for thy great name?" when God's
enemies boast of their victory.[70] In 2 Maccabees, the priests who pray for
God to spare their temple from desecration pray, "O holy Lord, from
whom is all hallowing, keep free from defilement forevermore this house
so lately cleansed, and shut every impious mouth" (2 Macc 14:36). These
texts affirm that God will act in accordance with God's holy name. When
we ask that God's name be hallowed, we are asking that God continue to
act in keeping with God's good nature.

THE EFFICACY OF PRAYER

Does prayer work? Beyond just making us feel better or even improving
our perspective, does prayer actually change situations? Luke would say
yes. In Luke, after Jesus prays, the Spirit falls on him and a voice from
heaven affirms him (Lk 3:22), he is transfigured (Lk 9:29), and an angel
appears in Gethsemane (Lk 22:43).

---

[68]Xenophon, *Mem.* 1.4.18.
[69]Pr. Azar. 20-21.
[70]2 Bar 5:1.

Luke's target audience would have been conditioned to expect that their ideal leaders would receive answers to prayer. Receiving omens of the gods' favor in response to prayer is common among ideal heroes.[71] The cause-and-effect relationship between prayer and divine action can be seen in Virgil's *Aeneid*. In response to Aeneas's prayers, the omen of a magnificent serpent appears.[72] Later Aeneas prays for a sign and "scarce had he so said when under his very eyes twin doves, as it chanced, came flying from the sky and lit on the green grass. Then the great hero knew them for his mothers' birds, and prays with joy: O be my guides, if any way there be, and through the air steer a course into the grove."[73] Likewise, when the Trojan ships are burning, Aeneas cries to Jupiter for help. Then, "Scarce had he uttered this when with streaming showers a black tempest rages unrestrained. . . . The ships are filled to overflowing, the half-burnt timbers soaked, till all the heat is quenched."[74] Later, Aeneas again prays and "at this, the almighty Father thundered thrice aloft from a clear sky, and with his own hand shook forth to view from heaven a cloud ablaze with shafts of golden light."[75] After Aeneas and a crowd of people hear the king's blessings on Aeneas and witness thunder and lightning flashing from a cloudless sky, the crowd steps back, but Aeneas "knew the sound and the promise of his goddess mother. Then he cries: 'Ask not, my friend, ask not, I pray, what fortune the portents bode; 'tis I who am summoned of Heaven.'"[76]

The Hebrew Bible also includes numerous examples of divine responses to prayer. While Daniel is praying, Gabriel comes to him and brings him a vision and a revelation (Dan 9:21). Samuel calls on God and God sends a thunderstorm magnificent enough to cause the people to fear God and Samuel (1 Kings 12:18). When Solomon finishes praying at the consecration

---

[71]In Xenophon's *Cyr.* 1.6.2, Cyrus prays before his expedition, and as he is on his way he sees thunder and lightning as a sign of the gods' favor. Plutarch narrates the story of Camillus, who "was sacrificing and praying the goddess to accept of their zeal . . . when the image, they say, spoke in low tones and said she was ready and willing." Plutarch, *Cam.* 6.2.

[72]Virgil, *Aen.* 5.85.

[73]Virgil *Aen.* 6.190.

[74]Virgil, *Aen.* 5.695.

[75]Virgil, *Aen.* 7.140.

[76]Virgil, *Aen.* 8.530.

of the temple, fire comes down from heaven and devours the sacrifices (2 Chron 7:1). Elisha prays and beholds a vision of a mountain full of horses and chariots of fire around him (2 Kings 6:17). He also prays for the people to be blinded, and then for them to see, and it is done immediately (2 Kings 6:20).

Josephus also illustrates the power of prayers with a direct fulfillment. After Moses prays, the Red Sea parts and God supplies manna.[77] While the biblical narrative also records these miracles, Josephus tends to highlight the immediacy of the answer and the cause-and-effect nature of Moses' prayers. Moses prays, "Prove that thou carest for those who would benefit the Hebrews, by pursuing with vengeance Abiram and Datham."[78] While Moses is still speaking, an earthquake swallowed up Datham and his followers, "furnishing an exhibition of God's mighty power."[79] Similarly, when some Israelites failed to follow through on their promise to provide sacrificial victims, the priests "prayed to God to exact satisfaction on their behalf from their countrymen; and He did not delay their punishment, but sent a mighty and violent wind to destroy the crops of the entire country."[80] After Joshua prays for victory during the conquest, he and his armies defeat their enemies.[81] Josephus then notes, "There too he was given to know of God's co-operation, manifested by thunder-claps, the discharge of thunder-bolts and the descent of hail of more than ordinary magnitude. Aye and moreover it befell that the day was prolonged."[82]

You may be thinking, that's very well and good to sketch out these cause-and-effect answers to prayer in the *Aeneid* or Josephus, and maybe even Jesus could expect this sort of response from God, but *I* have experienced nothing but God's silence in response to *my* fervent prayers. We might remember that even Jesus prays for the cup of his passion to pass, and he also must relinquish his will to God. I don't know why God doesn't always answer our prayers—especially when they are to save those whom

---

[77]Josephus, *Ant.* 2.339.2; 3.25.5-6.
[78]Josephus, *Ant.* 4.47, on the brothers who caused a rebellion against Moses in Num 16:1.
[79]Josephus, *Ant.* 4.51-52.
[80]Josephus, *Ant.* 12.28.
[81]Josephus, *Ant.* 5.42.
[82]Josephus, *Ant.* 5.61.

God loves from tragedy, suffering, or death. Theologies that subordinate God's omnipotence or omniscience to God's love seem as inadequate as they are well-intended. There have been times in the wake of horrific tragedies when I have muttered the "not your best day" sort of prayer in response to my perception of God's inaction and had to repent of it afterward. In those times, I find comfort in looking to Job, to Habakkuk, and to the psalmists for company as I wrestle with God, waiting for peace, if not resolution.

I have also been the recipient of the miraculous provision of God in response to prayer. A couple of months into her pregnancy, my mother discovered that her uterus was full of fibroid tumors. Every doctor she went to told her that there was no choice: she had to terminate her pregnancy. There was no way a healthy child could survive. My parents' entire church prayed fervently for a healthy birth. One night, my father had a dream. In it, a Scottish doctor was telling him, "Congratulations, Mr. Wright. You are the father of a little girl. She is small, but she's healthy." At the time, my mother wasn't seeing a Scottish doctor. Eventually she was transferred to a specialist, who happened to be from Scotland. The day finally arrived when he placed me in my father's arms, congratulating him on his premature but healthy infant daughter.

THE CORRELATION OF LIFE AND TEACHING REGARDING PRAYER

In Luke's world people felt that the best way to bring about moral change was by imitating a person who exemplified the kind of behavior that they sought to have themselves. They might have looked to several ideal heroes in Luke's literary world who guided others to piety through their own example of prayer and sacrifice. Xenophon points out that Socrates "benefited his companions, alike by actions that revealed his own character and by his conversation."[83] He points out that with respect to Socrates' attitude toward religion, "his deeds and words were clearly in harmony" with the teachings given by the priestess at Delphi concerning his sacrificial duty.[84] Xenophon remarks, "And so Socrates acted himself and counseled others to act. To take

---

[83]Xenophon, *Mem.* 1.3.1-2.
[84]Xenophon, *Mem.* 1.3.1-2.

any other course he considered presumption and folly."[85] Xenophon adds, "None ever knew him to offend against piety and religion in deed or word."[86]

Plutarch's Numa is another example of a pious hero who guides others through his own example of piety. Numa, who loved to spend all of his time in silent contemplation of the gods,[87] wandering alone in the country in the presence of the gods,[88] who at first shunned the throne because of his love of peace and solitude,[89] teaches his citizens the same habits he cherishes. Plutarch notes that he also taught them to pay special honors to one Muse in particular, "the silent one," to whom he ascribed much of his teaching, instructing them to practice the same patterns of withdrawal for private worship for which he was known:

> For, just as it is said that the Pythagoreans do not allow men to worship and pray to their gods cursorily and by the way, but would have them go from their homes directly to this office, with their minds prepared for it, so Numa thought that his citizens ought neither to hear nor see any divine service while they were occupied with other matters and therefore unable to pay attention.[90]

Numa, who "himself is said to have been the first" of the pontifices, regulates the worship of the people[91] by being able to "soften" the warlike nature of the city through his own example of worship:

> Numa, judging it to be no slight or trivial undertaking to mollify and newly fashion for peace so presumptuous and stubborn a people, called in the gods to aid and assist him. It was for the most part by sacrifices, processions, and religious dances, which he himself appointed and conducted . . . that he won the people's favour and tamed their fierce and warlike tempers.[92]

Because of their tremendous respect for his own example of piety, Numa's citizens follow his teaching and worship practices.[93] Plutarch sees this as a mark of an ideal philosopher king:

---

[85]Xenophon, *Mem.* 1.3.1-2.
[86]Xenophon, *Mem.* 1.1.11.
[87]Plutarch, *Num.* 3.6.
[88]Plutarch, *Num.* 4.1.
[89]Plutarch, *Num.* 5.4.
[90]Plutarch, *Num.* 14.2.
[91]Plutarch, *Num.* 7.1.
[92]Plutarch, *Num.* 7.1.
[93]Plutarch, *Num.* 15.1.

Not only was the Roman people softened and charmed by the righteousness and mildness of their king, but also the cities round about . . . and all of them were filled with a longing desire to have good government, to be at peace, to till the earth, to rear their children in quiet, and to worship the gods. . . . Honour and justice flowed into all hearts from the wisdom of Numa, as from a fountain. . . . Either fear of the gods, who seemed to have him in their especial care, or reverence for his virtue, or a marvellous felicity . . . made him a manifest illustration and confirmation of the saying which Plato, many generations later, ventured to utter regarding government, namely, that human ills would only then cease and disappear when, by some divine felicity, the power of a king should be united in one person with the insight of a philosopher, thereby establishing virtue in control and mastery over vice.[94]

This is an important point: Plutarch is saying that philosophers since the time of Plato despaired of finding an ideal hero who would lead through personal example. This, again, was the ideal for moral change. The problem was finding this exemplary a leader. Plutarch paints a portrait of Numa as this kind of leader. The strong parallels to Jesus in Luke would likely lead Luke's authorial audience to the conclusion that in fact Jesus *was* the kind of ideal hero who had long been awaited and that moral change was possible for them also through Jesus' example.

Most of us do not know how to pray as we ought. Luke's portrait of Jesus' exemplary prayer life invites us into deeper communion with God and increases our expectation for God to act. Jesus points to God's goodness and consistency as motivation for bold prayer. By illustrating the power of the Holy Spirit in Jesus' life and showing us the way in which Jesus' prayers open the door for God's activity, Luke bids us to imagine what the transformative work of prayer might accomplish in our own lives.

SUMMARY

Luke's authorial audience would have had examples of literary heroes whose prayer lives invited divine guidance and yielded spiritual strength. They would have been familiar with the ideal for philosopher-kings whose

---

[94]Plutarch, *Num.* 20.6-7.

superior rule was due to the divine guidance that marked their lives. Readers aware of Luke's literary culture would have also expected a unity of life and teaching from these heroes. In Luke, Jesus' teachings on prayer flow directly from his lifestyle of prayer, a mark of an ideal teacher.

Luke's intended audience would have been familiar with ideal heroes who seek the will of God (or the gods) in prayer. They would have appreciated Jesus' single-minded focus on the kingdom (Lk 11:2), his dependency on God's choice of his disciples (Lk 6:12), and his willingness to submit his own will to his Father's in Gethsemane (Lk 22:42). They would not have expected an ideal hero to insist on his or her own agenda. This could be instructive for enlarging the horizons of contemporary Western audiences who sometimes fail to see prayer as coming to a realization of God's purposes and submitting their own desires to them.

Luke's authorial audience would have known that spiritual strength comes from prayer and expected to see this in stories of their ideal heroes. They would have been familiar with stories of dramatic divine responses to prayer. Perhaps because of this, they might have expected more from prayer than do contemporary Western audiences. Luke invites us to consider again the importance and power of prayer. He shows us through Jesus' powerful example that prayer is both effective and essential to our spiritual lives.

We often struggle to find time for prayer in our overscheduled lives. As we have seen, Luke's literary culture helps us to recognize its necessity and power. We see these same themes as we move to the church's reception of Luke's texts on prayer. While we sometimes treat prayer as a brief acknowledgement to God before we attend to our tasks, we see in the early church a different portrait of prayer; just as Socrates or Numa would linger for extended periods in the company of the gods, so also we see Luke's earliest interpreters inviting us into a lifestyle of continual communion with God. For the early church, learning how to pray was imitating Jesus' example. We now turn to them for their help in that task.

9

LEARNING PRAYER WITH THE CHURCH

WE AREN'T ALWAYS ADEPT at taking abstract theoretical principles and trying to figure out how to live them out on our own. In Luke's day, many people thought that the most ideal kind of training in virtue would come from someone who embodied those qualities himself or herself and who could teach through personal example. Luke's intended audience would have recognized Jesus as this kind of teacher. When the patristic writers looked at his life and teachings about prayer, they also focused on his *example*. In part, this emphasis seems to stem from theological motivations: Jesus was God; therefore he didn't really *need* to pray for himself. Nonetheless, their emphasis on the exemplary quality of Jesus' life of prayer is consistent with Luke's own emphasis on the power of Jesus' personal example of prayer. For both Luke and the early church, modeling our own prayer lives after Jesus' is the means to spiritual strength.

JESUS' BAPTISM PRAYER (LUKE 3:21-22)

Within Luke's wider portrait of Jesus' prayer life, we can see this text highlighting Jesus' exemplary prayer habits. Here Luke begins to form the connection between prayer and revelation, causing Luke's readers to come to expect a connection between Jesus' prayers and the activity of God. The emphasis is on Jesus' example: if we desire the Spirit's transformative work, we should hear an invitation to bold prayer as well. Many in the early church also focus on Jesus' example, but their path to that conclusion takes a few different turns. As might be expected, patristic commentators are quick to insist that Jesus did not need to be baptized for his sins since he was sinless. For Ambrose, Jesus was baptized, "wishing not to be cleansed, but to cleanse the waters."[1] He points out that "He Who would need no remedies" provides justification for all: "For One immersed, but raised all; One descended, that we all may ascend; One assumed the sins of all, so that the sins of all were cleansed through Him."[2]

Cyril of Alexandria focuses on Jesus' example of both prayer and baptism:

> In order, therefore, that we may learn both the power itself of holy baptism, and how much we gain by approaching so great a grace, He commences the work Himself; and, having been baptized, prays that you, my beloved, may learn that never-ceasing prayer is a thing most fitting for those who have once been counted worthy of holy baptism.[3]

Cyril then urges, "Having taken, therefore, Christ as our pattern, let us draw near to the grace of holy baptism, that so we may gain boldness to pray constantly."[4] Christ's example, according to Cyril, should inspire us to bold, continual prayer. It is for the church's formation, and we who receive it should understand that the miraculous reception of the Holy Spirit that Jesus received at his baptism can be ours as well if we imitate Jesus. While Luke certainly emphasizes Jesus' *own* commissioning and empowerment, reading this story within the fuller context of Luke and Acts yields a parallel to the story of the earliest church waiting in prayer on the Holy Spirit at Pentecost.

JESUS PRAYS BEFORE CHOOSING HIS DISCIPLES (LUKE 6:12-16)

Tertullian emphasizes the effectiveness of Jesus' prayer: Jesus "spends a night in prayer, and He is indeed heard by the Father." Tertullian reads this text in light of Psalm 22:2: "Moreover, concerning the voice of His prayer to the Father by night, the Psalm manifestly says, 'O my God, I will cry in the day-time, and Thou shalt hear; and in the night season, and it shall not be vain to me.'"[5]

---

[1]Ambrose, *Exp. Luc.*, 71.
[2]Ambrose, *Exp. Luc.*, 76.
[3]Cyril of Alexandria, *Comm. Luke* 11, 80-81.
[4]Cyril of Alexandria, *Comm. Luke* 11, 81.
[5]Tertullian, *Marc.* 4.13, in *ANF* 3:364.

Some of Luke's earliest interpreters struggle with the idea that Jesus would need to ask for God's will if he was God. For Ambrose, Jesus isn't trying to discern God's will at all. Ambrose says, "The Lord prays, not to entreat for Himself, but to intercede for me."[6] The reason why Jesus retreats from the disciples for solitary prayer is because his conversation with God is above their comprehension. Ambrose notes, "Everywhere He entreats alone, for human prayers do not grasp the counsels of God . . . nor can anyone share with Christ in the inward mysteries."[7] For Cyril of Alexandria, too, Jesus "conversed with His Father and God in heaven in a way ineffable and beyond our powers of understanding, and such as is known solely to Himself."[8] Cyril supposes that an "enemy of truth" might suggest that Jesus' prayer is proof that he is not one with the Father. He asks, "Let then those who pervert the right faith teach us first of all, of what they imagine the Son to be in need? And what did He seek to obtain as not as yet possessing it?"[9] The motivation for emphasizing Jesus' example seems to be at least in part to avoid the charge that Jesus *needed* to pray to discern God's will. Ironically, perhaps, the emphasis on Jesus' example is also Luke's own.

Many in the early church focus on the fact that Jesus prayed all night, providing an example for believers to do likewise. Cyprian urges his hearers, "Let us urgently pray and groan with continual petitions" because "the Lord also Himself, the teacher of our discipline, and the way of our example, frequently and watchfully prayed."[10] For Cyprian, "Nor was it only in word, but in deeds also, that the Lord taught us to pray, Himself praying frequently and beseeching, and thus showing us, by the testimony of His example, what it behoved us to do."[11] He asks, "But if He prayed who was without sin, how much more ought sinners to pray; and if He prayed continually, watching through the whole night in uninterrupted petitions, how much more ought we to watch nightly in constantly repeated prayer!"[12]

---

[6]Ambrose, *Exp. Luc.*, 162-63.
[7]Ambrose, *Exp. Luc.*, 163.
[8]Cyril of Alexandria, *Comm. Luke* 23, 125.
[9]Cyril of Alexandria, *Comm. Luke* 23, 123-24.
[10]Cyprian, *Epistle* 7.5, in ANF 5:286.
[11]Cyprian, *Dom. or.* 20, in *ANF* 5:455.
[12]Cyprian, *Dom. or.* 20, in *ANF* 5:455.

Ambrose similarly observes, "It says, 'He passed the whole night in prayer'. . . a form is prescribed which ye must imitate."[13] For Cyril of Alexandria, Jesus prays in order to set "before us His conduct as a type of goodness unto the end, that as I said we may be earnest in following His footsteps."[14] Cyril pleads with his reader to heed the "pattern and example provided for us by Christ's acts . . . for thou hast heard that Jesus did not merely pray, but that He also passed the night in this duty."[15] The contemporary emphasis on Jesus' example is a little different. While we are likely to point out that if *Jesus needed* to pray, we certainly do as well; the emphasis of the early church is that it was Jesus' primary intent to provide an *example* for his disciples through his prayer. Cyprian makes the difference clear: "But the Lord prayed and besought not for Himself—for why should He who was guiltless pray on His own behalf?—but for our sins, as He Himself declared, when He said to Peter, 'Behold, Satan hath desired that he might sift you as wheat. But I have prayed for thee, that thy faith fail not.' And subsequently He beseeches the Father for all, saying, 'Neither pray I for these alone, but for them also which shall believe on me through their word.'"[16] Notice also the way that Cyril interprets Luke 22:31 through the lens of John 17:20.

The patristic interpreters tend to read Scripture canonically, with all of Scripture as the context for interpretation. If one reads the victorious confidence of Jesus' high priestly prayer in John into this text, for instance, it might be more difficult to see Jesus' own need for prayer. In John, Jesus does seem to be praying primarily for his disciples' benefit. So, are Luke's patristic readers right? Whatever their motivation, they do seem to have captured Luke's overall emphasis on Jesus' example of prayer. For Luke, however, the strength of this example also consists in the fact that Jesus *needs* to pray and that he *receives* what he needs through prayer. We have more than the appearance of an example; we have its reality. Luke provides us with more than just a picture of a praying Jesus from a distance. Luke provides a degree of transparency with respect to Jesus' own struggles for faithfulness and

---

[13]Ambrose, *Exp. Luc.*, 163.
[14]Cyril of Alexandria, *Comm. Luke* 23, 124.
[15]Cyril of Alexandria, *Comm. Luke* 23, 123.
[16]Cyprian, *Dom. or.* 20, in *ANF* 5:455.

discernment—and the example of Jesus' prayer life is that much more powerful because of it.

THE LORD'S PRAYER (LUKE 11:1-4)

In this text also, Cyril of Alexandria highlights Luke's own emphasis on Jesus' example. Cyril again stresses that Jesus doesn't really *need* to pray. He "Himself is absolutely in need of nothing; for He is *full*, as He said Himself." Rather, Christ prays "to teach us not to be slack in this matter, but rather to be constant in prayers, and very urgent."[17]

Cyprian urges that this prayer be used in corporate worship. He says that we should not pray

> singly and individually, as for one who prays to pray for himself alone. For we say not "My Father, which art in heaven," nor "Give me this day my daily bread;" nor does each one ask that only his own debt should be forgiven him; nor does he request for himself alone that he may not be led into temptation, and delivered from evil. Our prayer is public and common; and when we pray, we pray not for one, but for the whole people, because we the whole people are one.[18]

Cyprian's message is instructive for our Western culture since we tend to read the Bible with great individualism. Even when we pray the Lord's Prayer in church today, we all tend to be thinking about the circumstances of our own lives or our own spirituality. If we could take Cyprian's challenge to pray the Lord's Prayer as a community of faith, we might realize that together, we need to be about the work of God's kingdom, and that your request for daily bread is my own as well. We might think about the ways in which we act that dishonor God as a community and seek forgiveness collectively for that, and *together* we must ask for the strength that we need to face the trials that the followers of Jesus will surely encounter.

Father. Tertullian captures both the intimacy and boldness of calling God "Father." He says, "This form of address is one of filial love and at the same time one of power."[19] Origen similarly declares, "Nowhere have I found in a prayer the boldness claimed by the Savior in calling God

---

[17]Cyril of Alexandria, *Comm. Luke* 70, 298-99.
[18]Cyprian, *Dom. or.*, in *ANF* 5:449.
[19]Tertullian, *Or.* 2, in *FC* 60:160.

Father."[20] Cyril points out that Jesus commands us also "to take boldness" when we address God in the same way.[21]

Luke's early commentators are quick to point out that this address assumes that we will act as obedient children. Origen says, "We shall hesitate to offer this address to Him if we have not become genuine sons, lest we should somehow be guilty of the charge of impiety in addition to our other sins."[22] Cyril agrees that "if we call God Father, and have been counted worthy of so distinguished an honor, must we not necessarily lead holy and thoroughly blameless lives, and so behave as it pleasing to our Father."[23]

Hallowed be your name. How can we ask for God's name to be considered holy? Isn't that something only God can do? Many in the early church seem to have the same sort of question. Tertullian asks, "When is the name of God not holy and blessed in itself, when of itself it makes others holy?"[24] Augustine similarly asks, "Why, then, do you ask for the hallowing of what is already holy?"[25] For patristic interpreters, this request is really aimed at us. Tertullian notes, "We are asking that it be sanctified in us."[26] Origen points out that we may pray this rightly when we exalt God because we recognize God's holiness through God's actions.[27] Cyprian similarly thinks that this prayer is "not that we wish for God that He may be hallowed by our prayers, but that we beseech of Him that His name may be hallowed in us."[28] Augustine says that "when we say 'Hallowed be thy name,' we rouse ourselves to desire that His Name, which is always holy, should be held holy among men also, that is, that it be not dishonored."[29] For Cyril, this is not a request for "any addition to be made to God's holiness" but that the petitioner may "possess such a mind and faith, as to feel that His name is honorable and holy."[30]

---

[20]Origen, On Prayer, in An Exhortation to Martyrdom, Prayer and Selected Writings, Classics of Western Spirituality (New York: Paulist, 1979), 123.

[21]Cyril of Alexandria, Comm. Luke 71, 301.

[22]Origen, On Prayer, 124.

[23]Cyril of Alexandria, Comm. Luke 71, 301.

[24]Tertullian, Or. 3, in FC 60:161.

[25]Augustine, Sermon 56.5, in FC 11:243.

[26]Tertullian, Or. 3, in FC 60:161.

[27]Origen, On Prayer, 129-30.

[28]Cyprian, Dom. or. 20, in ANF 5:450.

[29]Augustine, Letter 130, in FC 18:392.

[30]Cyril of Alexandria, Comm. Luke 72, 304.

Ultimately, however, Luke's early commentators are right in that only God can "hallow" God's own name. They point to our responsibility—we are not to behave in a way that dishonors God. Contemporary scholars tend to see the Lukan request as an impetus to confidence in God: God will continue to act in ways that are in keeping with the divine nature. This should inspire the kind of boldness that the Lukan Jesus encourages in prayer and is in line with the portrait of the God who receives prayer elsewhere in Luke (Lk 18:1-8).

Your kingdom come. The request for God's kingdom asks not only for God's purposes to be realized on earth but assumes our participation in God's kingdom work. Several in the early church capture this emphasis. Tertullian understands the phrase "Thy kingdom come" to mean "May thy kingdom come 'in ourselves.'" He asks, "For when does God not reign?"[31] Similarly, Cyprian says, "We ask that the kingdom of God may be set forth to us, even as we also ask that His name may be sanctified in us. For when does God not reign, or when does that begin with Him which both always has been and never ceases to be?"[32] Origen agrees: "It is clear that the one who prays that the kingdom of God may come prays that the kingdom of God may spring up in him, bear fruit, and be rightly perfected."[33] Augustine points out that "when we say, 'Thy kingdom come,' it will come inevitably whether we wish it or not, but we stir up our desire for that kingdom, that it may come in us, and that we may deserve to reign in it."[34] Cyril of Alexandria, affirming that Christ "reigns over all with God the Father; nor can any addition be made to His kingly glory," argues that Jesus commanded his disciples to pray for the time when Christ comes as judge, "to make them know that they must live . . . as becometh saints."[35]

The early church's emphasis on our participation in God's kingdom work provides a necessary reminder to the contemporary church, which often underestimates the power of this request. We often ask for God's will to be done on earth like we have nothing to do with that work. Patristic interpreters

---

[31]Tertullian, *Or.* 5, in FC 60:163.
[32]Cyprian, *Treatise* 4, *On the Lord's Prayer* 20, in *ANF* 5:450.
[33]Origen, *On Prayer*, 132.
[34]Augustine, *Letter* 130, in FC 18:392.
[35]Cyril of Alexandria, *Comm. Luke* 73, 307.

understood that this is a powerful request to *participate* in God's kingdom work and to submit ourselves completely to God's transformative work in our lives so that we might be used for God's purposes.

Daily bread. According to LifeWay Research, 69 percent of church-goers agree with the statement, "God wants me to prosper financially."[36] Many of them believe that it is completely appropriate to pray for this sort of spiritual blessing. We have much to learn from the early church on this text.

First, some patristic readers express reluctance at even the thought of praying for material things that we *need*. They interpret Luke 11:3 as a promise of spiritual sustenance, not actual food. Origen expresses his intent to refute the "false opinion" of those "who suppose that we are told to pray for corporeal bread," asking how "the One who says we must ask for heavenly and great things" can "have us ask for bread to be given for our flesh, since that is not a heavenly thing nor is the request for it a great thing?" He says, "It would be as though He had forgotten his own teaching and ordered us to offer supplication to the Father for an earthly and small thing."[37] Rather, for Origen, "The true bread is He who nourishes the true Man, made in the image of God, and the one who has been nourished by it will come to be in the likeness of Him who created him."[38] Each person is nourished "in proportion to how he places himself in the power of the Word."[39]

Not all of Luke's early readers are reluctant to acknowledge God's provision for our human needs. Tertullian glories in the fact that "after the matters which pertain to heaven" there is a place "for our earthly needs, too!" However, he too thinks that we also should interpret this request "in a spiritual sense. . . . Therefore, when we ask for our daily bread, we are asking to live forever in Christ and to be inseparably united with His body."[40] Augustine takes this request literally—as asking for "the bread by

---

[36]LifeWay Research conducted the study on August 22-30, 2017. Bob Smietana, "Prosperity Gospel Taught to 4 in 10 Evangelical Churchgoers" *Christianity Today*, July 31, 2018, www.christianity today.com/news/2018/july/prosperity-gospel-survey-churchgoers-prosper-tithe-blessing.html.

[37]Origen, *On Prayer*, 137.

[38]Origen, *On Prayer*, 138.

[39]Origen, *On Prayer*, 142.

[40]Tertullian, *Or.* 6, in FC 60:164.

which the belly is filled and the body is nourished anew every day." It is
"necessary, for we could not live without it," and "it is not shameless to ask
Him for daily bread" because it is that which "enables you to live."[41] He also
points to another kind of bread, the "Word of God, which is dispensed to
us every day."[42]

Cyprian, too, thinks that the text has a dual meaning but stresses that
the prayer is only for what we *need*: "But it may also be thus understood,
that we who have renounced the world, and have cast away its riches and
pomps in the faith of spiritual grace, should only ask for ourselves food
and support, since the Lord instructs us, and says, 'Whosoever forsaketh
not all that he hath, cannot be my disciple.'"[43] Augustine also notes that
"it would be shameless for you to ask God for riches."[44] Cyril of Alexandria
similarly points out that this verse should not be taken as license to ask for
wealth. For Cyril, the very request for bread implies *need* on the part of
Christ's followers: "By this very command, therefore, inasmuch as they ask
what they have not, we may perceive, that He does not wish His disciples
to set their desire upon wealth."[45] He says, "When, therefore, they ask
food for the day, understand, that they offer the request as men free from
the desire of riches, and who count it their boast to be entirely destitute of
earthly things."[46] Cyril concludes that we should therefore "ask of Him
what sufficeth for life; food, that is to say, and clothing, and whatever is
sufficient for us, avoiding all wish to be rich, as that which threatens us
with destruction."[47]

Cyril's perspective can be instructive for the church today: God does
not wish us to set our desires on wealth but on God's kingdom. We are
invited to pray for what we actually *need*, not for a life of comfort and
privilege. We tend to focus on what God can do for us. The question that
the Lord's Prayer invites is, What can we do for God? Taken together

[41] Augustine, *Sermon* 56.9, in FC 11:247.
[42] Augustine, *Sermon* 56.9, in FC 11:248.
[43] Cyprian, *Dom. or.* 20, in *ANF* 5:452.
[44] Augustine, *Sermon* 56.9, in FC 11:247.
[45] Cyril of Alexandria, *Comm. Luke* 75, 312.
[46] Cyril of Alexandria, *Comm. Luke* 75, 313.
[47] Cyril of Alexandria, *Comm. Luke* 75, 314.

with Jesus' teachings on wealth and generosity (Lk 12:13-34), we can understand this request for daily bread as part of a life lived in dependence on God that enables us to invest ourselves completely in God's kingdom.

Forgive us our sins. For Luke's early interpreters, clearly implied in this request is a recognition of guilt. For Tertullian, "A prayer for pardon is an acknowledgement of sin."[48] Cyprian too notes that "we are admonished that we are sinners, since we are compelled to entreat for our sins, and while pardon is asked for from God, the soul recalls its own consciousness *of sin*! Lest any one should flatter himself that he is innocent . . . he is instructed and taught that he sins daily, in that he is bidden to entreat daily for his sins."[49] Cyprian's teaching invites the church to a prayer of examen, a prayer which Richard Foster notes is oddly lost to those who live in a time of "obsessive introspection."[50] Few Christians make time to reflect on a regular basis about the ways in which we have or have not responded to the voice of the Holy Spirit. We who have grown uncomfortable with the concept of sin are not always attentive to the ways in which we are or are not living according to kingdom principles. Foster says that this practice of doing a daily "spiritual inventory" must hold a middle ground between self-flagellation and justifying our actions but is a source of "immeasurable strength and empowerment."[51] For Cyril, those who "know themselves," are not "like that ignorant and haughty Pharisee" but acknowledge their faults, requesting forgiveness of their sins.[52] Cyril points out that this request implies an intended change: "It is not fitting for those who still continue in wickedness and wish to do so to the last, to say, Forgive us our sins; but for those rather, who have abandoned their former wicked deeds, and now earnestly desire to live as becometh saints."[53] For Cyril, this is a "fitting" prayer only for those "who have chosen a virtuous life."[54] It can be hard, in our society, to see guilt as a helpful part of life.

---

[48]Tertullian, *Or.* 7, in FC 60:165.

[49]Cyprian, *Dom. or.* 20, in *ANF* 5:453.

[50]Richard Foster, *Prayer: Finding the Heart's True Home* (San Francisco: HarperSanFrancisco, 1992), 27.

[51]Richard Foster, *Prayer*, 27.

[52]Cyril of Alexandria, *Comm. Luke* 76, 315-16.

[53]Cyril of Alexandria, *Comm. Luke* 76, 316-17.

[54]Cyril of Alexandria, *Comm. Luke* 76, 317.

Guilt, however, can be a reminder of our human limitations and our reliance on God's grace and forgiveness.

Do not bring us to the time of trial. Contemporary Christians sometimes see this verse as an invitation to pray for an easier path. Luke's early readers understand that this is not a prayer for trials to be removed. Rather, we should pray for the spiritual strength that we need to navigate life amid the storms that will inevitably come our way. Origen urges Christians to pray "that we be not encompassed with temptation, which is what happens to those who are enmeshed in it and conquered."[55] Origen then reminds us that the whole of human life on earth is temptation.[56] For Augustine, "When we say 'Lead us not into temptation,' we warn ourselves to ask not to be deprived of His help, not to consent to any temptation through deception, not to yield through tribulation." For Augustine, "The fact that this petition is placed last in the Lord's Prayer shows plainly that the Christian . . . beset by any kind of trouble, utters his groans by means of it, pours out his tears in it, begins, continues, and ends his prayer by it."[57] When we are faced with difficult circumstances, we often respond with resignation or escapism. Augustine rightly captures Luke's emphasis that the only way to emerge victoriously on the other side of trials is through persistent, insistent prayer.

THE FRIEND AT MIDNIGHT (LUKE 11:5-8)

Augustine points to the emphasis of this text: if even a human will answer a request from a friend, how much more so will God: "By this we are to understand that if a man, roused from sleep, is forced to give unwillingly in answer to a request, God, who does not know sleep, and who rouses us from sleep that we may ask, gives much more graciously."[58] Ambrose explains that this narrative teaches the need for continual prayer: Prayer is offered "not only by day, but also by night; for ye see that he who woke his friend at midnight demanding three loaves of bread and, persisting in his intention to obtain, is not denied in his supplications." The three loaves,

---

[55]Origen, *On Prayer*, 156.
[56]Origen, *On Prayer*, 152.
[57]Augustine, *Letter* 130, in FC 18:392.
[58]Augustine, *Letter* 130, in FC 18:388.

he goes on, are "the nourishment of the heavenly mystery"; we should be "continuing in prayer by day and by night" for this "bread of restoration." Then this bread "cannot be lacking for us, exhausted from the way, and tired out by the course of this age and the winding of this life."[59] Although Ambrose spiritualizes the parable, he captures the meaning of the text it explains: persistent prayer is the means through which we gain the resilience to remain faithful to the kingdom work we are called to do.

ASKING, SEEKING, KNOCKING (LUKE 11:9-13)

We live in a society that values immediate gratification; waiting in rush hour traffic, for a checkout line at Walmart on a Saturday, on hold with customer service, for multi-hour airline delays—this is a struggle for many of us. When I saw the movie *Zootopia* with my kids, my favorite scene was with Flash the sloth, the agonizingly slow clerk at the DMV—he waited on me also the last time I was there! We are so overscheduled that many of us chafe at the idea of waiting; we want to move quickly through the many stops of our day so that we can be more productive. We tend to import that mentality into our prayer lives too, many of us being entirely unaccustomed to prolonged periods of waiting on God in prayer.

Perhaps this is one place where we could benefit from reading Luke 11:9-13 with the early church. Cyprian promises, "'To him that knocketh also it shall be opened,' if only our prayers, our groanings, and our tears knock at the door; and with these we must be urgent and persevering, even although prayer be offered with one mind."[60] For Ambrose, prayer requires our full watchful attention: "Ye must always be watchful, for there are many snares for us. . . . So rise from your sleep that ye may knock on Christ's door."[61] Cyril of Alexandria says that the right kind of prayer is not to be done "wearily" or "lazily." He gives a bit of pastoral advice for those who are growing discouraged when they don't immediately hear from God. He would not have us be like those who when they are not heard after their first or second requests are tempted to "desist from their

---

[59]Ambrose, *Exp. Luc.*, 266-67.
[60]Cyprian, *Epistle* 7.2, in *ANF* 5:286.
[61]Ambrose, *Exp. Luc.*, 267-68.

supplications, as being unavailing to their benefit." He urges his audience, "That we may not experience this, nor suffer the injury that would result from such littleness of mind," to "diligently continue" in prayer, knowing "weariness in prayer is our loss, while patience therein is greatly to our profit; for it is our duty to persevere, without giving way to indolence." For Cyril, prayer is laborious. Acknowledging that "what is gained without toil, and readily won, is usually despised; whereas that which is gathered with labor is a more pleasant and abiding possession," he affirms that, "in telling us, therefore, to seek, [Christ] bids us labor." He affirms, "He who knocks, not once merely, but again and again, rattles the door" of heaven, imploring, "Knock, be urgent, ask. So must all act who ask any thing of God."[62]

Somewhere we have missed the point about prayer being urgent, persistent, and laborious. We need to cultivate the lost art of waiting on God, individually and corporately, sitting in God's presence, and like Jacob wrestling with the angel, refusing to fill the silence with our own imagined answers to prayer until *God* responds. This is not a process that we control. I was once at a spiritual retreat where we were given a few minutes to "lower our buckets" into our own spirits where Christ dwells before reporting back on what we had heard in the silence. This is becoming a fairly common practice in spiritual formation groups. The idea is that because God dwells in us, our thoughts are God's thoughts, and if we can quiet ourselves enough to hear this, we can hear the voice of God. In a sense, this is true: We become accustomed to hearing the voice of the indwelling Christ, and our thoughts and desires eventually are brought into line with Christ's. However, this does not mean that we can access the mind of God at will.

Discernment takes place on God's timetable, not ours. God is free and wholly Other, operating out of God's own volition. What does this mean for spiritual direction? I've participated in and led groups and individuals in spiritual direction. Sometimes I feel like I can discern the Spirit's direction during these meetings, and sometimes, in the twenty minutes or so allotted to silence, there's just silence. In those times, I think the best thing that we can do is be honest about the fact that we are speaking from

---

[62]All quotations of Cyril in this and the following paragraph are from Cyril of Alexandria, *Comm. Luke* 78, 321-22.

our own wisdom instead of hearing directly from God. Rarely have I experienced a situation in spiritual direction where on a subsequent meeting someone says, "I've been praying about your situation regularly over the past month, and this is what I've been hearing." I'm wondering if perhaps that practice fits Luke's directive a bit better.

Commenting on Luke 11:9-13, Cyril also deals with the reality of unanswered prayers. For him, God "loveth to be kind; and that very constantly." If one sees "that the gift of grace is delayed," one should "yield not to weariness; despair not of the expected blessing; abandon not the hope set before thee." Rather, one should trust that God's desires for our good supersede our own. He argues, "Rather think thus within thyself, that He who is the universal treasure house better knoweth our state than we do, in that He weigheth to every man what is due and suitable to him." One might ask "beyond thy measure" or for something "of which thou are not worthy." However, "The Giver Himself knoweth the time suitable for His gifts." Good human parents don't give their children everything they ask for without discretion. Neither does God. Sometimes "God knows that it would not be for their benefit to receive what they ask."

Finally, Cyril points his readers to the need to take a step of faith when they seem to be facing God's silence. He concedes that someone might say, "'I draw near frequently, making requests; but the vintage therefrom has wandered far away. I am not slothful in supplications, but persevering and very importunate: who will assure me that I shall receive?'" In response, Cyril declares that this scriptural promise "has the full force of an oath." He reminds his reader, "As, therefore, He makes this very promise on oath, it is not a thing free from guilt to disbelieve it."[63] We could perhaps use a bit of Cyril's faith. In the meantime, in those moments where we truly are hearing nothing, we should, as Thomas Merton says, take confidence "in the hidden One who prays within us even when we ourselves are not able to pray well, who asks for us the things we do not know we need, and who seeks to give us joys we would not dare to seek for ourselves."[64]

---

[63]Cyril of Alexandria, *Comm. Luke* 78, 321-22.
[64]Thomas Merton, *Life and Holiness* (New York: Image Books, 1963), 30-31.

THE WIDOW AND THE UNJUST JUDGE (LUKE 18:1-8)

Several of Luke's earliest interpreters use this text to appeal to the church to pray without ceasing. Tertullian observes that the judge "was compelled to listen to the widow, owing to the earnestness and importunity of her requests." For him, this text portrays God as "the avenger of His own elect, who cry day and night to Him."[65] Cyril of Alexandria, pointing out that of all the practices one could adopt, prayer "especially benefits those who practice it," urges us to not be "sluggish" in prayer but rejoice because of the "freedom of access" granted by God.[66]

For Origen, this text teaches that our prayer prompts God to action. Noting that Jesus "prays for those who pray and appeals along with those who appeal," Origen argues, "But He does not pray for servants who do not pray continuously through Him, nor will He be the Advocate with God for His own if they are not obedient to His instructions that they 'ought always to pray and not lose heart.'"[67] Similarly, for Cyril, this parable teaches us that "God will incline His ear to those who offer him their prayers, not carelessly nor negligently, but with earnestness and constancy."[68]

The early church is quick to point out the "how much more" argument of this text. Augustine, noting the "sheer persistence" of the widow, asks, "If the widow could not be treated contemptuously by an unjust judge because of her continual supplication, how much more will God hear us when we pray without ceasing?" For Augustine, this text shows us "how surely the merciful and just God hears us when we pray without ceasing." If the widow, "because of her continual petition, could not be treated with contempt even by an unjust and wicked judge," then "how willingly and kindly" will God satisfy "good desires" of God's children?[69]

In the narrative preceding the parable at hand, the disciples are growing frustrated with the suffering and injustice they are experiencing and wondering when they will experience the fullness of the kingdom. When faced with a persistent degree of injustice today also, we must not crumple in

---

[65]Tertullian, *Marc.* 4.36, in *ANF* 3:409-10.
[66]Cyril of Alexandria, *Comm. Luke* 119, 477.
[67]Origen, *On Prayer*, 101.
[68]Cyril of Alexandria, *Comm. Luke* 119, 478.
[69]Augustine, *Letter* 130, in *FC* 18:387-88.

defeat but partner with God in prayer as we seek to accomplish the work of the kingdom. When our society turns a blind eye to flagrant racial profiling, when our leaders slam our country's doors against suffering immigrants, when our society condones the objectification of women, we cannot despair. Cyril, urging us to not be divided by doubt when we pray, promises that "God will incline His ear to those who offer him their prayers, not carelessly nor negligently, but with earnestness and constancy." This parable "assures us" of it:

> For if the constant coming of the oppressed widow prevailed upon the unjust judge, who feared not God, neither had any shame at men, so that even against his will he granted her redress, how shall not He Who loveth mercy, and hateth iniquity, and Who ever giveth His helping hand to them that love Him, accept those who draw near to Him day and night.[70]

We cannot give up. We must work and hope, but above all, we must pray, because we do not do the work of the kingdom alone, and cannot do it in our own strength.

JESUS' PRAYER IN GETHSEMANE (LUKE 22:39-46)

For some of Luke's early interpreters, this text emphasizes Jesus' obedience—and motivates our own. As Tertullian says, with this phrase "we forearm ourselves for patient endurance since our Lord, too, willed to point out in His own flesh under the intensity of His Passion the weakness of the flesh." Jesus "surrendered Himself to the will of His Father to indicate the patient endurance which is rightly due."[71] Augustine observes that when Jesus uttered "not my will but yours" it was an act of "transforming the human will which He had taken in becoming man" so that "by the obedience of one, many are made just."[72]

Some in the early church wrestle with Jesus' anguished struggle for the will of God. Dionysius, the third-century patriarch of Alexandria, notes that the words "'If Thou be willing,' were demonstrative of subjection and docility, not of ignorance and hesitancy." He emphasizes that the words

---

[70]Cyril of Alexandria, *Comm. Luke* 119, 477-78.
[71]Tertullian, *Or.* 4, in FC 60:162.
[72]Augustine, *Letter* 130, in FC 18:397.

"'Let the cup pass,' does not mean Let it not come near me or approach me."[73] He admits that "some one may say that He is overborne and changes His mind, and asks presently something different from what He asked before, and holds no longer by His own will but introduces His Father's will. Well such truly is the case. Nevertheless He does not by any means make any change from one side to another; but He embraces another way, and a different method of carrying out one and the same transaction."[74] If that sounds confusing, Dionysius offers an analogy to help. He says that the transition from Jesus' request for the cup to be removed to his submission to God's will is like a runner grazed by a faster athlete who surpasses him; the former slows briefly, but both are heading in the same direction.[75] He notes that Jesus

> wished that the cup might come into His hands, and promptly pass from Him again very readily and quickly; but as soon as He spake thus, being strengthened in his Humanity by the Father's divinity, He urges the safer petition, and desires no longer that should be the case, but that it might be accomplished in accordance with the Father's good pleasure, in glory, in constancy, and in fullness. For John, who has given us the record of the sublimest and divinest of the Savior's words and deeds, heard Him speak thus: "And the cup which my Father hath given me, shall I not drink it?"[76]

Dionysius addresses the text's difficulty, but also leans into the more perhaps theologically comforting context of John.

Others struggle with the text so much that it is necessary to say that Jesus' sorrow is not for himself. Ambrose argues that this text "should not be explained away." Noting that Jesus "did not undertake the appearance of the Incarnation, but its reality," he allows that Jesus "must also undertake the grief, in order to overcome the sorrow, not exclude it." However, Ambrose argues that Jesus' grief was for humanity, not himself. He cries, "Thus, Lord, Thou art pained, not at Thy, but at my wounds, not at Thy Death, but at our

---

[73]Dionysius of Alexandria *II, The Gospel According to Luke* in *Exegetical Fragments on the Gospel of Luke*, trans. S. D. F. Salmond, *ANF* 6:38.
[74]Dionysius of Alexandria *III, On Luke XXII. 42, Etc.* in *Exegetical Fragments on the Gospel of Luke*, trans. S. D. F. Salmond, *ANF* 6:39.
[75]Dionysius of Alexandria *III, On Luke XXII. 42, Etc.*, *ANF* 6:39.
[76]Dionysius of Alexandria *III, On Luke XXII. 42, Etc.*, *ANF* 6:39.

infirmity."[77] For Ambrose, Jesus "was sorrowful, not because of His Own Passion, but because of our dispersion." When he asked for the cup to be removed from him, it was "not because the Son of God feared death, but because He was unwilling that even the wicked should perish."[78]

Cyril addresses his struggle directly to Christ:

> *He began*, it says, *to be grieved, and sore distressed*. For what reason, O Lord? Wast Thou also terrified at death? Didst Thou being seized with fear draw back from suffering? And yet didst not Thou teach the holy apostles to make no account of the terrors of death, saying *Fear not them who kill the body, but are not able to kill the soul*. Moreover, if any one were to say that the grace of spiritual fortitude is Thy gift to the elect, he would not err from the truth; for all strength is from Thee.[79]

Reading Luke with Mark's emphasis on Jesus' suffering and John's Christology, he adds,

> How, therefore, art Thou grieved, and sore distressed, and sorrowful, even unto death? For plainly Thou knowest, in that Thou art God by nature, and knowest whatsoever is about to happen, that by enduring death in the flesh Thou wouldst free from death the inhabitants of all the earth, and bring Satan unto shame . . . that Thou wouldst be known by every one, and worshipped as the God and creator of all. . . . For what reason, therefore, art Thou grieved and sore distressed?[80]

Cyril's solution is that Jesus grieves not for himself but for Israel.

> He says, not unbefittingly am I found thus in anguish. For I know indeed that by consenting to suffer the passion upon the cross, I shall deliver all. . . . But withal it grieveth Me for Israel the firstborn, that henceforth He is not even among the servants. . . . What shepherd would be so harsh and stern as, when his flock was perishing, to suffer nothing on its account? These are the causes of My grief; for these things I am sorrowful. For I am God, gentle, and that loveth to spare.[81]

---

[77] Ambrose, *Exp. Luc.*, 406-7.
[78] Ambrose, *Exp. Luc.*, 407-8.
[79] Cyril of Alexandria, *Comm. Luke* 146, 582.
[80] Cyril of Alexandria, *Comm. Luke* 146, 582.
[81] Cyril of Alexandria, *Comm. Luke* 146, 582-83.

Ironically, Cyril's profound struggle with the text only further highlights the awkwardness and agony of Jesus' suffering, and in so doing, he does the church a great service. We shun the ugliness and desperation of human suffering. Those expecting the bereaved or ill to put on a brave face of "faith" might consider that the Synoptic Gospels place no such lens over Christ's sufferings.

The *inclusio* of Luke 22:39-46 highlights the unity of Jesus' life and teaching, something that Cyril also notes. Jesus' life is a "pattern for thy conduct."[82] Cyril wants to be clear that Jesus had no need of prayer himself but that Jesus prays solely for our benefit: "And let no man of understanding say that He offered these supplications as being in need of strength or help from another . . . but it was that we might hereby learn."[83] However, it is the *reality* of Jesus' prayerful struggle for the will of God that provides a powerful example of the effectiveness of prayer for the church.

SUMMARY

The patristic readers struggled with the idea that Jesus would need to pray. For them, Jesus' prayer at his baptism (and Jesus' baptism itself) was not for Jesus' benefit but to provide an example for the church.[84] Jesus prays before choosing his disciples, not because he is seeking to learn God's will (for he already knows it) but to provide an example for us.[85] He prays alone not because he is seeking spiritual strength that he lacks but because his human disciples could never comprehend the conversation that he has with his Father.[86] As Cyril of Alexandria says, Jesus is "full" and "absolutely in need of nothing."[87] Because of this, he emphasizes the exemplary nature of Jesus' prayers. They are "for us." For the church, then, learning to pray is a matter of imitating Jesus' example. This emphasis is significant to Luke as well, but the early church capitalizes on it because of the discomfort with the notion that Jesus might actually need to pray. The

---

[82]Cyril of Alexandria, *Comm. Luke* 147, 585.
[83]Cyril of Alexandria, *Comm. Luke* 147, 584-85.
[84]Cyril of Alexandria, *Comm. Luke* 11, 80-81.
[85]Ambrose, *Exp. Luc.*, 162-63.
[86]Cyril of Alexandria, *Comm. Luke* 23, 125.
[87]Cyril of Alexandria, *Comm. Luke* 70, 298.

effect of this might somewhat diminish the power of the biblical example. In Luke, after all, Jesus *does* find the strength through prayer for his ministry and passion. In this respect, contemporary scholarship gets it right. If anything, though, Cyril's struggles reawaken for the contemporary reader the messy reality of Jesus' suffering. If Luke wanted to highlight Jesus' stoic resolve,[88] Cyril, in spite of himself, draws the church into the awkwardness and humbling nature of Jesus' suffering.

One thing Luke's early interpreters certainly get right is their depiction of the need for continual, fervent prayer. Contemporary Western readers, immersed in a culture of many wants, expect immediate satisfaction and struggle to grasp the nature of the kind of prayers that Jesus calls for in Luke. Jesus spent the whole night in prayer as prescription that the church must imitate.[89] We must pray with groanings and tears,[90] and not be weary or lazy in our prayers, and not desist from prayer when we don't receive an immediate answer.[91] We must labor in prayer, rattling the door of heaven.[92] Contemporary readers might take such descriptions as an invitation into the *work* of prayer.

Finally, Luke's patristic interpreters could also prompt the faith of contemporary Western readers so adept at satisfying their own desires that there is little expectation for God's miraculous activity. When facing God's silence, Cyril prompts us to faith, promising that the promises of Scripture have the "full force of an oath."[93] He urges us to go to God with expectancy and trust, knowing that God knows us more than we know ourselves and that God's desires for our good can be trusted.[94]

---

[88]Jerome Neyrey, *The Passion According to Luke* (New York: Paulist Press, 1985), 49-54.

[89]Ambrose, *Exp. Luc.*, 163.

[90]Ambrose, *Exp. Luc.*, 267-68.

[91]Cyril of Alexandria, *Comm. Luke* 78, 321.

[92]Cyril of Alexandria, *Comm. Luke* 78, 322.

[93]Cyril of Alexandria, *Comm. Luke* 78, 322.

[94]Cyril of Alexandria, *Comm. Luke* 78, 321-22.

EXPECTATIONS FOR AN IDEAL HERO

Luke's narrative intends not only to inform but also to transform. Luke's intended readers would have known that the best form of government was to have a virtuous ruler who ruled through personal example. Such a leader would be able to effect virtue in others. Luke's readers, knowing that philosophy was a lifestyle more than a set of theories, would have expected their ideal teachers to be models of virtue. Even if few individuals actually met the ideal, Luke's intended audience was familiar with it. They may have known stories of ideal kings and philosophers who had such a union with the gods that their lifestyles were powerful models of virtue for others. They would have recognized the unity of life and teaching as a mark of an ideal philosopher-king and knew that such an individual actually had the power to save others by the power of example.

Luke clearly presents Jesus as one who has a perfect unity of life and teachings. Luke describes his Gospel as a story of "all that Jesus did and taught" (Acts 1:1). Specifically, in each of the three areas of simplicity, humility, and prayer, Luke emphasizes the unity of Jesus' words and deeds. Jesus teaches his disciples to place their security in God (Lk 12:28) and abandon themselves to the kingdom (Lk 12:32) with no worries for the future (Lk 12:29). The wealthy must exercise generous benefaction (Lk 12:33). Jesus himself has no place to lay his head (Lk 9:58) but must himself depend on God's provision (Lk 6:1; 9:13; 10:4-5). With no wealth to give, Jesus devotes his life to bestowing freely the treasure of the kingdom (Lk 12:32). Jesus has sharp criticism for religious leaders whose lives are fueled by pride (Lk 20:45-47) and even his self-seeking disciples

(Lk 9:46-50; 22:26). He himself is actually worthy of all honor but still rejects the praises of others (Lk 11:27-28; 18:18-19) and models servant leadership for his disciples (Lk 22:27). Jesus' teaching about prayer is rooted in his own prayer practices. Jesus instructs his disciples about the necessity of prayer for their successful participation in the kingdom, depicting a God who is both generous and faithful to answer their requests (Lk 11:1-13; 18:1-8). Jesus himself prays constantly (Lk 9:18; 22:39) and before the critical moments of his ministry (Lk 4:14; 6:12; 9:28-29; 22:39), seeking the will of God and spiritual strength (Lk 22:39-46).

Luke's intended readers would have likely recognized in Jesus the marks of an ideal hero. Because of this, they would have responded to Luke's portrait of Jesus with a recognition of the formative power of Jesus' example in the areas of simplicity, humility, and prayer. Their attitudes and expectations for the text would have likely differed greatly from those of many contemporary academic readers of Luke who may approach the text as an object to be mined for information. Instead, they would have approached Luke's Gospel with an expectation to be transformed through their encounter with Jesus.

FIRST RECEPTIONS

Not only can our attitudes be markedly different from the sensibilities of Luke's target audience but our perspectives can be as well. Gaining familiarity with some of the expectations of Luke's intended readers provides an entry point into Luke's conceptual world and guards against reading contemporary concerns into an ancient text. While this is far from an exact science, our own horizons of understanding are enlarged by seeking entry into Luke's literary world. Luke wrote with certain assumptions about his intended audience's beliefs, knowledge, practices, and expectations. The closer we can get to their reading experience, the better we will be able to respond to Luke's invitations. For this reason, I began with a first reception of the text, asking how Luke's intended audience might have responded to his portraits of simplicity, humility, and prayer, and looking at the way in which ideal kings and philosophers practiced and taught on each of these topics within Luke's literary world.

Simplicity in Luke's literary world. There are a number of striking parallels between Jesus' teachings on simplicity and wealth and these ideas and ideals in Luke's literary world. The understanding that wealth is fleeting, that preoccupation with wealth can detract from more noble pursuits, and a knowledge of the moral corruption inherent in greed are all present in Luke's literary world. We also find there a redefinition of true wealth, praises for a simple lifestyle, and the ideal of generous benefaction. Luke's intended audience would not just have had their preconceptions affirmed, however. While Seneca urges disciples to seek philosophy first, "even though we starve,"[1] Jesus tells his disciples to "strive for his kingdom, and these things will be given to you as well" (Lk 12:31). For the Lukan Jesus, the motivation for simplicity rests on an awareness of God's gracious benefaction toward us. Further, the mandate for our own generous benefaction is made possible because God is our source of security (Lk 12:31-32). We are instructed in the lifestyle of simplicity and benefaction not just because it is a noble way to live but because such a lifestyle is an investment in God's kingdom, manifest also among the poor, who are in desperate need of our resources.

Contemporary readers have much to learn from a first reception of Luke's portrait of simplicity and benefaction. Because of our materialistic culture and individualistic mentality, we tend to spiritualize away many of Jesus' teachings on simplicity and wealth. Many in our culture tend to think that the wealthy in our culture have no real obligation toward the poor and that there is nothing undignified about an ostentatious lifestyle. What we glean from Luke's literary world is a different set of sensibilities. We get the impression that there is a certain responsibility that the wealthy have to care for the needy in their communities and that there is more honor that comes through the practice of benefaction than an amassing of goods for one's own benefit. The caricatures of ostentatious characters in Luke's literary world (which were surely matched in reality in Luke's actual cultural world) seem so garish that we would hardly idealize them. Reading through the lens of Luke's literary cohorts

---

[1]Seneca, *Ep.* 17.7.

retrains us to value what Luke values and tamps down the materialistic impulses of our own context.

Humility in Luke's literary world. Among first-century Mediterranean people, being humiliated was something to be feared, and there was nothing wrong with affirming the honors that one truly deserved. However, there are still a number of significant parallels between Jesus' teachings against pride and a general distaste for undeserved pride in Luke's literary world, and in both Luke and his milieu, a concern for a right relationship to honor. Those who engaged in relentless self-praise and who gloried in undeserved honors were the subject of mockery, both for Luke and his peers. Luke's readers would have certainly had the horizons of their understanding stretched, however. While there are some examples of a worthy person shunning superficial praise in Luke's literary world, it would still have been unthinkable to imagine an honorable person adopting the posture of a common servant (Lk 22:26-27). The parallels that are apparent between Luke and his literary world, however, would have caused Luke's intended readers to recognize Jesus as a person of integrity who exhibited personal and spiritual maturity.

Reading Luke in the context of his literary world gives us a bit more perspective on Luke's Gospel. We don't see humility as an essential quality in our leaders. Jesus, however, appears to. Reading through the lens of Luke's literary world enables us to catch the emphasis that those who, like the religious leaders (Lk 20:20, 24-26, 39-40, 45-47), bask in external, undeserved honors are essentially illegitimate leaders. Knowing, from Plutarch, that concern with these sorts of external trappings of status are the mark of a novice gives us a degree of patience with the status-seeking disciples but skepticism for the seasoned religious leaders' future.[2] When we see the Pharisee engaging in self-praise at the expense of the tax collector (Lk 18:9-14), we understand more of his predicament: he has no self-awareness or true self with which to respond to God, so *of course* he goes home unjustified. As we read Luke through the lenses of his literary world, we start to see how a willingness to acknowledge the truth about

---

[2]Plutarch, *Virt. prof.* 81c-d.

oneself is foundational to a person's basic maturity and spiritual development. Without it, such an individual is truly alone. Without a self that can be in relationship with God, the Pharisee must flatter himself because no one else will. He must deceive himself as to his righteousness because truly facing the alternative is unthinkable. He is entirely disqualified for leadership—a poseur at best.

Prayer in Luke's literary world. As we have seen, perhaps surprisingly, there are a number of parallels between Luke's depiction of Jesus at prayer and the prayer lives and teachings about prayer in Luke's literary world. While many leaders saw prayer as a part of their cultic duty, others felt sustained and nourished through their relationship with the gods. It was thought that an ideal philosopher-king in particular had a unique capacity to rule because of his relationship with the gods. Plutarch's Numa, for instance, is legendary for his contemplative prayer. Because of his friendship with the gods, he is not limited by his own understandings but is guided by the gods to form a people much like him—who are also contemplative and peace-loving in nature.[3] Just as Jesus prays before the critical events in his life and ministry, so Plato's Socrates appeals to the gods before speaking, reflecting, or beginning any activity.[4] Just as Jesus seeks the will of God and divine strength through prayer, so also do Xenophon's, Plato's, and Plutarch's heroes.[5]

What might contemporary readers glean from such a portrait? While the biblical texts sometimes seem too familiar to jostle me out of my habits, Timaeus's advice has often remained on my mind—to "call upon God always at the outset of every undertaking, be it small or great."[6] Texts like these help me to see Jesus' prayer habits in context and move me beyond academic observation to practice. Similarly, the image of Plutarch's Numa, lost in contemplation in the countryside, urging his citizens to not pray "cursorily" but with attentiveness, provides context for understanding Jesus' relentless dependence on God in prayer.[7] Those of us who might be tempted to think

---

[3]Plutarch, *Num.* 14.
[4]Plato, *Ep.* 8.352.e; *Critias* 108d; *Tim.* 27c.
[5]Xenophon, *Oec.* 5.19; *Cyr.* 1.6.46; Plato, *Critias* 106b; Xenophon, *Mem.* 4.8.11; Plutarch, *Lyc.* 29.2.
[6]Plato, *Tim.* 27c.
[7]Plutarch, *Num.* 4.1; 14.2.

of prayer as a few spoken words, who gloss over Luke's observations about Jesus' customary and continual prayer habits, might be prompted to a re-evaluation in light of texts like these. It is hard to emerge from a reading of these sorts of narratives with the understanding that prayer is a frivolous thing. Ideal heroes pray for divine aid in calming a warlike city,[8] for help when army or country is in peril,[9] for deliverance that vindicates the name of God (2 Kings 19:14-19),[10] or for a harmony of one's inner and outer life.[11] In one text, Socrates spends an entire day thinking before offering a prayer.[12] Reading Luke through this kind of literary context, noting his emphasis on the kingdom of God in the Lord's Prayer, teaches us that prayer is more about God's agenda than ours and, ironically perhaps, might even allow us to see prayer in a more sacred context. Finally, one of the features of prayer in both Luke and his literary world is that prayer is effective. There appears to be a cause-and-effect relationship between the prayers of ideal heroes and divine engagement that propels the plotline forward in many ancient Mediterranean biographies. So too with Jesus in Luke. Reading Luke's portrait of Jesus through the lens of Luke's literary world not only enables us to appreciate Luke's aims but also might create in us a desire not to pray only out of custom or occasional desperation but to be the kind of people with whom God would want to consort,[13] who lead a life of contemplation, listening for the direction of God in the silence of their lives, who are as dependent on God as on air, for whom divine engagement is not a cause for astonishment but a natural outcome of a life spent in intimate friendship with God.

Subsequent Receptions

Biblical scholars have grown accustomed to approaching Scripture as an object for study. It is how many of us were trained. We approached the text with our exegetical toolbox, not wanting to color what we thought of as

---

[8]Plutarch, *Num.* 7.1.
[9]Virgil, *Aen.* 5.695.
[10]Pr. Azar. 20-21.
[11]Plato, *Phaedr.* 279b-c.
[12]Plato, *Symp.* 220d.
[13]Plutarch, *Num.* 4.3.

our semiscientific results with the biases of personal faith. Eventually, the assumption that the right method could yield objective truth gave way to an awareness that we all approach the text with biases. Additionally, some began to question whether checking our biases at the door (if that were even possible) would result in better interpretations. Operating from a perspective of detached neutrality seemed not only impossible but also undesirable. People understood that if we are really to understand literature, the text must engage us—it must have its intended effect on our lives. If the biblical text was written to form the people of God, perhaps we ought to interpret it in that way as well.

Over the last twenty years, a growing number of scholars have begun to advocate the practice of reading the biblical text as Christian Scripture—that is, with a view to the formation of the church. While this is more a posture and attitude than a method, many of these scholars use reception theory in order to widen the circle of their potential interpretive partners to include the historic and global church. Reading the biblical text through the lens of the early church does more than unveil previously forgotten interpretations. It teaches us to read Scripture as Scripture. We inherit from the church fathers and mothers new attitudes toward the biblical text. Instead of standing over the text as an object to be dissected, we stand under its authority, allowing ourselves to be formed by it. We discover that this is actually good practice, hermeneutically, for we are approaching scriptural texts in the same spirit that they were given in, seeking to respond to the prompts that the text originally sought to elicit.

Learning simplicity with the church. Particularly because we are immersed in a materialistic culture, we have a lot to learn from the early church about simplicity and generosity. The church mothers and fathers took seriously Jesus' mandate to care for those in need. As "granaries for the poor," when the wealthy spend their money solely on themselves, they are stealing both from the poor and from God. Luke's earliest Christian interpreters knew that money had the potential to prevent people from full participation in the kingdom and saw much virtue in a radically simplistic lifestyle. They boldly proclaimed a generous God, however, and knew that God was the only true source of security for the Christian.

Reading about Jesus' teachings and lifestyle of simplicity through the eyes of the church forces us to take Luke's mandates more seriously. Our tendency to spiritualize the strongest commands to dispossession are tempered somewhat by the early church's ascetic perspective. At the very least, this should cause us to reign in our rampant consumerism, consider how we could cultivate a habit of generosity, and question the moral choices of our leaders who often appear to be fueled by desires for financial gain.

Learning humility with the church. The early church recognized that pride was the mark of a spiritually bankrupt person and saw humility as the foundational virtue on which all others depend. Knowing that humility and self-knowledge go hand in hand, they understood pride as having the potential to shipwreck a life. Because they are apt to read Luke through the lens of the rest of the New Testament, they see the ultimate expression of Christ's humility through the lens of Philippians 2:6-11. The remarkable humility of characters in Luke, like the centurion of Luke 7:1-10, pale in comparison to Jesus' own humility, which Luke's earliest commentators repeatedly hold up as the church's example. The early church takes very seriously the disciples' status-seeking behavior; such attitudes are a "snare of death."[14] The patristic interpreters recognize that the prideful religious leaders essentially lack self-knowledge. In fact, the abiding example of the Pharisees' tragic lives is so significant that the Fathers and Mothers use *Pharisee* and *publican* as synonyms for *pride* and *humility*. Finally, early Lukan scholars sometimes actually practice humility in the way in which they identify with characters in Luke's story. They are quick to point to any tendencies toward pride in their own lives because they recognize its destructive power.

The contemporary church in North America today has simply lost this lesson. We misunderstand humility as weakness and don't particularly care whether those in positions of responsibility in the church or in government are prideful or not. We don't understand what is at stake. Because we don't see humility as a foundational virtue the way the church mothers and fathers did, we don't understand that pride masks the lack of a true self, and that without a true self, any level of maturity—spiritual or

---

[14]Cyprian, *Treatise* 10.10, in *ANF* 5:493-94.

otherwise—is impossible. The caricature of the pompous leader who engages in self-flattery isn't comical; such a person will resort to anything to maintain his or her fragile ego. Patristic readings of the status-seeking disciples should be instructive for us as well: we should recognize the danger inherent in a desire for power and position at any cost. Instead, we need to have the courage to look at ourselves in the mirror, individually and corporately, and commit ourselves again to be people of integrity.

Learning prayer with the church. One rather fascinating thing that we see among many of Luke's early interpreters is their inability to acknowledge Jesus' need to pray. Typically, they see Jesus' prayers as functioning as a model for the church. Particularly when Jesus is praying for spiritual strength or to discern the will of God, they feel a need to highlight Jesus' example. Luke emphasizes Jesus' example, holding him up as a model for prayer, so ironically, perhaps, the early church catches this emphasis. Jesus' example lacks power, however, if his struggle for prayer is not real. In Luke, Jesus' Gethsemane narrative is the watershed of the passion narrative—it is there where Jesus wrestles like an athlete for the will of God in prayer and there where he rises victoriously, resolute to fulfill his divine mission. His example has authority for us because it is rooted in the reality of his own experience.

We do have much to learn from the early church as we read Luke through their eyes. We who gravitate toward immediate gratification lack the patience for perseverant prayer. We may be unaccustomed to spending entire nights in prayer, wrestling for the will of God, praying fervently with tears and groanings, and remaining in prayer when God is silent. We lack the early church's deeply rooted confidence in God's ability to answer prayer and their trust in God's character to act in ways that are for our good. The early church has captured rightly Luke's emphasis on the power of prayer. We who are entirely too independent of the supernatural need to sit at the feet of the church mothers and fathers, expectantly waiting with them for God to act.

An ancient path. Luke's contemporaries knew that the best way to effect change in people was to present them with a model to copy. This is precisely what Luke has provided for the church through Jesus' example of simplicity, humility, and prayer. The unity of Jesus' life and teaching in these areas would have caused Luke's intended readers to recognize Jesus as an ideal leader—the legendary philosopher-king who could effect real change in people through his personal example. There was power in that identification: they knew that only such a person who lived in unity with God could bring them to a point of transformation. The early church also recognized the power of Jesus' example. For them, every Gospel story seems to hold up Jesus as a model for emulation. The fathers and mothers of the church didn't just analyze Jesus' example from an objective distance either. They very personally and intimately apprenticed themselves to the living Jesus, placing themselves under the authority of his instruction and the power of his life. The invitation stands for us to do the same.

DISCUSSION QUESTIONS

PART 1: SIMPLICITY

1. In the first century when someone would give a gift, there were often strings attached, such as the expectation of loyalty. In what ways do people give to others today with an expectation of receiving something back? Does this ever happen in the church? How might we fight against that tendency?

2. In Luke, Jesus has a lot to say about our attitudes toward money, but he is even more concerned that we actually embrace a lifestyle of simplicity and give to the poor. Luke provides us an example of what this kind of simple and generous lifestyle looks like in Acts 2:45 and Acts 4:32-37. Do you think the church takes Jesus' teachings on generosity seriously enough today? How might we do a better job of that?

3. Jesus tells his followers to seek the kingdom first and that God will provide for them. Does this teaching seem unrealistic in a context where so many people today have lost their jobs and have no idea how to pay their rent and put food on the table? How might we deal theologically with extreme financial insecurity?

4. We sometimes hold back from giving because we are unsure how the recipients of our gift will spend "our" money. What might we learn from the early church about this attitude?

Part 2: Humility

1. Most of us probably don't regularly boast about our accomplishments. However, we probably do engage in a constant comparison of ourselves to others, which is also rooted in a deep insecurity. How might we address this problem theologically? What does Luke have to say about it?

2. We might look with disdain on the disciples' overt strivings for status. However, we also want to be important. We want to achieve great things and be recognized for our accomplishments. We certainly don't want to be "ordinary." In the TV series *The Good Place*, Eleanor sometimes leveled the greatest insult she could at a person: "Ya basic." Why might this be so devastating? What might our attempts to overcome our own insignificance convey about our spiritual condition?

3. I once had a particularly gifted student who I was sure would go to grad school and then become a professor. After graduation, he went to work full time on his family's farm and had no plans beyond that. At the time, I questioned his ambition and potential "waste" of talent. How might a theological perspective on humility correct this attitude?

4. What can we learn from the early church about the importance of humility? Why is humility so critical for the life of faith? What does it mean to have a true sense of self and why is that so important for our relationships with God and each other?

PART 3: PRAYER

1. One inescapable conclusion that we reach from reading Luke's Gospel is that Luke genuinely expected concrete answers to prayer. That is apparent in Jesus' teaching and experience, in the experience of the early church in Acts, in Luke's cultural world, and in the church's reception of Luke. Do we really expect our prayers to be answered (other than perhaps an improvement in attitude or in our relationship with God)? Richard Foster complained that when we come to prayer, instead of praying boldly for a healing, we give God an "out" by asking God to heal someone if is in God's will. What do you think about this practice? Is it appropriate, or too timid?

2. In Luke, Jesus invites us to pray for what we need, but we also see that prayer is fundamentally oriented around God and God's kingdom. Within Luke's cultural context we see examples of Socrates and Numa who pray for themselves or for their people to be moved toward virtue. What might it look like to emphasize God's agenda in our prayer lives?

3. How would you describe Jesus' own spiritual discipline of prayer in Luke? What can the context of Numa or Socrates' example teach us about prayer? How did the early church appropriate Jesus' example of prayer?

4. According to Luke, prayer is essential for spiritual strength. Even Jesus must rely upon communion with God to receive the strength that he needs to embrace his mission. How did the early church wrestle with Jesus' need for prayer? (Is Jesus' struggle for the will of God real?) How does Luke effectively present Jesus as a model to copy in prayer?

BIBLIOGRAPHY

Primary Sources

1 (Ethiopic Apocalypse of) Enoch. Translated and introduced by E. Isaac. In *The Old Testament Pseudepigrapha.* Vol. 1 of *Apocalyptic Literature and Testaments.* Edited by James H. Charlesworth. Peabody, MA: Hendrickson, 1983.

2 Baruch, or The Syriac Apocalypse of Baruch. Translated and introduced by R. H. Charles. In *The Apocrypha and Pseudepigrapha of the Old Testament in English: With Introductions and Critical Explanatory Notes to the Several Books.* Vol. 2 of *Pseudepigrapha.* Edited by R. H. Charles. Oxford: Clarendon, 1913.

Ahiqar. Translated and introduced by J. M. Lindenberger. In *The Old Testament Pseudepigrapha.* Vol. 2 of *Expansions of the "Old Testament" and Legends, Wisdom and Philosophical Literature, Prayers, Psalms, and Odes, Fragments of Lost Judeo-Hellenistic Works.* Edited by James H. Charlesworth. Peabody, MA: Hendrickson, 1983.

Ambrose. *Exposition of the Holy Gospel According to Saint Luke.* Translated by Theodosia Tomkinson. Etna, CA: Center for Traditionalist Orthodox Studies, 1998.

———. *Letters 1-91.* Translated by Sister Mary Melchior Beyenka. In *The Fathers of the Church: A New Translation.* Vol. 26. 127 Vols. Washington, DC: Catholic University of America Press, 1954.

———. "On the Duties of the Clergy." In *Selected Works and Letters.* In *Nicene and Post-Nicene Fathers,* Series II. Edited by Philip Schaff. Vol. 10. 14 vols. Grand Rapids: Christian Classics Ethereal Library. New York: Christian Literature, 1886.

Aquinas, St. Thomas. *Summa Theologiae.* Translated by Fathers of the English Dominican Province. New York: Benziger Brothers, 1947.

Aristotle. *Nicomachean Ethics.* In *Benefactor: Epigraphic Study of a Graeco-Roman and New Testament Semantic Field.* Edited by Frederick W. Danker. St. Louis: Clayton, 1982.

Athanasius. *Festal Letters of Fasting, and Trumpets and Feasts.* In *Nicene and Post-Nicene Fathers,* Series II. Edited by Philip Schaff. Vol. 1. Grand Rapids: Christian Classics Ethereal Library. New York: Christian Literature Publishing Co., 1886.

———. *The Resurrection Letters.* Paraphrased and introduced by Jack N. Sparks. Nashville: Thomas Nelson, 1979.

Augustine. *The Confessions and Letters of St. Augustine, with a Sketch of His Life and Work.* In *Nicene and Post-Nicene Fathers,* Series I. Edited by Philip Schaff. Vol. 1. 14 vols. Grand Rapids: Christian Classics Ethereal Library; New York: Christian Literature, 1886.

———. *Letters, Vol. II (83-130)*. Translated by Sister Wilfrid Parsons. In *The Fathers of the Church: A New Translation*. Vol. 18. 127 vols. Washington, DC: Catholic University of America Press, 1953.

———. *Sermons on the Liturgical Seasons*. Translated by Sister Mary Sarah Muldowney. In *The Fathers of the Church: A New Translation*. Vol. 38. 127 vols. Washington, DC: Catholic University of America Press, 1959.

———. *The Works of Saint Augustine: A Translation for the 21st Century*. Edited by John E. Rotelle, Edmund Hill, and Augustinian Heritage Institute. Brooklyn: New City, 1990.

Basil. *Exegetic Homilies*. Translated by Sister Agnes Clare Way. In *The Fathers of the Church: A New Translation*. Vol. 46. 127 vols. Washington, DC: Catholic University of America Press, 1963.

———. "I Will Tear Down My Barns." In *On Social Justice*. Translated by C. Paul Schroeder. Yonkers, NY: St. Vladimir's Seminary Press, 2009.

———. "On Humility." In *Ascetical Works*. Translated by Sister M. Monica Wagner. In *The Fathers of the Church: A New Translation*. Vol. 9. 127 vols. Washington, DC: Catholic University of America Press, 1962.

———. "To the Rich Ruler." In *On Social Justice*. Translated by C. Paul Schroeder. Yonkers, NY: St. Vladimir's Seminary Press, 2009.

Benedict. *The Holy Rule of St. Benedict*. Translated by Rev. Boniface Verheyen. Grand Rapids: Christian Classics Ethereal Library, 1949.

The Book of Jubilees. Translated and introduced by R. H. Charles. In *The Apocrypha and Pseudepigrapha of the Old Testament in English: With Introductions and Critical Explanatory Notes to the Several Books*. Vol. 2 of *Pseudepigrapha*. Edited by R. H. Charles. Oxford: Clarendon Press, 1913.

Cassian, John. *The Conferences of John Cassian*. Translated by Edgar C. S. Gibson. In *Nicene and Post-Nicene Fathers*, Series II. Edited by Philip Schaff. Vol. 11. 14 vols. Grand Rapids: Christian Classics Ethereal Library. New York: Christian Literature, 1894.

Chrysologus, Peter, and Valerian. *Saint Peter Chrysologus: Selected Sermons; and Saint Valerian: Homilies*. Translated by George E. Ganss. In *The Fathers of the Church: A New Translation*. Vol. 17. 127 vols. Washington, DC: Catholic University of America Press, 1953.

Chrysostom, John. "An Exhortation to Theodore After His Fall." Translated by W. R. W. Stephens. In *On the Priesthood; Ascetic Treatises; Select Homilies and Letters; Homilies on the Statutes 1-2*. In *Nicene and Post-Nicene Fathers*, Series I. Edited by Philip Schaff. Vol. 9. 14 vols. Grand Rapids: Christian Classics Ethereal Library. New York: Christian Literature, 1886.

———. *Homilies on Galatians, Ephesians, Philippians, Colossians, Thessalonians, Timothy, Titus, and Philemon*. In *Nicene and Post-Nicene Fathers*, Series I. Edited by Philip Schaff. Vol. 13. 14 vols. Grand Rapids: Christian Classics Ethereal Library. New York: Christian Literature, 1886.

———. *Homilies on the Acts of the Apostles and the Epistle to the Romans*. In *Nicene and Post-Nicene Fathers*, Series I. Edited by Philip Schaff. Vol. 11. 14 vols. Grand Rapids: Christian Classics Ethereal Library. New York: Christian Literature, 1886.

———. *Homilies on the Gospel of Saint Matthew.* In *Nicene and Post-Nicene Fathers,* Series I. Edited by Philip Schaff. Vol.10. 14 vols. Grand Rapids: Christian Classics Ethereal Library. New York: Christian Literature, 1886.

———. *Homilies on the Gospel of St. John and the Epistle to the Hebrews.* In *Nicene and Post-Nicene Fathers,* Series I. Edited by Philip Schaff. Vol. 14. 14 vols. Grand Rapids: Christian Classics Ethereal Library. New York: Christian Literature, 1886.

———. "Homily Concerning Lowliness of Mind; And Commentary on Philippians I. 18." Translated by R. Blackburn. In *On the Priesthood; Ascetic Treatises; Select Homilies and Letters; Homilies on the Statutes 1-2.* In *Nicene and Post-Nicene Fathers,* Series I. Edited by Philip Schaff. Vol. 9. 14 vols. Grand Rapids; Christian Classics Ethereal Library. New York: Christian Literature, 1886.

———. *On Wealth and Poverty.* Translated by Catharine P. Roth. Crestwood, NY: St. Vladimir's Seminary Press, 1984.

Clement of Alexandria. *The Instructor.* In *The Ante-Nicene Fathers: Translations of the Fathers down to AD 325.* Edited by The Rev. Alexander Roberts and James Donaldson. Vol. 2. 9 vols. Grand Rapids: Eerdmans, 1971.

———. *The Rich Man's Salvation.* Translated by G. W. Butterworth. LCL. Cambridge: Harvard University Press, 1919.

———. *The Stromata, or Miscellanies.* In *The Ante-Nicene Fathers: Translations of the Fathers down to AD 325.* Edited by The Rev. Alexander Roberts and James Donaldson. Vol. 2. 9 vols. Grand Rapids: Eerdmans, 1971.

Cyprian. *The Epistles of Cyprian.* In *The Ante-Nicene Fathers: Translations of the Fathers down to AD 325.* Edited by The Rev. Alexander Roberts and James Donaldson. Vol. 5. 9 vols. Grand Rapids: Eerdmans, 1971.

———. "On Jealousy and Envy." In *The Treatises of Cyprian.* In *The Ante-Nicene Fathers: Translations of the Fathers down to AD 325.* Edited by The Rev. Alexander Roberts and James Donaldson. Vol. 5. 9 vols. Grand Rapids: Eerdmans, 1971.

———. "On the Lord's Prayer." In *The Treatises of Cyprian.* In *The Ante-Nicene Fathers: Translations of the Fathers Down to AD 325.* Edited by The Rev. Alexander Roberts and James Donaldson. Vol. 5. 9 vols. Grand Rapids: Eerdmans, 1971.

Cyril of Alexandria. *A Commentary on the Gospel of St. Luke.* Translated by R. Payne Smith. Studion, 1983.

Didache. In *The Ante-Nicene Fathers: Translations of the Fathers down to AD 325.* Edited by The Rev. Alexander Roberts and James Donaldson. Vol. 7. 9 vols. Grand Rapids: Eerdmans, 1970.

Dio Cassius. *Roman History, Volume VII: Books 56-60.* Translated by Earnest Cary, Herbert B. Foster. LCL. Cambridge: Harvard University Press, 1917.

Dio Chrysostom. *Discourses.* Translated by H. Lamar Crosby. LCL. Cambridge: Harvard University Press, 1964.

Diogenes Laertius. *Lives of Eminent Philosophers, Volume II: Books 6-10.* Translated by R. D. Hicks. LCL. Cambridge: Harvard University Press, 1925.

Diotogenes. *Concerning a Kingdom.* In *Political Fragments of Archytas, Charondas, Zaleucus, and Other Ancient Pythagoreans Preserved by Stobaeus.* Translated by Thomas Taylor. Chiswick: C. Whittingham, 1822.

Dionysius. *Exegetical Fragments on the Gospel of Luke.* Translated by S. D. F. Salmond. In *The Ante-Nicene Fathers: Translations of the Fathers down to AD 325.* Edited by

The Rev. Alexander Roberts and James Donaldson. Vol. 7. 9 vols. Grand Rapids: Eerdmans, 1988.

Ecphantus. *On a Kingdom.* In *Political Fragments of Archytas, Charondas, Zaleucus, and Other Ancient Pythagoreans Preserved by Stobaeus.* Translated by Thomas Taylor. Chiswick: C. Whittingham, 1822.

Epictetus. *Discourses, Books 1-2.* Translated by W. A. Oldfather. LCL. Cambridge: Harvard University Press, 1925.

———. *Discourses, Books 3-4. Fragments. The Encheiridion.* Translated by W. A. Oldfather. LCL. Cambridge: Harvard University Press, 1928.

———. *The Stoic and Epicurean Philosophers.* Translated by Whitney J. Oates. New York: Random House, 1940.

The Epistle of Barnabas. In *The Ante-Nicene Fathers: Translations of the Fathers down to AD 325.* Edited by The Rev. Alexander Roberts and James Donaldson. Vol. 1. 9 vols. Grand Rapids: Eerdmans, 1973.

Fathers of the Second Century, Macarius Chrysocephalus: Parable of the Prodigal Son, Luke XV, Oration on Luke XV, Towards the Close. In *The Ante-Nicene Fathers: Translations of the Fathers down to AD 325.* Edited by The Rev. Alexander Roberts and James Donaldson. Vol. 2. 9 vols. Grand Rapids: Eerdmans, 1971.

Isocrates. *To Demonicus.* Translated by George Norlin. LCL. Cambridge: Harvard University Press, 1928.

Jerome. "Against the Pelagians." In *The Principal Works of St. Jerome.* Translated by W. H. Freemantle. In *Nicene and Post-Nicene Fathers,* Series II. Edited by Philip Schaff. Vol. 6. 14 vols. Grand Rapids: Christian Classics Ethereal Library. New York: Christian Literature, 1892.

———. *The Homilies of Saint Jerome,* Volume 2. Translated by Sister Marie Liguori Ewald. In *The Fathers of the Church: A New Translation.* Vol. 57. 127 vols. Washington, DC: Catholic University of America Press, 1966.

———. "Letter II. To Theodosius and the Rest of the Anchorites." In *The Principal Works of St. Jerome.* Translated by W. H. Freemantle. In *Nicene and Post-Nicene Fathers,* Series II. Edited by Philip Schaff. Vol. 6. 14 vols. Grand Rapids: Christian Classics Ethereal Library. New York: Christian Literature, 1892.

———. "Letter XVI. To Pope Damasus." In *The Principal Works of St. Jerome.* Translated by W. H. Freemantle. In *Nicene and Post-Nicene Fathers,* Series II. Edited by Philip Schaff. Vol. 6. 14 vols. Grand Rapids: Christian Classics Ethereal Library. New York: Christian Literature, 1892.

———. "Letter LXXVII. To Oceanus." In *The Principal Works of St. Jerome.* Translated by W. H. Freemantle. In *Nicene and Post-Nicene Fathers,* Series II. Edited by Philip Schaff. Vol. 6. 14 vols. Grand Rapids: Christian Classics Ethereal Library. New York: Christian Literature, 1892.

———. "Letter CXXII. To Rusticus." In *The Principal Works of St. Jerome.* Translated by W. H. Freemantle. In *Nicene and Post-Nicene Fathers,* Series II. Edited by Philip Schaff. Vol. 6. 14 vols. Grand Rapids: Christian Classics Ethereal Library. New York: Christian Literature, 1892.

Josephus. *The Jewish Antiquities.* Translated by H. St. J. Thackeray, Ralph Marcus, Allen Wikgren, and Louis H. Feldman. 9 vols. LCL. Cambridge: Harvard University Press, 1930–65.

Lactantius. *The Divine Institutes Book V*. In *The Ante-Nicene Fathers: Translations of the Fathers down to AD 325*. Edited by The Rev. Alexander Roberts and James Donaldson. Vol. 5. 9 vols. Grand Rapids: Eerdmans, 1971.

Letter of Aristeas. Translated and introduced by R. J. H. Shutt. In *The Old Testament Pseudepigrapha*. Vol. 2 of *Expansions of the "Old Testament" and Legends, Wisdom and Philosophical Literature, Prayers, Psalms, and Odes, Fragments of Lost Judeo-Hellenistic Works*. Edited by James H. Charlesworth. Peabody, MA: Hendrickson, 1983.

The Life of Secundus the Philosopher. Translated by B. E. Perry. Chapel Hill, NC: American Philological Association, 1964.

Lucian. *Demonax*. Translated by A. M. Harmon. Vol. 1. 8 vols. LCL. Cambridge: Harvard University Press, 1913.

———. *The Passing of Peregrinus*. Translated by A. M. Harmon. LCL. Cambridge: Harvard University Press, 1936.

———. *A Professor of Public Speaking*. Translated by A. M. Harmon. LCL. Cambridge: Harvard University Press, 1925.

Origen. *Against Celsus*. In *The Ante-Nicene Fathers: Translations of the Fathers down to AD 325*. Edited by The Rev. Alexander Roberts and James Donaldson. Vol. 4. 9 vols. Grand Rapids: Eerdmans, 1907.

———. *Commentary on Matthew*. In *The Ante-Nicene Fathers: Translations of the Fathers down to AD 325*. Edited by The Rev. Alexander Roberts and James Donaldson. Vol. 9. 9 vols. Grand Rapids: Eerdmans, 1912.

———. *Origen: An Exhortation to Martyrdom, Prayer and Selected Works*. Translated by Rowan A. Greer. New York: Paulist, 1979.

Philo. *On Abraham, On Joseph, On Moses*. Translated by F. H. Colson. Vol. 6. 10 vols. LCL. Cambridge: Harvard University Press, 1935.

———. *On Sobriety*. Translated by F. H. Colson, G. H. Whitaker. LCL. Cambridge: Harvard University Press, 1930.

———. *On the Migration of Abraham*. Translated by F. H. Colson, G. H. Whitaker. LCL. Cambridge, MA: Harvard University Press, 1932.

———. *On the Special Laws, Book 4*. Translated by F. H. Colson. LCL. Cambridge: Harvard University Press, 1939.

———. *On the Virtues*. Translated by F. H. Colson. Vol. 8. 10 vols. LCL. Cambridge: Harvard University Press, 1939.

Plato. *Euthyphro, Apology, Crito, Phaedo, Phaedrus*. Translated by Harold North Fowler. Vol. 1. 12 vols. LCL. Cambridge: Harvard University Press, 1914.

———. *Laws*. Translated by R. G. Bury. Vols. 10–12. 12 vols. LCL. Cambridge: Harvard University Press, 1926.

———. *Republic*. Edited and translated by Christopher Emlyn-Jones, William Preddy. Vol 1. 2 Vols. Cambridge: Harvard University Press, 2013.

———. *Statesman*. Translated by W. R. M. Lamb. Vol. 8. 12 vols. LCL. Cambridge: Harvard University Press, 1925.

———. *Symposium*. Translated by W. R. M. Lamb. Vol. 3. 12 vols. LCL. Cambridge: Harvard University Press, 1925.

———. *Timaeus. Critias. Epistles*. Translated by R. G. Bury. Vol. 9. 12 vols. LCL. Cambridge: Harvard University Press, 1929.

Pliny the Elder. *Natural History*. Translated by H. Rackham. LCL. Vol. 9. 10 vols. Cambridge: Harvard University Press, 1952.

Plutarch. *Agis and Cleomenes*. In *Lives*. Translated by Bernadotte Perrin. Vol. 10. 11 vols. LCL. Cambridge: Harvard University Press, 1921.

———. *Alexander*. In *Lives*. Translated by Bernadotte Perrin. Vol. 7. 11 vols. LCL. Cambridge: Harvard University Press, 1919.

———. *How to Tell a Flatterer from a Friend. How a Man May Become Aware of His Progress in Virtue*. In *Moralia*. Translated by Frank Cole Babbitt. Vol. 1. 16 vols. LCL. Cambridge: Harvard University Press, 1927.

———. *Lycurgus, Numa*. In *Lives*. Translated by Bernadotte Perrin. Vol. 1. 11 vols. LCL. Cambridge: Harvard University Press, 1914.

———. *On the Control of Anger*. In *Moralia*. Translated by W. C. Helmbold. Vol. 6. 16 vols. LCL. Cambridge: Harvard University Press, 1939.

———. *On Praising Oneself Inoffensively*. In *Moralia*. Translated by Phillip H. De Lacy, Benedict Einarson. Vol. 7. 16 vols. LCL. Cambridge: Harvard University Press, 1959.

———. *Themistocles and Camillus. Cimon and Lucullus*. In *Lives*. Translated by Bernadotte Perrin. Vol. 2. 11 vols. LCL. Cambridge: Harvard University Press, 1914.

———. *Timoleon*. In *Lives*. Translated by B. Perrin. Vol. 6. 11 vols. LCL. Cambridge: Harvard University Press, 1918.

Psalms of Solomon. Translated and introduced by R. B. Wright. In *The Old Testament Pseudepigrapha*. Vol. 2 of *Expansions of the "Old Testament" and Legends, Wisdom and Philosophical Literature, Prayers, Psalms, and Odes, Fragments of Lost Judeo-Hellenistic Works*. Edited by James H. Charlesworth. Peabody, MA: Hendrickson, 1983.

Sentences of Pseudo-Phocylides. Translated and introduced by P. W. van der Horst. In *The Old Testament Pseudepigrapha*. Vol. 2 of *Expansions of the "Old Testament" and Legends, Wisdom and Philosophical Literature, Prayers, Psalms, and Odes, Fragments of Lost Judeo-Hellenistic Works*. Edited by James H. Charlesworth. Peabody, MA: Hendrickson, 1983.

Seneca. *De Beneficiis*. In *Moral Works*. Translated by John W. Basore. Vol 3. 3 vols. LCL. Cambridge: Harvard University Press, 1935.

———. *Epistles*. Translated by Richard M. Gummere. Vol. 1. 3 vols. LCL. Cambridge: Harvard University Press, 1917.

Sentences of the Syriac Menander. Translated and introduced by T. Baarda. In *The Old Testament Pseudepigrapha*. Vol. 2 of *Expansions of the "Old Testament" and Legends, Wisdom and Philosophical Literature, Prayers, Psalms, and Odes, Fragments of Lost Judeo-Hellenistic Works*. Edited by James H. Charlesworth. Peabody, MA: Hendrickson, 1983.

Suetonius. *Lives of the Caesars, Volume I: Julius. Augustus. Tiberius. Gaius. Caligula*. Translated by J. C. Rolfe. LCL. Cambridge: Harvard University Press, 1914.

Sibylline Oracles. Translated and introduced by J. J. Collins. In *The Old Testament Pseudepigrapha*. Vol. 1 of *Apocalyptic Literature and Testaments*. Edited by James H. Charlesworth. Peabody, MA: Hendrickson, 1983.

Tertullian, Cyprian, and Origen. *Against Marcion Book 4*. In *The Ante-Nicene Fathers: Translations of the Fathers down to AD 325*. Edited by The Rev. Alexander Roberts and James Donaldson. Vol. 3. 9 vols. Grand Rapids: Eerdmans, 1973.

———. *Disciplinary, Moral, and Ascetical Works.* Translated by Rudolph Arbesmann, Sister Emily Joseph Daly, Edwin A. Quain. In *The Fathers of the Church: A New Translation.* Vol. 40. 127 vols. Washington, DC: Catholic University of America Press, 1959.

———. *On Idolatry.* In *The Ante-Nicene Fathers: Translations of the Fathers down to AD 325.* Edited by The Rev. Alexander Roberts and James Donaldson. Vol. 3. 9 vols. Grand Rapids: Eerdmans, 1973.

———. *On Modesty.* In *The Ante-Nicene Fathers: Translations of the Fathers down to AD 325.* Edited by The Rev. Alexander Roberts and James Donaldson. Vol. 4. 9 vols. Grand Rapids: Eerdmans, 1907.

———. *On Prayer.* In *The Ante-Nicene Fathers: Translations of the Fathers down to AD 325.* Edited by The Rev. Alexander Roberts and James Donaldson. Vol. 3. 9 vols. Grand Rapids: Eerdmans, 1973.

———. *On the Lord's Prayer.* Translated by Alistair C. Stewart. Crestwood, NY: St. Vladimir's Seminary Press, 2004.

Testament of Isaac. Translated and introduced by W. F. Stinespring. In *The Old Testament Pseudepigrapha.* Vol. 1 of *Apocalyptic Literature and Testaments.* Edited by James H. Charlesworth. Peabody, MA: Hendrickson, 1983.

Testament of Jacob. Translated and introduced by W. F. Stinespring. In *The Old Testament Pseudepigrapha.* Vol. 1 of *Apocalyptic Literature and Testaments.* Edited by James H. Charlesworth. Peabody, MA: Hendrickson, 1983.

Testament of Job. Translated and introduced by R. P. Spittler. In *The Old Testament Pseudepigrapha.* Vol. 1 of *Apocalyptic Literature and Testaments.* Edited by James H. Charlesworth. Peabody, MA: Hendrickson, 1983.

Testaments of the Twelve Patriarchs. Translated and introduced by H. C. Kee. In *The Old Testament Pseudepigrapha.* Vol. 1 of *Apocalyptic Literature and Testaments.* Edited by James H. Charlesworth. Peabody, MA: Hendrickson, 1983.

Virgil. *Aeneid: Books 1-6.* Translated by H. Rushton Fairclough. Revised by G. P. Goold. LCL. Cambridge: Harvard University Press, 1916.

———. *Aeneid: Books 7-12.* Translated by H. Rushton Fairclough. Revised by G. P. Goold. LCL. Cambridge, MA: Harvard University Press, 1918.

Vision of Ezra. Translated and introduced by J. R. Mueller, G. A. Robbins. In *The Old Testament Pseudepigrapha.* Vol. 1 of *Apocalyptic Literature and Testaments.* Edited by James H. Charlesworth. Peabody, MA: Hendrickson, 1983.

Ward, Benedicta. *The Sayings of the Desert Fathers: The Alphabetical Collection.* Rev. ed. Cistercian Studies Series; v. 59. Kalamazoo, MI: Cistercian Publications, 1975.

Xenophon. *Cyropaedia.* Translated by Walter Miller. Vol. 1. 2 vols. LCL. Cambridge: Harvard University Press, 1960.

———. *Memorabilia and Oeconomicus.* Translated by E. C. Marchant. LCL. Cambridge: Harvard University Press, 1923.

SECONDARY SOURCES

Bailey, Kenneth Ewing. *Poet and Peasant: A Literary Cultural Approach to the Parables in Luke*. Grand Rapids: Eerdmans, 1976.

Bock, Darrell L. *Luke*. The IVP New Testament Commentary Series. Downers Grove, IL: InterVarsity Press, 1994.

Bovon, François. *Luke 1: A Commentary on the Gospel of Luke 1:1–9:50*. Edited by Helmut Koester. Translated by Christine M. Thomas. Hermeneia. Minneapolis: Fortress Press, 2002.

———. *Luke 2: A Commentary on the Gospel of Luke 9:51–19:27*. Edited by Helmut Koester. Translated by Donald S. Deer. Hermeneia. Minneapolis: Fortress Press, 2013.

———. *Luke 3: A Commentary on the Gospel of Luke 19:28–24:53*. Edited by Helmut Koester. Translated by James E. Crouch. Hermeneia. Minneapolis: Fortress, 2012.

Braun, Willi. *Feasting and Social Rhetoric in Luke 14*. Cambridge: Cambridge University Press, 1995.

Burkert, Walter. *Greek Religion: Archaic and Classical*. Translated by John Raffan. Ancient World. Oxford: Blackwell, 1985.

Cassidy, Richard. *Jesus, Politics, and Society: A Study of Luke's Gospel*. Maryknoll, NY: Orbis, 1978.

Chesnut, Glenn. "The Ruler and the Logos in Neopythagorean, Middle Platonic, and Late Stoic Political Philosophy." In *Aufstieg und Niedergang der Römischen Welt: Geschichte und Kultur Roms im Spiegel der neueren Forschung, II*. Teil (*Principat*), Band II 16: Religion. Edited by Hildegard Temporini and Wolfgang Haase. Berlin: Walter de Gruyter, 1978.

Clarke, M. L. *The Roman Mind: Studies in the History of Thought from Cicero to Marcus Aurelius*. Cambridge, MA: Harvard University Press, 1965.

Conzelmann, Hans. *The Theology of St. Luke*. Translated by Geoffrey Buswel. New York: Harper & Row, 1960.

Culy, Martin M., Mikeal C. Parsons, and Joshua J. Stigall. *Luke: A Handbook on the Greek Text*. Baylor Handbook on the Greek New Testament. Waco: Baylor University Press, 2010.

Danker, Frederick W. *Benefactor: Epigraphic Study of a Graeco-Roman and New Testament Semantic Field*. St. Louis: Clayton, 1982.

Darr, John A. *On Character Building: The Reader and the Rhetoric of Characterization in Luke-Acts*. Louisville: Westminster/John Knox, 1992.

Dunn, James C. "Spirit and Kingdom." *Expository Times* 82, 1970.

Edwards, James R. *The Gospel According to Luke*. Pillar New Testament Commentary. Grand Rapids: Eerdmans, 2015.

Fitzmyer, Joseph A. *The Gospel According to Luke*. 2 vols. Anchor Bible. Garden City, NY: Doubleday, 1981–1985.

Foster, Richard J. *Prayer: Finding the Heart's True Home*. 1st ed. San Francisco: HarperSanFrancisco, 1992.

Foulcher, Jane. *Reclaiming Humility: Four Studies in the Monastic Tradition*. Cistercian Studies Series. Collegeville, MN: Cistercian Publications, 2015.

Fuhrman, Charles M. "A Redactional Study of Prayer in the Gospel of Luke." PhD diss., Southern Baptist Theological Seminary, 1981.

Garland, David E. *Luke.* Zondervan Exegetical Commentary on the New Testament. Grand Rapids: Zondervan, 2011.

Gordon, Richard. "The Veil of Power: Emperors, Sacrifices and Benefactors." In *Pagan Priests: Religion and Power in the Ancient World.* Edited by Mary Beard and John North. London: Duckworth, 1990.

Gowler, David B. *Host, Guest, Enemy, and Friend: Portraits of the Pharisees in Luke and Acts.* Emory Studies in Early Christianity. Vol 2. New York: Peter Lang, 1991.

Green, Joel B. *The Gospel of Luke.* The New International Commentary on the New Testament. Grand Rapids: Eerdmans, 1997.

———. *Seized by Truth: Reading the Bible as Scripture.* Nashville: Abingdon, 2007.

Gregory of Nyssa. "On the Love of the Poor 1: On Good Works." In *The Hungry Are Dying: Beggars and Bishops in Roman Cappadocia.* Oxford Studies in Historical Theology. New York: Oxford University Press, 2001.

———. "On the Love of the Poor 2: On the saying, 'Whoever Has Done It to One of These Has Done It to Me.'" In *The Hungry Are Dying: Beggars and Bishops in Roman Cappadocia.* Oxford Studies in Historical Theology. New York: Oxford University Press, 2001.

Grundmann, Walter. *Das Evangelium nach Lukas.* Berlin: Evangelische Verlagsanstalt, 1961.

Holgate, David A. *Prodigality, Liberality and Meanness in the Parable of the Prodigal Son: A Greco-Roman Perspective on Luke 15.11-32.* Journal for the Study of the New Testament Supplement Series 187. Sheffield, Sheffield Academic Press, 1999.

Jackson, B. Darrell. "The Prayers of Socrates." *Phronesis* 16, no. 1 (1971): 14-37.

Jauss, Hans Robert. *Toward an Aesthetic of Reception.* Translated by Timothy Bahti. Minneapolis: University of Minnesota Press, 1982.

Jeremias, Joachim. *The Parables of Jesus.* New York: Charles Scribner's Sons, 1963.

Johnson, Luke Timothy. *The Gospel of Luke.* Edited by Daniel J. Harrington. Sacra Pagina. Collegeville, MN: Liturgical Press, 1991.

Klostermann, Erich. *Das Lukasevangelium.* Tübingen: J. C. B. Mohr, Paul Siebeck, 1929.

Malherbe, Abraham J. *The Cynic Epistles: A Study Edition.* Missoula, MT: Scholars Press, 1977.

Manning, Brennan. *Abba's Child: The Cry of the Heart for Intimate Belonging.* Colorado Springs: NavPress, 1994.

Marshall, I. Howard. *The Gospel of Luke: A Commentary on the Greek Text.* New International Greek Testament Commentary. Grand Rapids: Eerdmans, 1978.

Merton, Thomas. *Life and Holiness.* New York: Image Books, 1963.

———. *New Seeds of Contemplation.* New York: New Directions, 1961.

Moxnes, Halvor. *The Economy of the Kingdom: Social Conflict and Economic Relations in Luke's Gospel.* Overtures to Biblical Theology. Philadelphia: Fortress, 1988.

Neyrey, Jerome H. *The Passion According to Luke: A Redaction Study of Luke's Soteriology.* Theological Inquiries. New York: Paulist Press, 1985.

Nolland, John. *Luke.* 3 vols. Word Biblical Commentary. Dallas: Word, 1989–93.

Palmer, Parker J. *Let Your Life Speak: Listening for the Voice of Vocation.* San Francisco: Jossey-Bass, 2000.

Parris, David Paul. *Reception Theory and Biblical Hermeneutics.* Princeton Theological Monograph Series 107. Eugene, OR: Pickwick, 2009.

Parsons, Mikeal C. *Luke.* Paideia. Grand Rapids: Baker Academic, 2015.

Plymale, Stephen F. *The Prayer Texts of Luke-Acts.* American University Studies. New York: Peter Lang, 1991.

Pulleyn, Simon. *Prayer in Greek Religion.* Oxford: Clarendon, 1997.

Rabinowitz, P. J. "Truth in Fiction: A Reexamination of Audiences." *Critical Inquiry* 4, no. 1 (1977):121-41.

———. "Whirl Without End: Audience Oriented Criticism." In *Contemporary Literary Theory.* Edited by G. D. Atkins and L. Morrow. Amherst: University of Massachusetts Press, 1989.

Reid, Barbara E. "Prayer and the Face of the Transfigured Jesus." In *The Lord's Prayer and Other Prayer Texts from the Greco-Roman Era.* Edited by James H. Charlesworth, Mark Harding, and Mark Kiley. Valley Forge, PA: Trinity Press International, 1994.

———. *The Transfiguration: A Source- and Redaction-Critical Study of Luke 9:28-36.* Paris: J. Gabalda et Cie Éditeurs, 1993.

Rengstorf, Karl Heinrich. *Das Evangelium nach Lukas.* NTD 3. Göttingen: Vandenhoeck & Ruprecht, 1965.

Rohrbaugh, Richard L. "The Pre-Industrial City in Luke-Acts: Urban Social Relations." In *The Social World of Luke-Acts: Models for Interpretation.* Edited by Jerome H. Neyrey. Peabody, MA: Hendrickson, 1991.

Schmidt, Thomas E. *Hostility to Wealth in the Synoptic Gospels.* Sheffield, England: JSOT Press, 1987.

Schneider, Gerhard. *Das Evangelium nach Lukas.* 2 vols. Würzburg: Echter-Verlag, 1984.

Schweitzer, Eduard. *The Good News According to Luke.* Translated by David E. Green. Atlanta: John Knox Press, 1984.

Soards, Marion L. *The Passion According to Luke: The Special Material of Luke 22.* Journal for the Study of the New Testament. Supplements Series 14. Sheffield: JSOT Press, 1987.

Talbert, Charles H. *Literary Patterns, Theological Themes, and the Genre of Luke-Acts.* Missoula, MT: Scholars Press, 1974.

———. *Reading Luke: A Literary and Theological Commentary on the Third Gospel.* Reading the New Testament Series. New York: Crossroad, 1982.

———. *Reading Luke-Acts in Its Mediterranean Milieu.* Supplements to Novum Testamentum. Leiden: Brill, 2003.

———. *What Is a Gospel?: The Genre of the Canonical Gospels.* Philadelphia: Fortress Press, 1977.

Tannehill, Robert C. *Luke.* Abingdon New Testament Commentaries. Nashville: Abingdon Press, 1996.

———. *The Narrative Unity of Luke-Acts: A Literary Interpretation.* Vol. 1 of *The Gospel According to Luke.* Philadelphia: Fortress Press, 1986.

Wengst, Klaus. *Humility: Solitary of the Humiliated: The Transformation of an Attitude and Its Social Relevance in Graeco Roman, Old Testament Jewish and Early Christian Tradition.* Philadelphia, PA: Fortress, 1988.

Wright, Addison G. "The Widow's Mites: Praise or Lament?—A Matter of Context." *CBQ* 44, 1982.

ANCIENT AUTHOR INDEX

INDEX OF APOCRYPHA AND PSEUDEPIGRAPHA

MODERN AUTHOR INDEX

SCRIPTURE INDEX